D0835125

The Dark Side 2

THE DARK SIDE

2

CRITICAL CASES ON THE

DOWNSIDE OF BUSINESS

Edited by Pauline Fatien Diochon,
Emmanuel Raufflet and Albert J. Mills

© 2013 Greenleaf Publishing Limited
Unless where otherwise stated

Published by Greenleaf Publishing Limited
Aizlewood's Mill
Nursery Street
Sheffield S3 8GG
UK
www.greenleaf-publishing.com

Printed in the UK on environmentally friendly, acid-free paper
from managed forests by CPI Group (UK) Ltd, Croydon

Cover by LaliAbril.com

All rights reserved. No part of this publication may be reproduced, stored
in a retrieval system, or transmitted, in any form or by any means, electronic, mechanical, photocopying, recording or otherwise, without the
prior permission in writing of the publishers.

British Library Cataloguing in Publication Data:
  A catalogue record for this book is available from the British Library.

ISBN-13: 978-1-906093-92-1 [paperback]
ISBN-13: 978-1-906093-97-6 [hardback]
ISBN-13: 978-1-909493-90-2 [PDF ebook]
ISBN-13: 978-1-907643-80-4 [ePub ebook]

Contents

Introduction
Dark side cases: challenging the 'bright side' bias of mainstream management education

Pauline Fatien
Menlo College, CA, USA

Emmanuel Raufflet
Department of Management, HEC Montreal, Canada

Albert Mills
Saint Mary's University, Canada

> It ain't what you don't know that gets you into trouble. It's what you know for sure that just ain't so.
>
> Mark Twain

Rationale

Beyond the mere focus on 'bad apples'

The "dark side" of organizations is often associated with "exceptional," "abnormal," "dysfunctional," or "pathological" aspects of human behaviors (Linstead, Maréchal and Griffin, 2010), the intentional or unintentional conduct of isolated "bad apples." The individual focus that reduces the explanation of problematic and dysfunctional situations to individual deficiencies leads to an individualization of the problems. Thus, framing the issue at an individual level implicitly protects the inherent morality of the system and allows for education practices that aim to correct, prevent, or "reeducate" the individual through the acquisition of "proper" behaviors to conform to more "ethical" norms. For critical management scholars (CMS), this dominant "bad apples" approach has several limitations for business education.

The first limitation is that getting out of the dark (becoming ethical) is reduced to a normative process of obeying instructions, predetermined ethical rules, and codes. By drawing clear boundaries around what is ethical, such a mechanistic approach both simplifies the complexity of organizational life and deprives subjects of their own discretion and discernment. Rather than sustaining the development of moral reasoning, it undermines it. The second limitation is that this process restricts the ethical decision-making process to a cognitive one that disregards the embodied, compassionate dimension of the ethical building process (Kjonstad and Willmott, 1995). As a result, the dominant "bad apple" view constitutes an impoverished understanding of ethics that reinforces prevailing and discredited relations of power in an organization (Wray-Bliss, 2009), since

> the privileging of abstract, depersonalized, and individualistic moral reasoning, and associated qualities such as duty and justice have been means by which women and non-Western peoples have historically been written out of the category of moral subjects or assimilated within masculinist or Western notions of moral agency (p. 269).

This leads to the third limitation, which concerns basic assumptions about society and gender. The ethical universal mask supports the universalization of an alienating, atomized, or one-dimensional subjectivity (Wray-Bliss, 2009). The fourth limitation of this "bad apple" view is that it impedes business educators from revisiting some problematic basic assumptions about what should be taught in business education. In his posthumous article, Ghoshal (2005, p. 76) writes:

> Business schools are blamed for focusing too narrowly on technical business prowess, efficiency, and profit maximization; for being poor endorsers of professional standards and norms of conduct; and for promoting "amoral theories ... that have actively freed their students from any sense of moral responsibility.

In all, "bad apples" approaches tend to simplify the complexity of organizations' lives and definitely prevent a systemic analysis of the problems. They also prevent these behaviors from being seen as just "normal."

Up-to-date cases to support critical, reflective moral development

Reflective thought: "active, persistent, and careful consideration of any belief or supposed form of knowledge in the light of the grounds that support it and the further conclusions to which it tends" (John Dewey, 1909, re-ed 1997, p. 7).

The view we promote in this book is a rejoinder to Linstead, Maréchal, and Griffin (2010), who suggest considering the dark sides of our organizations as "normal" organizational aspects. This is why we hope Dark Side cases will help students discuss the complexity of organizational ethics by differentiating complex from simple and complicated issues (Raufflet and Mills 2009). We hope this set of cases will contribute to achieving two main objectives. The first is that these cases will support students' moral development as an essential "personal quality." As such, morality cannot be abstracted from the individual actor, but is constructed through the actor's real-life interactions with his/her environment and fellows. Hopefully, the material in this book will allow for self-reflection and peer discussion as ethical maturity is developed by confronting oneself and others (Carroll and Shaw, 2013). We also expect these cases to sustain "empowering ethics" that lead to the emancipation of students and future employees, managers, and leaders who feel a sensorial responsibility towards ethics that become sensorial, corporeal, carnal, and somatic (Wray-Bliss, 2009). This is the uncertain and "frail but vital condition of ethics."

The second objective is to provide high-quality, up-to-date, international, and well-documented teaching material that will help train students and practitioners in reflective and critical thinking. There is clear evidence that the improvement of reflective and critical thinking is a condition that goes beyond the hidden assumptions of business curricula from the perspectives of ethics (Giacalone and Thompson, 2006) and sustainable development (Kearins and Springett, 2003).

Dark Side case competitions

The cases selected for this book have reached the final stage of the Dark Side Competition at the Academy of Management (AOM). Established in 2001 by the Critical Management Studies Division of the AOM, organized by the Representatives at Large of the CMS Division, and sponsored by the Sobey School of Business at Saint Mary's University in Halifax, Nova Scotia, Canada, this competition is designed to encourage and acknowledge the development of cases that provoke reflection and debate on the "dark side" of contemporary organizations. The competition rewards critical teaching cases that challenge the taken-for-granted assumptions and practices of contemporary organizations and offer alternatives to mainstream corporate and management conceptual frames, mental models, values, paradigms, practices, processes, and systems.

Cases have been selected based on the following criteria:

- The use of a critical perspective that provides an alternative to mainstream management analyses

- The importance, from a critical perspective, of the issues raised

- The quality of the underlying research: we encourage solid background research consistent with the nature and purpose of the case

- The quality of the presentation and the originality of the pedagogical supports

- The utility of the accompanying teaching note

This book

Each of these 14 outstanding cases was either a finalist or a winner of the Dark Side Case Competition at the Academy of Management over the 2009–2012 period. Each of them was thoroughly documented, has been peer-reviewed, and edited. These 14 cases cover four continents (Asia, the Americas, Europe, and Oceania) and business and public organizations. The industries range from extractive industries, the energy industry, consumer products, pulp and paper, movies, media, municipal affairs, academia, banking, and the drug industry.

This book is divided into three sections:

Section A, "Community and environment," focuses on the relationships between business organizations, local communities, and the environment. Representing various industries and countries, the cases in this section deal with how private growth may hurt local public good. Three cases in this section address the environmental impact of energy industries in three different countries, Ireland, India, and Canada. The remaining two cases highlight how the profit-seeking strategies of firms have unintended consequences on vulnerable communities or ethnic groups in America and New Zealand. The last case concerns long-term relationships between a company and a local milieu (San Rafael, Mexico).

Section B, "Human rights and business," concerns the relationships between firms and workers in several contexts around several issues, including workplace safety issues (Kraft in Argentina, the Bhopal tragedy in India), and human rights in the global supply chain (textile industry) and in the movie industry (The battle for Middle Earth).

Section C, "Ethics and policy," includes cases that discuss the larger question of ethics in private firms and in public organizations, including universities. These cases provide material for discussion on the blurry boundaries between the Dark Side and/or "business as usual" in the strategies and practices of business and public organizations. The *"News of the World"* case exposes the process of the moral and economic bankruptcy of one of the world's dominant newsgroups. The "Alicia in Obesity-land" case questions advertising aimed at children of specific ethnic backgrounds and its connections to the increase in obesity rates. The Olivieri case highlights the delicate balance between journalistic/research ethics and public information/good. The "Monkey business in Canada" case explores the recent ethical backdrop and erosion of the democratic process of the Halifax Regional Municipality in Canada. The "Academia accommodating plagiarism: surely not!" case reveals the well-hidden and complex problem of the institutionalization and incentivization of academic research. Finally, the "Milk or wine come rain or shine" case deals with the grey area of organizational conflict in cross-border mergers and acquisitions.

Synopsis

Section A: Community and environment

1. Shell in Ireland: a community destroyed
Sheila Kilian and Francis O'Donnell

This case deals with issues of relative power and accountability and explores the boundaries of a company's responsibilities to a community fractured by its presence.

Ireland, Shell, gas industry	Leadership, ethical decision-making Stakeholder engagement Change management

2. Of gods and demons: the sacred hills of Niyamgiri and Vedanta Aluminium Ltd (VAL)
Nimruji Jammulamadaka and Sandeep Bhattacharjee

This case analyzes how a company tries to get away with violating norms and whether Corporate Social Responsibility (CSR) handouts can be used as compensation to absolve oneself of corporate misdeeds. It also explores how a local struggle becomes potentiated with cross-national allies and eventually becomes a political issue and a part of vote-bank electoral politics.

India, indigenous people	CSR Corporate community

3. The dark side of light-handed regulation: Mercury Energy and the death of Folole Muliaga
Todd Bridgman

This case highlights the tensions between economic and social responsibilities in profit-seeking organizations operating in a capitalist system.

New Zealand, Mercury Energy	Corporate social performance Policy-making process

4. San Rafael
Emmanuel Raufflet

This case examines the political, economic, cultural, and organizational factors that affected the relationship between the village of San Rafael and an eponymous corporation, the local major employer for three eras covering a century of operations.

Latin America, pulp industry, trade union, community relations	Labor movements and policies Corporate-community relationship CSR from life cycle of firm perspective

Section B: Human rights and business

5. Kraft Foods Argentina: the H1N1 disparity
Susan Myrden and Kathy Sanderson

Through a series of incidents that involved workers' rights at an international factory belonging to a US multinational company, this case explores the effect of leadership styles, communication barriers, and the treatment of employees on individuals, families, communities, and the organization.

developing countries, multinational companies, Argentina	Leadership, espoused and enacted values, motivation, communication, organizational structure, ethics, human rights, organizational politics, conflict, negotiation, power, and employee rights

6. When clothes for children are made by children
Guillaume Delalieux

Intense competition in labor-demanding industries forces Western firms to relocate to developing countries. One such firm, DISTRI, works with the very criticized Burmese regime and adopts questionable practices in its manufacturing process. The case also presents the justification given by the firm owner for adopting such a policy.

DISTRI, CSR, textile industry, France, labor-intensive	Ethical angles of supply chain management Trade with authoritarian regimes Strategies and challenges in labor-intensive industries CSR

7. Bhopal Gas tragedy: revisited after twenty-five years
Debapratim Purkayastha and Hadiya Faheem

This case explains the sequence of events that led to the gas leak at the Union Carbide factory in Bhopal. It analyzes several cases of negligence, both corporate and government, before and after the incident concerning industrial safety, compensation, and prosecution.

Industrial safety, Bhopal Gas, relief and rehabilitation	Regulatory loopholes in emerging countries Corporate governance Liability of management versus workers Negative externality Corruption: corporate and government collusion

8. The battle for Middle Earth: New Zealand's bid to save *The Hobbit*
Todd Bridgman and Colm McLaughlin

Through the analysis of an international boycott on the filming of *The Hobbit*, this case explores the power of multinational corporations and their influence over national-level policy. It covers issues such as economic efficiency versus workers' rights and local and international workers' unions versus global capital.

New Zealand, media, policy-making process, government, labor organizations	Power Conflict theory Labor unions

Section C: Ethics and policy

9. Ethical breaches at *News of the World*
Debapratim Purkayastha and AJ Swapna

This deals with the closure of the *News of the World*, the 168-year-old UK tabloid and discusses the questionable practices common at the tabloid, which eventually led to its demise.

phone hacking, bribery, surveillance, press, News of the World, UK	Ethics theories—utilitarianism, deontological moral theory, virtue ethics, etc. White collar crimes, bribery Managing ethics internally

10. Monkey Business: the Black Eyed Peas in Halifax
Lawrence T. Corrigan and Jean Helms Mills

This explores the recent ethical backdrop and erosion of the democratic process of the Halifax Regional Municipality in Canada. Through a series of seemingly mundane decisions, the mayor and senior government officials were allowed to make unquestioned decisions that affected the city's citizens.

Canada, music industry, Black Eyed Peas, not-for-profit	Culture, groupthink, leadership and ethical decision making, bureaucracy, structure, communications and corporate social responsibility

11. Academia accommodating plagiarism? Surely not!
Belinda Luke and Kate Kearins

This examines academic ethics and leadership through the dilemmas faced by a senior lecturer when she realized her work had been plagiarized.

academia, plagiarism	Work ethics Plagiarism Author rights Power dynamics

12. Milk or wine come rain or shine: culture and politics in a Dutch–Belgian banking group after an international takeover
Alexandra Bristow

Through the journey of an intern, this case explores some of the consequences of the seemingly unstoppable drive for the internationalization of the workforce of a European banking group.

Europe (Belgium, Holland, UK), banking sector, internship	Organizational power and politics, structure, culture, power, resistance and change

13. 'Alisha in Obesity-land' Is food marketing the Mad Hatter?
Sonya A. Grier and Guillaume D. Johnson

This explores the aggregate influence of corporate marketing practices on public health through the examination of the role of target marketing strategies (here, to ethnic minority children) in the obesity epidemic of the food and beverage industries.

continued

obesity, marketing, children's market, ethnic minorities	Individual versus social responsibility Public policy Target marketing Vulnerable consumers CSR programs
14. The Olivieri case: an ethical dilemma of clinical research and corporate sponsorship *Heide Weigand and Albert J. Mills*	
This highlights the case of a protracted conflict between medical researchers and pharmaceutical companies over the ethics of clinical trials. It describes the challenges and ambiguities involved in fighting corporations over invalid scientific data.	
medical research, Canada, clinical trials, pharmaceutical industry	Theoretical aspects of ethics and bioethics Information asymmetry of consumers Policy and regulation in research-based industries

Acknowledgments

We would like to acknowledge the CMS Representatives at Large who organized the competitions from which the cases for this book were selected: Mary Godwyn, Jessica Heineman-Pieper, Marianna Fotaki, and Pauline Fatien Diochon. We would also like to thank Siddarth Mazumbar, PhD candidate at HEC Montréal, for his enthusiastic and professional assistance in this process. Last, Emmanuel Raufflet would like to thank Direction de la Recherche, HEC Montréal, for financial support.

References

Carroll, M., & Shaw, E. (2013). *Ethical maturity in the helping professions. Making difficult life and work decisions*. Philadelphia, PA: Jessica Kingsley Publishers.

Dewey, J. (1997). *How we think*. Mineola, NY: Dover Publications. (Original work published 1907).

Ghoshal, S. (2005). *Bad management theories are destroying good management practices*. Academy of Management Learning & Education, 4(1), 75–91.

Giacalone, R., & Thompson, K. (2006). Special issue on ethics and social responsibility. *Academy of Management Learning and Education*, 5(3), 261–265.

Kearins, K., & Springett, D. (2003). Educating for sustainability: Developing critical skills. *Journal of Management Education*, 27(2), 188–204.

Kjonstad, B., & Willmott, H. (1995). Business ethics: Restrictive or empowering? *Journal of Business Ethics*, 14, 445–464.

Linstead, S., Maréchal, G. & Griffin, R. (2010) Special issue of Organization Studies 31(7).

Raufflet. E., and Mills, A.J. (2009) *The Dark Side: Critical Cases on the Downside of Business*, Sheffield: Greenleaf Publishing.

Wray-Bliss, E. (2009). Ethics: Critique, ambivalence, and infinite responsibilities (unmet). In M. Alvesson, T. Bridgman, & H. Willmott (Eds.), *The Oxford handbook of critical management studies* (pp. 267–285). New York, NY: Oxford University Press.

Section A
Community and environment

1

Shell in Ireland
A community destroyed

Sheila Killian
Kemmy Business School, University of Limerick

Francis O'Donnell

This case deals with the efforts of an Irish subsidiary of Royal Dutch Shell to establish a gas refinery in a remote location in Ireland, with resistance to the project by local people and with the role of government in the dispute.

In 2001, an Irish subsidiary of Royal Dutch Shell was granted planning permission for a pipeline and refinery to develop the Corrib Gas fields off the North West coast of Ireland. Their plan was to refine the gas in a remote and beautiful location near the village of Rossport, in North Mayo. Ten years on, the community remains bitterly divided about the project, and the refinery is still not operational. Opposition to the project has been on a scale not previously seen in Ireland. In 2005, five local men, known nationally as the Rossport 5 served almost three months in prison for non-violent opposition to the development. Their struggle against the refinery has received international recognition, with one being awarded the prestigious Goldman Environmental Prize. In 2008, another retired schoolteacher spent ten days on hunger strike in opposition to the laying of the pipeline. In 2010, a local fisherman was imprisoned for his protests. Shell has been forced on a continuous basis to review its respective planning applications by the independent planning authority in Ireland as a result of appeals by local community groups and individuals.

Equally significantly, the community of Rossport has been all but destroyed by the project. Previously, this windswept line of coast was home to a rural, close-knit community, mainly farmers and fishers, where everybody was on first-name terms and doors were rarely locked at night. Now it is populated by large numbers of police and private security guards, and a regular haunt of the security correspondents of national media outlets. Parts of the beach have been fenced off from locals. Neighbours who have been friends since childhood are no longer on speaking terms, children have been withdrawn from a local school; a bitterness has been created by the project before it even becomes operational, which may take generations to heal.

The case is organised in two parts, each covering a period of some years, and culminating with some decision points on the part of the main actors. The material is laid out as follows: initially, students are provided with background information for both parts of the case, describing the place, the issues and the main actors. Phase One spans the period from 2001 to 2005, covering initial engagement with the community and culminating with the imprisonment of the Rossport 5. Phase Two runs from 2007 to early 2011, starting with the coming to power of a new government, with a Green Party minister given responsibility for the controversial development. Questions follow each section, and online resources are also supplied. A short epilogue brings students up to date, and facilitates their speculation on how the dispute will develop.

Background information

The place

Erris, County Mayo, is a remote area on the west coast of Ireland with a declining population and no industry to speak of. The largest town is Belmullet, with a population of some 1200 people. The area suffered particularly badly during the Irish famines of the 1840s, when even the limited assistance given to the starving population in other parts of the country was not always made available to the people of Erris. When Britain ruled Ireland, under the leadership of Oliver Cromwell, Irish peasants were forced away from more fertile parts of the country into the wider Connaught area including Erris, where they lived mostly as tenant farmers for absentee English landlords. An influential land-based peasant movement was instigated[1] in the area shortly after The Famine, and there is a strong folk memory of resistance to landlords and defence of the land rights in the area. This is the place that gave the world the word "Boycott", after a protest against an English landlord of that name who attempted to evict long-standing tenant farmers. The idea of land and property rights in Erris is therefore intrinsically connected to ideas of resistance to outside rule, and to the overthrowing of an external threat.

It is also a spectacularly beautiful place, and ecologically important in a European and global context. The landscape is dominated by blanket bog and is home to several unique species. The area as a whole has been designated by the EU as a Special Area of Conservation, and additional protection status has been

---

1   Michael Davitt's founding of the Land League in 1879.

awarded to some locations on the Erris peninsula under the European Birds Directive. Those areas are classified as Special Protected Areas. In part, this is also due to the troubled history of the place: it is one of the few parts of Europe which was never really industrialised.

Rossport is the village on which the dispute relating to the gas pipeline centres, and until recently, it was a tight-knit community where traditional occupations of farming and fishing predominated. Now, attitudes to the development and the protests have fractured these previously close relations. Neighbours who grew up together now pass each other on the road without speaking. Doors which were left open for hundreds of years are now locked at night. The local priest has described the situation as being similar to the divisions in Irish society caused by the Irish civil war. The area has been populated by police and private security guards. There have been complaints of police brutality during peaceful protests, a phenomenon almost unknown in Ireland where the police force is unarmed. The community has been torn apart.

The players

Royal Dutch Shell is one the largest oil and gas producers in the world, with profits of $18.6 billion in 2010. It has a history of poor environmental and community engagement, with most controversy centring on its involvement with the Ogoni people in Nigeria in the 1990s. At the time, Shell was the largest oil producer in Nigeria, working closely with the government. The indigenous Ogoni people mobilised themselves against Shell's activity on their tribal hunting lands. The government brutally suppressed anti-Shell protests by this movement, eventually executing the leader of the Ogoni people, the internationally known writer Ken Saro-Wiwa, and eight other Ogoni activists in November 1995.

The families of those executed by the Nigerian government then brought legal proceedings against Shell, accusing the company of having collaborated in the execution of Ken Saro-Wiwa and eight other community leaders opposed to its development in the area. In April 2009, Judge Kimba Wood of the U.S. District Court rejected Royal Dutch Shell's motion to dismiss the case being brought against it, and charged the company with complicity in the torture and killing of the Ogoni leaders. The case was settled out of court in April 2010, when the company paid over $15 million in settlement.

Since 1997, Shell has reported annually in relation to its business operations by way of an annual sustainability report in which it reiterates its support for the UN Global Compact and its ten principles covering areas such as human rights, labour, environment and anti-corruption. In the introduction of the 2009 sustainability report, Shell's CEO, Peter Voser, says: "Safety, environmental and social performance are now closer to the core of our business plans and decisions."[2]

---

2   http://reports.shell.com/sustainability-report/2009/servicepages/downloads/files/all_shell_sr09.pdf.

Shell is a very large organisation with a distinct and strong corporate culture. As one officer of Shell in Ireland put it: "It's a whole thing of boxes that need ticking. There's a whole load of boxes. We, Shell, are like a big civil service . . . you have to adhere to Shell law, Shell standards, Shell guidelines".[3]

Willie Corduff, who became one of the Rossport 5, has lived in Erris all his life farming the land he inherited from his father. This kind of continuity is important to Willie and to his wife Mary, who hails from a nearby village. Willie is passionate about the natural environment and the job of protecting it for future generations. He describes the peacefulness of his native place as

> food for the soul [which] must be protected for my children, for their children and for every Irish person and foreign visitor to the area . . . I want this to be here for others to enjoy as I have done and my family before me has done. Nobody has the right to destroy such beauty, not Shell, not anybody. How can our government allow this development in an area that has received maximum European environmental protection.

Willie works very hard on a small farm with his family and will never leave the area. "No amount of Shell's money will buy me as I am not for sale." The place means a lot to him. He works on the land, improving it, trying "to turn a field green that's brown, to improve it as my father did. And I like to do that, because it's the land that reared us."

His son hopes one day to take over the farm, but Willie would prefer him to leave for the city and find well-paid work. However, Willie adds:

> I cannot change his mind as he has the same love for the land and its beauty as I do. It's the love for one's place if you understand; I will die if necessary to protect this place. I have no choice. Otherwise my imprisonment and my standing up to big business and corrupt government officials will have been in vain.

Two national politicians, **Frank Fahey** and **Eamon Ryan** served at key times throughout the dispute as the Government Minister responsible for Energy, Communications and Natural resources. **Frank Fahey** is a member of Fianna Fáil, the dominant government party in Ireland over the last twenty years. He lives in Galway City, in the West of Ireland, a few hours from the Erris area. His main focus in politics is on the economy and employment, and in particular on the work of attracting multinational companies to locate in his area. He describes how the government facilitate such investment:

> The key economic driver since the 60s is bringing in international investment, particularly from the US. And in general terms the state has kind of rolled out whatever was necessary to ensure that you had the companies involved facilitated in the right way.

3 Unless otherwise indicated, all quotes are taken from interviews with one or other of the authors in the period 2007 to 2010.

In 2001, at the start of Phase One of this case, he held the key government portfolio with responsibility for the proposed Corrib development. He describes the discovery of gas as a sort of windfall:

> ...the Corrib Gas, which is something that wasn't planned, it just happened. And obviously there was great celebration . . . everybody at an official level was hugely enthusiastic about this development. There was an assumption that it was going to be greeted with great welcome in North West Mayo.

The second national political player is **Eamon Ryan**, a member of the Green Party, which was a small opposition party during Phase One of this case, but joined government at the start of Phase Two. In opposition, Mr Ryan was a strong opponent of the Corrib Gas development, and a supporter of the grassroots protest movement which became known as Shell to Sea. He attended many of their public demonstrations and marches, and issued a public statement widely carried in the national media condemning the lack of consultation with locals, and the role of Frank Fahey as minister in particular. In 2007, the Green Party joined a coalition government together with Frank Fahey's party, and Eamon Ryan was appointed as Minister for Communications, Energy and Natural Resources, the portfolio with responsibility for the Corrib Gas project.

The issue

Gas was discovered in the Corrib field 50 miles off Erris in 1996, by a British-owned company, Enterprise. In 2001, the company's Irish subsidiary was granted planning permission by the local council for an onshore refinery near the village of Rossport, in Erris, and an associated pipeline to bring ashore untreated gas at high pressure. The refinery was planned for a 400-acre site owned by the state forestry company. There was no consultation with locals prior to the granting of this permission, and it was immediately appealed. That year, Minister Frank Fahey introduced regulations empowering him to grant Compulsory Acquisition Orders (CAOs) for upstream pipelines, which was the first time in Irish history that such powers were available to a private company. In 2002, Shell acquired Enterprise, and from then on controlled the development of the gas field, refinery, and associated pipeline, all of which were contested by locals and environmental activists.

Phase One: 2001 to 2005

Permission

Willie Corduff's life and that of his family and neighbours changed one day in 2001 when agents attached to Enterprise, the company who first received planning permission to bring gas ashore, called at his door. They were holding maps of the local area showing their intended route of the pipeline. Until then, he and his family had been unaware that the pipeline would pass within metres of their house and those of their neighbours. He was shocked to see that the map showed the pipe running through his land, although no permission for this had been sought. His neighbours were similarly taken aback at the development. The agents offered compensation to the landowners, but explained that in order to maximise this, they would need to sign up within 21 days. Otherwise, they warned, the land would be compulsory purchased and the landowners would have to take whatever was offered by the company at that point. Willie describes it like this: "That's what they did in the beginning. They came, telling us what they were going to do. They never asked us at any stage for permission."[4]

This lack of consultation is confirmed by senior officers in Shell Ireland, who said "From an engineering perspective this is like just building a normal house. But, we forgot about the community. We had a simple engineering task. We were just bulldozing ahead. But we learned our lesson."

This is echoed by Frank Fahey, who as the relevant minister did not see a role for government at the time in promoting consultation: "The one thing that we didn't do was we didn't consult the people on the ground. And in actual fact the department officials didn't feel there was any necessity to do so."

The local landowners could hardly believe what was happening. Compulsory purchase orders were not unknown in Ireland, but until this time had only been available to the state, and were most commonly used in the building of motorways. The idea that an oil and gas company would have this power seemed outrageous to them. When Frank Fahey introduced these regulations, it was the first time in Irish history that a privately owned company had the power to make such purchases compulsory. Parallels were quickly drawn with powers of eviction held by landlords during famine times.

Locals also took the lack of consultation as a slight, a sign that they were held in contempt by the figures of authority. Willie Corduff sums it up as follows:

> They thought we were simple people, small farmers who were uneducated who didn't know any better. That may have been the case initially, but by god we weren't long educating ourselves about Shell . . . They asked the wrong people in the community. They asked business people, and people who they thought were important players and movers. Those people told them we would be glad to get the money. Why did they not come to us? We are the people most affected by the development. More importantly we own the land.

Shortly after Shell took over the venture, the original decision to grant planning permission was appealed to An Bord Pleanála (the Irish independent appeals board) by local residents living along the proposed route of the pipeline, on health and safety grounds. In 2002, Mr Kevin Moore, a senior inspector with

---

4   From *The Pipe*, award winning documentary. See www.thepipethefilm.com.

An Bord Pleanála, recommended refusal of planning permission on a number of grounds, memorably criticising the development as follows:

> From a strategic planning perspective, this is the wrong site; from the perspective of Government policy which seeks to foster balanced regional development, this is the wrong site; from the perspective of minimising environmental impact, this is the wrong site; and consequently, from the perspective of sustainable development, this is the wrong site.[5]

Following this appeal, in July 2002, the Committee of the Managing Directors of Shell met in private to discuss the situation. Five years later, through an unrelated court case, the minutes of this confidential meeting became public. It was revealed that the directors had pondered whether or not Shell had created enough influence within the planning departments, regulators and Irish government to deal with this setback, and that they made a plan to contact the authorities to explore their options. That September, Shell officials secured a private meeting with the then Taoiseach (Prime Minister) and three senior government ministers. Four days later they met with An Bord Pleanála, and then submitted a slightly amended planning application. In April 2004 that permission to build a pipeline was granted. In October, an appeal by local residents against this was rejected by An Bord Pleanála. Shell had their permissions, and prepared to start construction of the pipeline.

Protest and imprisonment

Despite the compulsory purchase orders, some local landowners continued to peacefully resist the development, obstructing the access of Shell workers to their land. In 2005, Shell issued legal proceedings against some Rossport landowners including Willie Corduff, compelling them to cooperate with the development. They refused. In April of that year, Shell secured a temporary order from the courts prohibiting any interference with the laying of the pipeline. In June, five local landowners were found to be in contempt of the order, and were imprisoned. They could only be released if they gave an undertaking to allow the pipeline to go ahead.

The imprisonment of peaceful protestors for defending their land rights struck a chord with the public, and the men became known nationally as the Rossport 5. A grassroots campaign quickly developed in support of the men under the loose banner Shell to Sea, demanding their release and also campaigning for the refinery to be moved offshore so that the controversial pipeline did not run through the village of Rossport. A conscious decision was taken not to structure the Shell to Sea group in a formal or hierarchical way, as it was thought that a loose network would allow all participants to choose the level of their own involvement.[6] Three months later, in the face of a massive public

---

5   An Bord Pleanála's Inspectors report No 1 (126/R126073) 2002.
6   For a discussion on this, see *Our Story, the Rossport 5*, edited by Mark Garavan, Small World Media, 2006.

reaction, Shell changed its mind and dropped the injunction against the five men. They were released to a heroes' welcome, and the experience had left them more determined than ever to resist the development. One of the men, Micheál Ó'Seighin, said:

> I know this area will be destroyed if Shell's project comes through. The future of this area will be gone. I don't make any distinction between area and people or between people and environment . . . There is continuity here from the Bronze Age or even earlier. To see that continuity destroyed . . . it affects me . . . for something so trivial as more money for already rich people.[7]

Frank Fahey, no longer in office at the time of the imprisonment of the Rossport 5, later commented:

> The fatal mistake by Shell was just to go put the guys in jail, and then that changed the whole thing. Then it became a question of martyrdom and obviously the whole thing became hugely emotional, with massive support for the idea of guys being put in jail for standing up for their rights and whatnot. In hindsight that was all a great mistake.

Questions on Phase One

1. What errors did Shell make in their initial community engagement?
2. What could/should political leaders have done differently?
3. What is the impact of the local culture and history on the dispute?
4. What can this case so far tell us about the nature of leadership?
5. What aspects of this case address the concept of accountability?

Phase Two: 2007 to 2011

A new beginning?

In 2007, following a general election that produced a coalition government, Eamon Ryan of the Green Party became Minister for Communications, Energy and Natural Resources. The most controversial issue on his desk remained the Corrib Gas project. Prior to entering government, he had campaigned on the streets on this issue, most famously posing for a photograph in front of the national parliament holding a Green Party placard reading "Support Rossport

---

7 Source: *Our Story, the Rossport 5*, edited by Mark Garavan, Small World Media, 2006.

Five". His outlook on the environment was very different to his predecessor, and his previous involvement with the protests led many to believe he would be well placed to relate to all the parties to the dispute.

The situation had not moved closer to resolution since 2005. In the immediate aftermath of the release of the Rossport 5, the Irish government appointed a well-known Dublin-based trade union figure, Peter Cassells, to mediate between the parties to the dispute. At that time, however, the protestors had become radicalised by the imprisonment of the Rossport 5, and were distrustful of the mediation process. After seven months of discussions, Mr Cassells reported that no agreement could be reached between the parties. The Irish government next commissioned an independent review of safety associated with the project from a UK company, British Pipeline Agency (BPA). It later emerged that the firm was part-owned by Shell, further undermining the faith locals held in both Shell and the Irish government. Following this controversy, the government then commissioned a new independent appraisal of BPA's report. The reporting firm, Advantica, recommended key changes to the planned pipeline, including a reduction in the gas pressure and its relocation to at least 140 m from the nearest houses. Shell and the government accepted Advantica's recommendations, but local residents were not satisfied with the Advantica report, saying the terms of reference were too narrow. They commissioned their own research, using a firm called Accufacts, which was critical of the proposed pipeline, highlighting a number of locations worldwide where similar pipes had ruptured with loss of life.

Before the 2007 election, the Green Party had campaigned on a policy of seeking a full independent review of the Corrib project. However, this was not included in the programme for government they helped to shape in coalition. Eamon Ryan visited the Rossport 5 shortly after his appointment as the Minister for Communications, Energy and Natural Resources. Local activists were somewhat disappointed in his visit. As one of the Rossport 5 put it:

> In August 2007, Eamon Ryan came here shortly after he was appointed
> as Minister for Communication, Energy and Natural Resources. I got
> the impression that the purpose of his visit was to gauge if our position
> had altered or if our determination had weakened in any way.

Later in 2007, Eamon Ryan and another government minister convened a forum in the Rossport area to address issues around the development. Ironically, there was no community consultation in the formation of the forum, and as its terms of reference excluded revisiting any planning issues, it was boycotted by many of the locals including the leaders of the Shell to Sea movement.

The battle for hearts and minds

By now, the Shell to Sea movement had gained international support. The case was highlighted at the World Social Forum in Nairobi in 2006, and in 2007, Willie Corduff received the prestigious Goldman Environmental Prize for environmental activism. Messages of support poured in from all over the world, including from

Archbishop Tutu of South Africa, and Ogoni leaders from Nigeria. In response to their support, the Shell to Sea movement erected a set of crosses bearing the names of those executed by the Nigerian Government outside the gates of the proposed refinery outside Rossport.

In response, Shell launched a series of high-profile CSR developments. In 2009, they had seven to ten full-time community liaison officers working in the relatively small area of Erris, engaged, as a Shell official put it in: "literally out walking, talking, every club, every women's group, every children's group, everything in the community, the landowners, everybody continuously".

The grants made were small by reference to the profitability of Shell, but enormous in the context of Erris, a small community with little employment outside of fishing and farming. For example, the community investment programmes include grants for third level education, for which there is considerable competition at the local school. The development fund made a grant of €200,000 to a local voluntary sports club, enabling it to redevelop its facilities. This would have been a near-impossible sum to raise locally without the money from Shell. The Royal National Lifeboat Institution (RNLI) based locally also received funding of €200,000.

The fact that these local groups would even accept a donation from Shell was seen by the company as representing success in terms of their CSR efforts. One company official put it like this:

> If we go back to 2005 when the guys were in prison, I mean people wouldn't even talk to us never mind take a donation for a local club. So it actually shows how we have actually—not completely and we will never probably completely turn the tide—but we definitely have turned the corner on this in my view.

Perhaps as a result of these donations, some of the local people ended their opposition to development. Despite the previous closeness of the community, this became the breaking point in community relations. Neighbours who had known each other since childhood stopped speaking because of their different reactions to Shell's CSR campaign. Some parents withdrew their children from a local school which was sponsored by the company. New community groups were formed, such as Pro Gas Erris, comprising a group of business people who were supportive of the refinery, emphasising the need for economic development in the area. Other groups emerged from the banner of Shell to Sea with slightly different perspectives. In particular, Pobal Chill Chomáin (People of Kilcommon) and Pobal Le Chéile (People Together) both came out as opposing the refinery and the pipeline route, but supporting a new compromise proposal which came from local church leaders.

The Glinsk proposal

In this part of Ireland the population is overwhelmingly Catholic, and the church plays a pivotal role in guiding public thought. In 2007 three local priests wrote to Eamon Ryan as the key government minister dealing with the dispute. They suggested rerouting the controversial pipeline away from the village of Rossport by relocating the refinery to the unpopulated area of Glinsk. This proposal was supported by most of the local population, and was seen as a viable compromise which would allow the development to proceed without impacting on the local population. Both Pobal Chill Chomáin and Pobal Le Chéile were in favour of it, while Shell to Sea remained adamant that the refinery could only be located offshore. Eamon Ryan did not respond to the suggestion, and Shell never really engaged with the Glinsk proposal. As a company official said in 2008: "I mean the terminal is 70% complete now as well, so it's not going to move at this stage. To be brutally honest it's not going to move at this stage."

Ongoing opposition

Opposition to the development continues to polarise the community. Maura Harrington is a retired local schoolteacher, and an important influence in the Shell to Sea group. In 2008, when Shell brought their vessel *The Solitaire* into Broadhaven Bay to lay the offshore section of the pipeline, she went on public hunger strike in a location beside the beach, only calling off her protest when *The Solitaire* left Irish waters for repairs. Pat O'Donnell is a local commercial fisherman who has fished in Broad Haven bay since childhood. He is seen as a local leader, nicknamed "The Chief". He actively campaigned against the laying of the gas pipe by *The Solitaire* across his traditional fishing grounds, and in 2009 was imprisoned for seven months for allegedly obstructing the police and breaching the peace. When Willie Corduff was assaulted by masked men while protesting the development, suspicion fell on the large number of private security personnel employed by Shell in the area. A 2010 report by the human rights group, Frontline, recommended that this incident be reinvestigated by local police. Minister Eamon Ryan welcomed this report without responding to its contents, noting to a national newspaper: "Independent oversight is always welcome, and we take this report seriously. The more neutral observers the better, if this helps to give people confidence."[8]

As Ireland entered recession in late 2008 and 2009, many groups campaigning on the issue and some who were previously uninvolved have called on Eamon Ryan to revisit the original terms under which the Corrib partners led by Shell were granted their exploration licence. In particular, the fact that the Irish state takes no royalties from gas from the Corrib field became a source of controversy. Speaking to the state radio station in July 2000, Eamon Ryan agreed that the terms were unusual: "Yes, I thought that we were too cheap, that the terms were too favourable."[9]

However, he ruled out changing the terms, explaining to a national newspaper that:

8 The *Irish Times*, Thursday, April 29, 2010, Lorna Siggins.
9 Radio interview on RTE, July 1, 2009.

What we didn't want to do and what the State is reluctant to, particularly when you're dealing with corporation tax, is to start changing deals that you've already done. If we started shifting our tax rates all over the place, particularly on projects already signed and projects that have already been agreed, it would have a reputational damage for the State.[10]

In early 2011 the Irish National Trust (An Taisce) called on Minister Ryan and his Green Party colleague Minister for the Environment, John Gormley, to delay the granting of the foreshore licences for the final stages of the development in order to allow it to carry out a full review. This request was not granted.

Questions from Phase Two

1. How best could Shell have responded to the publicity garnered by the Rossport 5?

2. Could the CSR strategy which was intensified in 2006 have been done differently so as to minimise the divisions within the community?

3. What might government have done differently?

4. What future do you see for this dispute?

5. What, if anything, does Shell seem to have learned from its involvement in this dispute?

Epilogue

In January 2011 the offshore pipe was laid, and the final section of the onshore pipeline leading to the refinery in its original location received planning permission from An Bord Pleanála. Another planning body, An Taisce, is at the time of writing pursuing a judicial review on points of law pertaining to An Bord Pleanála's decision. That review will focus on areas surrounding national and European law.

At a general election in Ireland at the end of February 2011, Frank Fahey lost the parliament seat which he had held since 1997. Eamon Ryan also lost his seat, as did every one of the Green Party's six members of parliament. The Green Party now has no representation in the Irish parliament.

---

10   The *Irish Examiner*, Thursday, July 02, 2009, Juno McEnroe.

About the authors

Dr **Sheila Killian** is the Assistant Dean of Research at the Kemmy Business School, University of Limerick, Ireland. Prior to joining the KBS she worked as a tax advisor with Ernst & Young, KPMG and Arthur Andersen & Co., in the aviation finance industry as a leasing analyst, and as a programmer in both the educational software and industrial sectors. More recently, she taught at the University of the Witwatersrand in Johannesburg, Rhodes University in Grahamstown, South Africa, and Helsinki School of Economics in Mikkeli, Finland. Sheila has a primary degree in mathematics, a master's degree in business studies and a PhD in taxation. She qualified as a chartered accountant in 1992 (national prizewinner in the final admitting exams) and as an associate of the Institute of Taxation in Ireland in 1989. She has published widely in academic journals, and is the author of *Corporate Social Responsibility: A Guide with Irish Experiences* (Chartered Accoutnants Publishing, 2012).

Francis O'Donnell is an ecologist and business graduate from the Republic of Ireland. His current area of interest is the development of corporate social responsibility (CSR). He considers culture a serious impediment to CSR's potential to reduce social and environmental conflict in an Irish context. His first book, *Corporate Social Responsibility and Shell in Ireland: A Thin Veneer* (Cambridge Scholars Publishing, 2011) evaluates Shell's stated commitments to society and the environment in Ireland. It also explores how weak regulation and political facilitation may have influenced Shell to act as poor corporate citizens there. The book deals with issues of relative power and accountability, and explores the boundaries of a company s responsibilities to a community fractured by its presence.

Teaching notes for this case are available from Greenleaf Publishing. These are free of charge and available only to teaching staff. They can be requested by going to:
www.greenleaf-publishing.com/darkside2notes

2

Of gods and demons[1]
The sacred hills of Niyamgiri and Vedanta Aluminium Ltd (VAL)

Nimruji Jammulamadaka
Indian Institute of Management Calcutta (IIMC)

Sandeep Bhattacharjee
Usha Martin Academy, India

The case recounts the ongoing conflict between Vedanta Aluminium Ltd (VAL) in Niyamgiri, Orissa, and the indigenous people and environmentalists over the mining and refining of aluminium in India. VAL is a subsidiary of FTSE listed Vedanta Resources Plc. The company acquired a license for mining alumina from the state owned Orissa Mining Corporation and began work on the project that would make it the largest integrated producer of aluminium. Since the very beginning, this project has faced stiff resistance from the endangered indigenous tribes of the area and the environmentalists for its adverse impact. The case depicts the several ups and downs of both the company and the resistance movement and the methods employed by each of them during the decade-old struggle that has been fought over continents and is now a very charged political issue in the country. The case also illustrates the manner in which the state and political leadership work, at times supporting the people and at times the corporate interests.

---

1 A version of this case appeared as "Smart Strategy or Great Tragedy? Vedanta Alumina and the Dongria Kondhs" by Nimruji Jammulamadaka, *Journal of Business Ethics Education* 9 (2012), pp. 431-446.

A March 17th 2010 editorial in the highly influential newspaper *Economic Times* ran:

> In the long-term interest of internal security, survival of an endangered
> primitive tribe and justice and fairness, the government should withhold
> clearance to the bauxite mining project spread over Orissa's Kalahandi
> (South) and Rayagada forest divisions, proposed by minerals major
> Vedanta . . . India can progress with some of its bauxite continuing to lie
> underground for some more time. India cannot progress with a growing
> internal security threat, fed by the state's failure to live up to its commit-
> ment to the common people.[2]

The editorial seemed to be echoing popular public sentiment against his company's operations, and troubles for Anil Agarwal, the czar of Sterlite Industries
that owned Vedanta Aluminium Ltd (VAL), seemed far from over. The respite
given by a Supreme Court order that permitted VAL to proceed with its bauxite
mining and refining project provided it plowed back at least 5% of it profits for
conservation and tribal welfare[3] appeared to be just that, a respite, a temporary
one at best. The resentment had its genesis almost 15 years ago when Sterlite
Industries signed a lease agreement with state-owned Orissa Mining Corporation (OMC) for building an aluminium refinery at Lanjigarh, Orissa;[4] and, with a
quickening in the pace of the project, this resentment only seemed to be getting
louder and more vociferous and universal.

The tribals of remote Niyamgiri had found comrades in arms all across the
globe and investors were getting wary of Vedanta. The Norwegian Pension Fund
had boycotted Vedanta in 2007;[5] in February 2010, the Church of England sold
of its shares worth £3.8m saying "we are not satisfied that Vedanta has shown,
or is likely in future to show, the level of respect for human rights and local
communities that we expect".[6] Over the next few days The Joseph Rowntree
Charitable Trust had sold its £1.9m stock. Susan Seymour, chair of the Trust
said, "the behaviour may be legal but it is morally indefensible".[7]

Sterlite Industries

VAL is a subsidiary of Vedanta Resources Plc. and Sterlite Industries (also held
by Vedanta Plc.) (Exhibits 1 and 2). Vedanta Plc. headquartered in London and

2 http://economictimes.indiatimes.com/Opinion/Stop-the-Vedanta-Project-in-Orissa/article-
   show/5692364.cms

3 http://www.orissalinks.com/orissagrowth/topics/court-judgements

4 http://www.amnesty.org/en/library/asset/ASA20/001/2010/en/0a81a1bc-f50c-4426-9505-
   7fde6b3382ed/asa200012010en.pdf

5 http://www.bloomberg.com/apps/news?pid=newsarchive&sid=aBuTgWgXKuCU&refer=in
   dia

6 http://www.guardian.co.uk/business/2010/feb/05/vedanta-niyamgiri-orissa-church-of-england

7 http://online.wsj.com/article/SB10001424052748703315004575073580361583678.html

listed on the LSE in the FTSE 100, has its extraction and refining operations in aluminium, copper, zinc, iron ore and lead in India, Zambia and Australia. Vedanta is India's largest non-ferrous metals and alloys company.[8]

Sterlite Industries, owned by non-resident Indian businessman Anil Agarwal began its existence in the late 1980s as a firm supplying copper cables for telecom companies in India. Soon, it moved into the non-ferrous metals space and acquired properties for processing and refining these metal ores at several places in India. In 1994, it imported a decommissioned copper smelter from Australia and began operating it in Tuticorin much to the chagrin of environmentalists and the State Pollution Control Board.[9]

Over the years, amongst the several businesses acquired by Sterlite was the state owned Bharat Aluminium Company (BALCO) in 2001. By 2002, Sterlite was controlling about half of (42%) of India's copper market, 21% of aluminium output and a staggering 62% of zinc production.[10] In early 2001, Sterlite rechristened itself as Vedanta Resources Plc. It soon got on board Brian Gilbertson as the chair of Vedanta. Gilbertson had engineered the Billiton-BHP merger and was quite a well known figure in the mining industry. While the Agarwal family held 54% of the stake in Vedanta Resources through Volcan Investments Ltd., it offered the remaining to the public on the London Stock Exchange in December 2003. It was the second biggest offer that year and the first for an Indian company. The *Financial Times* observed that Vedanta would fill the gap between the big three—BHPBilliton, Rio Tinto, Anglo American—and smaller companies which exploit a single commodity.[11]

Gilbertson, a lifelong minerals man, brought much needed exposure and recognition to Vedanta across the globe. Soon after joining, in November 2003, he observed:

> To be quite honest, I had never thought of India as a resource country at all ... I went along and found to my surprise that there is actually a great deal happening ... the country is very rich in resources. For example, it's the sixth-largest reserve in the world of bauxite. And then it also has the fourth- or fifth- largest reserves of iron ore in the world and those two commodities ... are kind of like the holy grail of mining at this time, because the markets have been so strong for the past two or three years.[12]

He was excited by the prospect of utilizing a highly educated workforce for a fraction of the Westerner's wages. Agarwal and Gilbertson (who left the company in 2004) set in motion a US\$ 2b plan to "expand current operations ... and develop a portfolio of attractive greenfield projects".[13]

8 http://www.vedantaresources.com/who-we-are.aspx
9 http://www.indiaresource.org/issues/globalization/2005/RavagesThroughIndia28.pdf
10 http://www.indiaresource.org/issues/globalization/2005/RavagesThroughIndia28.pdf
11 http://www.indiaresource.org/issues/globalization/2005/RavagesThroughIndia28.pdf
12 http://www.indiaresource.org/issues/globalization/2005/RavagesThroughIndia28.pdf
13 http://www.indiaresource.org/issues/globalization/2005/RavagesThroughIndia28.pdf

Like any other ambitious concern, they saw the opportunity in India and aluminium. The Indian government's growing ease with privatization and disinvestment only made the process so much more enticing.

Bauxite and aluminium prospects

Aluminium is produced from bauxite ore. 3 tonnes of bauxite produces 1 tonne of alumina, an intermediate; 2 tonnes of alumina produces 1 tonne of aluminium.[14] In 2000–01, known global reserves of bauxite were 23 million MT with an estimated reserve base of 32 million MT (Exhibit 3). Of this India had the fifth largest reserve where only about 7000 MT had been mined out of a known reserve of 770,000 MT. The costs of aluminum production also dropped significantly during the decade of the nineties and Asia had one of the lowest costs of production. India's cost appeared to be lesser than that of China (Exhibit 4).

The demand for aluminium, which is used in a variety of applications like power transmission and distribution, aircraft and space craft manufacture, kitchenware, architectural fittings, grain silos, industrial explosives and automobiles, was only expected to go up dramatically with increasing economic growth. Demand for aluminium globally had been projected to grow strongly at a compound rate of 5.7% between 2007 and 2020 according to Brook Hunt, with India and China projected to grow at 8.2% and 9.7%, respectively in the same period.[15]

Bauxite and aluminium prospects in India

It had been estimated in 1999–2000 that the reserves of high grade bauxite in India are to the tune of 3.037 million MT (proved + probable + possible). Of this, recoverable reserves had been placed at 2.5 million MT with proved and probable being 1.2 million MT. These reserves were expected to last for over 350 years at an anticipated consumption rate of 7 million tonnes per year. The most interesting opportunity lay in the fact that while reserves accounted for 7.5% of global deposits, production capacity was only 3%.[16] The installed capacity for alumina and aluminium production in India as of 1999–2000 are given in Exhibit 5. While Bauxite deposits are found in Orissa, Andhra Pradesh, Madhya Pradesh, Gujarat, Maharashtra and Bihar, major resources are concentrated in the East Coast Bauxite deposits of Orissa and

14 http://mines.nic.in/archp5.html
15 http://www.vedantaresources.com/uploads/vedantaar2008.pdf
16 http://mines.nic.in/archp5.html

Andhra Pradesh.[17] Deposits in Orissa were estimated to be to the tune of 1.5 million MT.[18]

Vedanta's plans

Vedanta planned on seizing this opportunity by leveraging its Indian connections and emerging as a leader in aluminium. Their plans were to reach 2500 ktpa of refining capacity by 2013. Vedanta focused on Orissa to tap into the rich bauxite deposits (named as Khondalite after the local Kondh tribes) of Niyamgiri Hills. The top of Niyamgiri Hills was shown to contain very rich deposits of bauxite. In fact, the very low over-burden (unwanted soil, rock and clay that covers the ore) was believed to significantly reduce the cost of production from the open-cast mine.[19] (This implied mining the mountain top; removing the entire top soil and vegetation to gain access to the ore beneath, an environmentally unsound and discouraged practice.) It aimed at setting up a 1.4 mtpa greenfield alumina refinery project with an associated 90 MW captive power plant, at Lanjigarh in Kalahandi district along with another greenfield 500,000 tpa aluminium smelter (in two phases of 250,000 tpa each), together with an associated 1,215 MW captive power plant, in Jharsuguda again in Orissa. It had planned on commissioning these projects by 2007 (Exhibit 6). The company also noted that the vast coal reserves of Orissa (about 62 billion tonnes in Orissa alone) would also lead to significant savings in costs of power generation for the project.[20]

The whole project would make Vedanta the largest integrated aluminium producer—right from mining, to extraction of alumina and its purification to aluminium along with captive power generation, catapulting it into the big league. While it was engaged in all three phases in the existing BALCO and Madras Aluminium Company (MALCO), the scale of operations was small compared to what was now planned. BALCO was operating mines in Chattisgarh that produced about 565,300 tpa of bauxite in 2005–06 and MALCO had a refinery capacity of 80,000 tpa of alumina and a smelter of 40,000 tpa of aluminium.[21]

In pursuance of its plans, it obtained mining leases from the state-owned Orissa Minining Corporation (Constitution of India prohibits sale of tribal land to non-tribals) for setting up a 1.4 million tpa alumina refining plant at Lanjigarh and mining bauxite from the neighboring Niyamgiri Hills for the next 25 years.

17 http://www.geologydata.info/bauxite_deposits.htm
18 http://www.freewebs.com/epgorissa/MIUpdate/StatusPaperonMiningLeases.pdf
19 http://www.sterlite-industries.com/investor_relations/PDFs/Investors_Visit_Presentation_
    Lanjigarh_mar09.pdf
20 http://www.sterlite-industries.com/investor_relations/PDFs/Investors_Visit_Presentation_
    Lanjigarh_mar09.pdf
21 http://www.indiaresource.org/issues/globalization/2005/RavagesThroughIndia28.pdf

Its agreement compelled the Orissa state government to provide Vedanta with bauxite mines with reserves of at least 150 million tonnes.[22] Vedanta's estimates showed that within a 60 km radius of Lanjigarh, there were deposits of 900 MT of bauxite.

Conflict begins

Controversy was not new for either Anil Agarwal or Vedanta. From the days when it began operations with a second-hand decommissioned smelter in Tuticorin, Vedanta often found itself on the wrong side of law on various fronts—whether insider trading, political corruption, labour disputes, environmental damage, violations of permissions or non-compliance of pollution and forest laws. Almost each of its operations in India and abroad seemed to have a history of malfeasance.[23] The experience in Orissa, though, was quite different. This was unprecedented.

Facets of opposition

Niyamgiri Hills was home to an endangered tribe, the Dongria-Kondhs, who had a population of less than 6000. The tribe believed the mountain top to be the abode of its patron deity, Niyam Raja. The proposed mine meant that the mountain top would have to be destroyed and the tribe did not want their religious beliefs to be desecrated. Accordingly they opposed the project.

The company had initially signed the lease with Orissa Mining Corporation in April 1997, but this was quickly followed by the landmark *Samata* judgment by the Supreme Court of India in July 1997 which upheld the rights of tribals over their land. The judgment prohibited the transfer of such land known as Scheduled Area by way of lease for mining and other purposes to non-tribals. The judgment effectively annulled the lease.[24]

In early 2002, the government of Orissa took the view that it was not bound by the *Samata* judgment as it pertained to another state and went ahead with the lease for Lanjigarh-Niyamgiri Hills. It was widely believed that Anil Agarwal's political connections were instrumental for the transformations.[25]

The government estimated that 12 villages would be negatively impacted by the project, sixty families would need to be "relocated" and five times as many would be adversely affected by land acquisition. In July 2002, land acquisition was started for the Lanjigarh refinery. The district collector of Kalahandi

22 http://www.metalworld.co.in/newsletter/2013/jan/infocus1-0113.pdf
23 http://www.indiaresource.org/issues/globalization/2005/RavagesThroughIndia28.pdf
24 http://www.mynews.in/Blog/Vedanta_rebuts_Amnesty_report_on_mining_project_impact_B558.html
25 http://www.indiaresource.org/issues/globalization/2005/RavagesThroughIndia28.pdf

wherein lay Lanjigarh and Niyamgiri Hills served a notice for land acquisition on June 6, 2002 and 'invited' the community to register their opinions/complaints. On June 22nd, nearly 1000 people assembled at the Revenue office and submitted a memorandum opposing the project. Two hundred other protest petitions were also filed. In neighbouring Batelima, the villagers called for cancellation of the project. Several visits by government officials to convince the population to accept compensation and hand over land were largely fruitless. The villagers had earlier successfully resisted corporate plans to trespass on another deposit at neighbouring Kashipur and drew their strength from this experience. There was also a section of the population, predominantly of non-tribals and local elite that favoured the project in the hope that it would bring growth, employment and development to the poverty stricken region.[26]

Quickening pace

Meanwhile Vedanta continued its work at a rapid pace. A rapid environment impact assessment that it had commissioned in 2002 was ready by early 2003 and it began seeking environmental clearances. The rapid environment impact assessment was commissioned by Vedanta for acquiring land, using water from the Vamsadhara river and dumping overburden and wastes. Along with this, it continued work at the site, acquiring land for the project's road, air strip and railroad and construction of the refinery. In some cases land was acquired after serving encroachment and eviction notices on Kandha tribals who had been cultivating the said land for generations. In October 2003 it obtained permission from the state government for drawing 30,000 cu.mts of water per day from the River Tel. Vedanta secured environmental clearance in September 2004 and it stated that the project did not involve any diversion of forest land. But of the (723.343 ha + 721.323 ha) land required for the project, applications for the diversion of 58.943 ha and 672.018 ha of forest land were still pending with the ministry. However, it circumvented the problem by projecting the mining and refining phases as delinked projects instead of an integrated one.[27] On 5 October 2004, Vedanta signed a renewed lease agreement with Orissa Mining Corporation for setting up an integrated aluminium project at Lanjigarh.[28]

In line with its corporate approach, Vedanta also started CSR activities at Lanjigarh during the period. From the project's inception in 2004 until 2008, Vedanta's CSR interventions were spread over 53 villages in Lanjigarh block and they had resettled 118 families from three villages in the area. Their interventions involved providing skill training to youth and employment with the company, child care centers with mid-day meal facility, primary health care and vaccination support and support for enhancing local civic infrastructure

26 http://www.indiaresource.org/issues/globalization/2005/RavagesThroughIndia28.pdf
27 http://kashipursolidarity.tripod.com/id4.html
28 http://www.mynews.in/Blog/Vedanta_rebuts_Amnesty_report_on_mining_project_impact_B558.html

and agriculture.[29] All these activities, though, did nothing to pacify the anger of the tribals.

While Vedanta was busy implementing the plans from the drawing board, the community too was vociferously protesting. In 2002 they set up an organisation called Niyamgiri Suraksha Samiti. Lingaraj Azad, a local leader of the protest, was arrested in April 2003 but public siege by 250 unarmed men, women and children led to his release. The returning protestors were attacked and their houses and belongings destroyed by goons who they alleged belonged to Vedanta. In June 2003, they damaged the project's foundation stone.[30]

The project faced opposition from not only the local tribals but also several environmentalists. Niyamgiri Hills was declared as a wild life sanctuary in December 1998. It was part of an elephant corridor and home to several exotic species of animals like sambhars, leopards, tigers, barking deer and others, many of whom were on the endangered species list. Its lush forest cover (75% of the land was covered by forests with an average density of 0.6) were the genetic repository of over 300 species. Six of these species were listed in the IUCN Red Data book on endangered species. The Hills, which had an altitude of over 4000 feet, were also the source of several perennial streams and the Nagavalli and Vamshadhara rivers that provided water to South Orissa and north Andhra Pradesh. The special properties of the bauxite laden soil enabled it to retain moisture and provide water to the rivers even during the lean summer months. Environmentalists feared that the destruction of the Hills for the mines would not only destroy the flora and fauna of the region but also irreparably damage the water system of the entire region, not to mention the damage caused by pollution.[31]

The protests gathered steam and in late 2004, three activists, Biswajeet Mohanty of Wildlife Society of Orissa, Prafulla Samantara of Lok Shakti Abhiyan and Academy of Mountain Environics, approached the Supreme Court stating that the project violated the provisions of Schedule V of the Indian Constitution, the *Samata* judgment and the country's forest and environment laws. The Supreme Court began hearings in November 2004 and constituted a Central Empowered Committee (CEC) to investigate the matter and advice the Court.[32]

Protest gathers support

Niyamgiri Suraksha Samiti's cause soon found support among various local and international agencies. Green Kalahandi, a local environmental group supported them and paved the way for greater exposure to the issue.[33] Massive efforts were launched by civil society to build public opinion against the abuse of human rights of the tribals and the environmental impact of the project. There

29   http://www.vedanta.co.in/uploads/sdr2008.pdf
30   http://www.indiaresource.org/issues/globalization/2005/RavagesThroughIndia28.pdf;
       http://www.actionaid.org.uk/doc_lib/vedanta_report.pdf
31   http://kashipursolidarity.tripod.com/id4.html
32   http://kashipursolidarity.tripod.com/id4.html
33   http://www.boloji.com/analysis2/0173.htm

were several signature campaigns aimed at the President and Prime Minister of India. International agencies like Amnesty International, Green Peace, Action Aid and Human Rights Foundation got involved with the protestors. The international agencies not only wrote to the Indian government asking it to stop the project, but were actively engaged in persuading investors to back out of Vedanta. ActionAid and Bianca Jagger of World Future Council were particularly focusing on the human rights violations.[34]

While the CEC continued to investigate the allegations, the Orissa Mining Corporation commissioned another EIA. The Ministry of Environment and Forests ordered Vedanta to stop construction at the site in May 2005. Vedanta withdrew its application for diversion of forest land and went back with a revised EIA on the refinery in September 2005.[35] Independent reports by the Wildlife Institute of India and the Central Mine Planning and Design Institute presented a damaging picture of the consequences of the project. Several other independent reports by national and international agencies continued to indict VAL's Lanjigarh project. They simultaneously highlighted the various environmental and human rights violations like mountain-top mining, forcible eviction, lack of safety and compensation at Vedanta's other operations like MALCO in India and abroad in Zambia and Armenia.[36]

Supreme Court orders stay of work

At Vedanta, though, business continued during 2006 to 2008, construction continued, trials were completed and production had begun (see Exhibit 7 for share price performance). Lanjigarh refinery had begun production from a single stream and produced 267,000 tonnes; it was expected to stabilize by end of fiscal 2009. In October 2007, Vedanta applied for clearance for expanding the refining capacity by six times and continued work for this expansion. Phase I of Jahrsuguda smelter too was commissioned one year ahead of schedule in May 2008. The entire project was expected to be online by end of 2010.[37]

The CEC report which came out in February 2007 lambasted both Vedanta and the Ministry of Environment and Forests. The report found several counts of wrong doing by Vedanta, including concealment of forest land use, forcible acquisition of land, lack of compensation, dumping of toxic wastes along Vamsadhara river, violation of stop orders and construction of project without due permissions. It also noted that the project had severe environmental and human consequences and should not be pursued.[38] Orissa Pollution Control Board's periodic testing of water, air and soil samples in the vicinity showed alarming

34 http://www.outlookindia.com/article.aspx?264249
35 http://www.amnesty.org/en/library/asset/ASA20/001/2010/en/0a81a1bc-f50c-4426-9505-7fde6b3382ed/asa200012010en.pdf
36 http://www.indiaresource.org/issues/globalization/2005/RavagesThroughIndia28.pdf
37 http://www.vedantaresources.com/uploads/vedantaar2008.pdf
38 http://kashipursolidarity.tripod.com/id4.html

rates of pollution and confirmed the community's protests.[39] The Supreme Court ordered a stay on mining operations in November 2007.[40]

The protestors saw the stay as a victory and continued their campaign. The international campaign was also gaining momentum. The Norwegian pension fund, the largest sovereign investment fund, started taking note of Niyamgiri and was considering pulling out of Vedanta.[41] The British government and press too found Vedanta to be at fault.[42] The Government of India also enacted an enabling legislation, The Scheduled Tribes and Other Traditional Forest Dwellers (Recognition of Forest Rights) Act, which came into effect from January 2008. The Act recognized the community's right to the common property resources and managing them.[43]

This Vedanta case before the Supreme Court was not an isolated one. There were several complaints from Orissa itself, for example, against the South Korean major company POSCO dealing with land acquisition for mining/industrialisation and its consequences. All of these were particularly pitched as struggles between development interests and unrelenting tribals. The Court therefore decided to a take a long-term view.

In its judgment in August 2008, the Supreme Court observed that it was true that the region was extremely backward and belonged to the tribals and that the project also had adverse consequences but it felt that development was necessary and therefore it permitted Vedanta to go ahead with the project subject to the condition that Vedanta would have to give money for forest destruction, wildlife management and tribal development totaling around $180 million. Other conditions included handing over 5% of pre-tax profits annually from its mining projects across India to the Orissa government. Vedanta would also have to set up a 'special purpose vehicle' to ensure that environmental regulations were met, the court said.[44]

Work resumes: Vedanta's renewed CSR

After the court judgment, Vedanta received a shot in the arm and went ahead full steam with its expansion plans. By April 2009, it had also received an "in principle" approval from Union Ministry of Environment and Forests (MOEF).[45] It now planned to increase the project's capacity to 3 mtpa.

After the judgment, VAL scaled up its CSR interventions (Exhibit 8). It constituted a special CSR Board for VAL, Lanjigarh, and also set about creating a

39 http://www.amnesty.org/en/library/asset/ASA20/001/2010/en/0a81a1bc-f50c-4426-9505-7fde6 b3382ed/asa200012010en.pdf
40 http://www.amnesty.org/en/library/asset/ASA20/001/2010/en/0a81a1bc-f50c-4426-9505-7fde6 b3382ed/asa200012010en.pdf
41 http://www.guardian.co.uk/commentisfree/2010/feb/18/vedanta-mining-battle-plans
42 http://ibnlive.in.com/news/investor-sells-vedanta-shares-over-human-rights-violations/110335-7 .html?from=rssfeed
43 http://fra.org.in/
44 http://www.orissalinks.com/orissagrowth/topics/court-judgements
45 http://kalahandia.blogspot.com/2007_11_01_archive.html

Special Purpose Vehicle for developing the area.[46] The CSR programmes it hitherto carried out through its in-house staff and associate "Vedanta Foundation" also became more focused on the Dongria-Kondhs and Kutia Kondhs tribes' needs.[47] These tribes were affected by the project. It named the Special Purpose Vehicle (SPV) as Lanjigarh Project Area Development Foundation (LPADF), and formed it jointly with the Orissa government, Sterlite Industries India Ltd (SIIL) and Orissa Mining Corporation (OMC) as stakeholders for initiating programmes for uplift of Kutia Kondh and Dongria-Kondh community on a priority basis.[48]

The special CSR advisory board boasted intellectuals and famous personalities (Exhibit 9).[49] Working along with government welfare schemes run through district administration and local and international NGOs like Shakti, ASHA, Lepra Society, White Ribbon Alliance and TB Control Society, it initiated various activities like informal education and day care for children (Bal Chetna Yojana), skill training programme for women through Jeevika. A primary health awareness programme along with immunization and mobile health checkups was also undertaken. Self Help Groups of men and women were encouraged along with sharing of agriculture best practices with the local farmers.

Senior management of VAL including the COO, Dr. Mukesh Kumar, Mr. Umesh Mehta, the Vice President, Ms Chaamundi, General Manager, Vedanta Foundation, along with a CSR managerial team comprising managers and assistant managers, were leading the various projects.[50] In spite of receiving praise from the Governor of Orissa, Mr Bhandare, who in an award ceremony giving the St. John Ambulance Award to Vedanta suggested that "Other industrial organizations must follow the path shown by Vedanta"[51] resentment towards Vedanta from the locals, environmentalists and human rights groups continued.

Undeterred by the Supreme Court judgment, the communities petitioned the National Environmental Appellate Authority against the license to Vedanta.[52] They continued to engage various governmental statutory bodies on violations by Vedanta along with increasing interaction with global supporters. Consequently, taking cognizance of continued pollution and the expansion activity of Vedanta, the Orissa Pollution Control Board ordered Vedanta to stop construction in January 2009.[53] The Environment Ministry initiated investigations into the expansion project.[54] The Golden Peacock Award given by World

46   http://kalahandia.blogspot.com/2007_11_01_archive.html
47   http://blog.vedantaaluminium.com/sendComments.aspx?eventid=28, accessed 21 April 2010
48   http://blog.vedantaaluminium.com/sendComments.aspx?eventid=28, accessed 21 April 2010
49   http://www.kalingatimes.com/business_news/news2/20081025-Vedanta-holds-first-CSR-advisory-board-meet.htm, accessed 21 April 2010
50   http://www.orissadiary.com/ShowBussinessNews.asp?id=11414
51   http://www.indiaprwire.com/pressrelease/mining-metals/2009020319078.htm, 7 June 2010
52   http://www.amnesty.org/en/library/asset/ASA20/001/2010/en/0a81a1bc-f50c-4426-9505-7fde6
     b3382ed/asa200012010en.pdf
53   http://www.amnesty.org/en/library/asset/ASA20/001/2010/en/0a81a1bc-f50c-4426-9505-7fde6
     b3382ed/asa200012010en.pdf
54   http://www.amnesty.org/en/library/asset/ASA20/001/2010/en/0a81a1bc-f50c-4426-9505-7fde6
     b3382ed/asa200012010en.pdf

Environment Foundation for good environmental practices was withdrawn for the year 2009 from Vedanta.[55]

Vedanta went ahead full steam with its operations, and now started releasing full page advertisements in prominent newspapers and maintaining strong online presence through blogs defending its case and highlighting the Supreme Court verdict and the development initiatives it was carrying out from time to time. Some of the employees also seemed to believe that the protests of the environmentalists were misplaced (casual conversation with the case writer) because the Supreme Court had given them permission. The tribals looked at new constitutional means for taking the struggle forward. Taking cue from the villagers of Dhinkia at POSCO's site, the Dongria Kondhs planned to make use of the new Forest Act (2008) and pass a resolution in their *gram sabha* (all men and women in the village who are above 18 years of age) declaring Niyamgiri as their common property resource so that the government also could not acquire that land without consent of the *gram sabha*.[56]

With constant public gaze on the Environment Ministry's bungling and the foreign investors' discomfort at being unable to start their projects as scheduled, the mining projects in Orissa and the popular struggles against them assumed political importance. The Congress party ruling at the Centre, which had been positioning itself as pro-poor, saw an opportunity to score against the regional party government in Orissa. Its leader Rahul Gandhi had led a protest at Niyamgiri in 2010. In August 2010, the Environment Ministry withdrew the mining license to Vedanta citing several violations.[57] But the struggle was not over; the next day, 5000 people working on the project were served retrenchment notices and the company put the blame on the government decision.[58]

55   http://southasia.oneworld.net/todaysheadlines/award-to-vedanta-withdrawn-amidst-controversy
56   http://infochangeindia.org/index2.php?option=com_content&do_pdf=1&id=7279
57   http://timesofindia.indiatimes.com/business/india-business/Centre-rejects-Vedantas-Niyamgiri-mining-proposal/articleshow/6429038.cms
58   Personal email Subrat, 1 September 2010.

EXHIBIT 1 Corporate structure

Source: http://vedantaresources.com/uploads/vedantafixedincomeinvestorpresentation–january2010.pdf

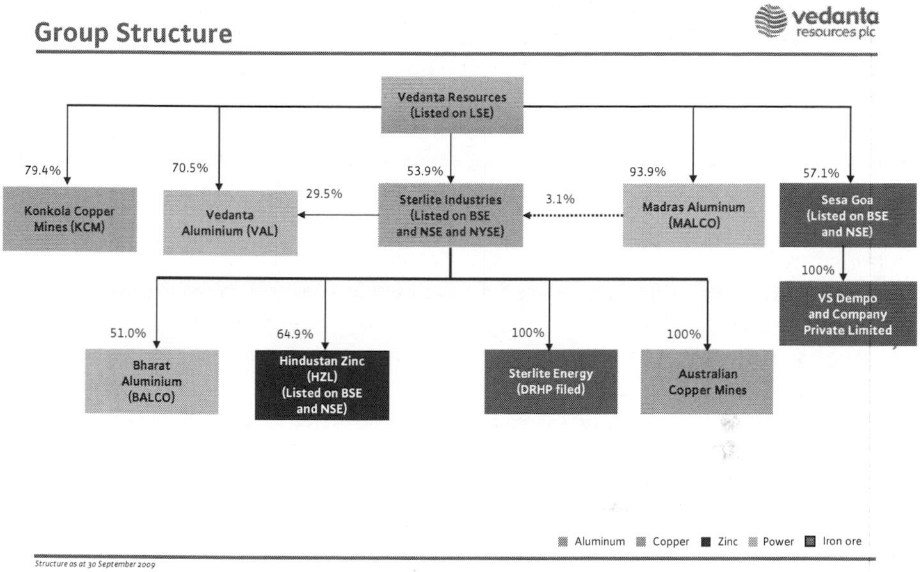

Group Structure

vedanta
resources plc

Vedanta Resources
(Listed on LSE)

79.4% → Konkola Copper Mines (KCM)

70.5% → Vedanta Aluminium (VAL)

29.5%

53.9% → Sterlite Industries (Listed on BSE and NSE and NYSE)

3.1%

93.9% → Madras Aluminum (MALCO)

57.1% → Sesa Goa (Listed on BSE and NSE)

100% → VS Dempo and Company Private Limited

51.0% → Bharat Aluminium (BALCO)

64.9% → Hindustan Zinc (HZL) (Listed on BSE and NSE)

100% → Sterlite Energy (DRHP filed)

100% → Australian Copper Mines

Aluminum   Copper   Zinc   Power   Iron ore

Structure as at 30 September 2009

Exhibit 2 Vedanta's global presence

Source: http://www.sterlite-industries.com/investor_relations/PDFs/Investors_Visit_Presentation_Lanjigarh_mar09.pdf

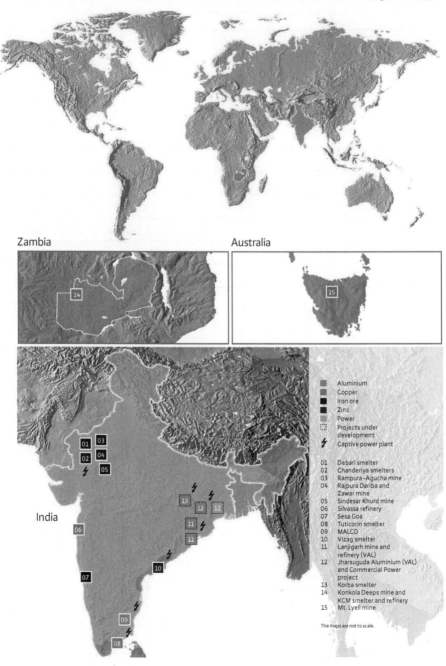

The maps are not to scale.

Exhibit 3 Global production: world bauxite mine production, reserves, and reserve base (2000–2001) (x1000 tonne)

Source: http://www.geologydata.info/bauxite_deposits.htm.

COUNTRIES	MINE	PRODUCTION	RESERVES	RESERVE BASE
Australia	53,800	53,500	3,800,000	7,400,000
Guinea	15,000	15,000	7,400,000	8,600,000
Brazil	14,000	14,000	3,900,000	4,900,000
Jamaica	11,100	13,000	2,000,000	2,500,000
India	7,370	8,000	770,000	1,400,000
China	9,000	9,200	720,000	2,000,000
Russia	4,200	4,000	2,000,000	250,000
Suriname	3,610	4,000	5,80,000	600,000
United States	NA	NA	20,000	40,000
Venezuela	4,200	4,400	320,000	350,000
Other countries	10,800	10,200	4,100,000	4,700,000
World total (rounded)	1,33,080	1,35,300	2,39,45,300	3,27,40,000
(NUMBERS FOR 2001 estimated				

Note: The geologist Pierre Berthier named bauxite after the village les Baux de Provence in Southern France, where it was first discovered in 1821.

Exhibit 4 Production costs

Source: http://ftp.jrc.es/EURdoc/JRC40221.pdf.

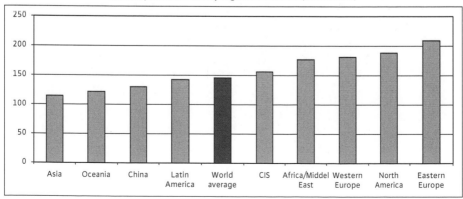

Alumina production cost by region (nominal USD/tonne, 2002)

EXHIBIT 5 Installed capacity in India

Source: Metalworld Research Team Aluminium Industry Poised for Exorbitant Growth, 26 October 2007, Metalworld.

Trends in installed capacity, aluminium production of primary producers (`ooo tonnes)							
FY	**2001**	**2002**	**2003**	**2004**	**2005**	**2006**	**2007**
Installed capacity– *Alumina*	1712	2487	2487	2797	2970	3015	3015
Nalco	800	1575	1575	1575	1575	1575	1575
Hindalco	350	350	350	660	1145	1160	1160
Indal *	312	312	312	312	–	–	–
Balco **	200	200	200	200	200	200	200
Malco **	50	50	50	50	50	80	80
Installed capacity – *Aluminium*	714	714	714	875	932	891	1185
Nalco	230	230	230	288	345	345	345
Hindalco	242	242	242	345	345	345	345
Indal *	117	117	117	117	117	–	–
Balco **	100	100	100	100	100	100	345
Malco **	25	25	25	25	25	36	40
Production – *Aluminium*	641	634	689	816	883	999	1152
Nalco	231	232	245	298	338	359	359
Hindalco	251	261	267	323	409	429	443
Indal	44	41	51	65	–	–	–
Balco **	87	70	95	97	100	174	313
Malco **	29	29	31	32	36	37	38

EXHIBIT 6 Project cost

Source: http://vedantaresources.com/uploads/vedantafixedincomeinvestorpresentation-january2010.pdf

in US$million, except as stated

Sector	Project	Capacity	Country	Expected completion date	Project cost	Spent to 30 September 2009
Alumina	Lanjigarh I Alumina Refinery	1.4 mtpa	India	Q4 FY2009	1,015.3	874.6
	Debottlecking Lanjigarh I	0.6 mtpa	India	March–2010	150.0	35.6
	Lanjigarh II Alumina Refinery	3.0 mtpa	India	Mid 2011	1,570.0	411.5
Aluminium	Korba III Smelter	325 KT	India	September–2011	1,820.0	483.5
	Jharsuguda I Smelter	0.5 mtpa				
		1,215 MW CPP	India	FY 2010	2,112.8	2,103.0
	Jharsuguda II Smelter	1.25 mtpa	India	September–2012	2,920.0	960.0

EXHIBIT 7 Share price movement of Vedanta plc (September 2005 to March 2010)

Source: http://www.lse.co.uk/ShareChart.asp?sharechart=VED&share=Vedanta.

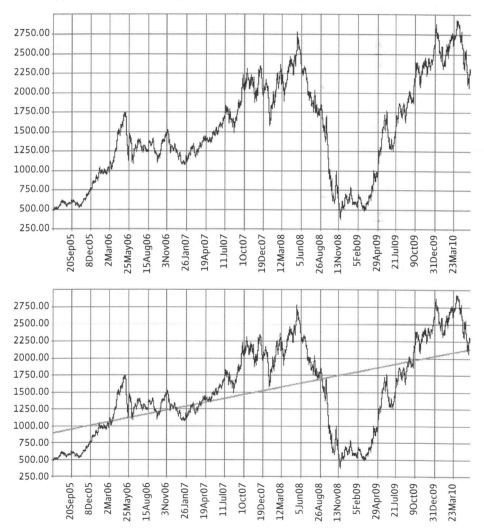

EXHIBIT 8 CSR activities of Vedanta in India

Source: Annual Report of Vedanta.

	2008–09	2007–08
Education		
Company run schools and colleges	27	16
Number of Child Care Centres	83	93
Number of Angawadi centres	937	900
Number of children enrolled in Angawadi centres	30,347	25,000
Number of persons enrolled in computer education and adult literacy programmes	44,313	55,000
Health		
Company run hospitals	18	8
Total patients treated in Company run hospitals	0.64 million	0.5 million
Total health outreach through health posts/clinics, mobile health units, camps	0.84 million	1 million
Number of Mid-day meal kitchens	6	6
Number of children covered by the Mid-day meal programme	180,000	180,000
Livelihoods		
Farmers covered: training/cultivation/water she activities/ soil testing/providing seeds and fertilisers	3,360	1,650
Total land covered under agriculture and watershed programme	3,225 acres	3,120 acres
Cattle covered under veternary health initiatives	121,676	65,540
Total women SHGS	1,337	781
Number of women members in SHGs	18,583	10,055
Our Reach		
Villages we work in	427	373
Villages with in the integrated Village Development Programme	75	70
Total population reached (million)	2.5	2.5
Our NGO partners	82	72
CSR Personnel	96	93
CSR Coordinators/volunteers/extensionworkers	454	1031
Total spend on CSR activities (million USD)	24.6	20

EXHIBIT 9 CSR Advisory Board of Vedanta Aluminium Ltd

Source: http://www.kalingatimes.com/business_news/news2/20081025-Vedanta-holds-first-CSR-advisory-board-meet.htm, accessed 21 April 2010

P.K. Jena, Chairman, Institute of Advance Technology & Environmental Studies
S.B. Mishra and Sahadev Sahoo (both former Chief Secretaries of Government of Orissa)
O.N. Mohanty, Vice-Chancellor, Biju Patnaik University of Technology
A.B. Tripathy, retired Director General of Police
A.B. Ota, Director SC &ST Research and Development Centre, Government of Orissa
Bijay Mohanty, actor
Rita Ray, Professor, Department of Sociology, Utkal University
Namita Panda, Chairperson State Women Commission
Pratibha Ray, writer

About the authors

Dr **Nimruji Jammulamadaka** is an Assistant Professor of Behavioral Sciences at the Indian Institute of Management, Calcutta. She holds a doctorate degree in Industrial Engineering from the Indian Institute of Technology, Kanpur. Dr Jammulamadaka has significant experience in the non-profit sector in India.

Mr **Sandeep Bhattacharjee** is currently working as a faculty of marketing research in the Usha Martin Education & Solutions Group. He has more than six years of experience. His research areas include applied data-mining in marketing and other social areas of development.

Teaching notes for this case are available from Greenleaf Publishing. These are free of charge and available only to teaching staff. They can be requested by going to:
www.greenleaf-publishing.com/darkside2notes

3

The dark side of light-handed regulation
Mercury Energy and the death of Folole Muliaga[1]

Todd Bridgman
Victoria Management School, University of Wellington, New Zealand

On 29 May 2007, Folole Muliaga died following the disconnection of her home power supply for an overdue bill of $NZ168 (US$87). This apparent act of heartlessness by her state-owned electricity supplier, Mercury Energy, generated intense media interest in New Zealand and was picked up by international news agencies. Mrs Muliaga had been receiving oxygen therapy at home for treatment of breathing difficulties associated with her obesity, and the cessation of oxygen caused by the disconnection led directly to her death. Mercury Energy initially denied any wrongdoing, but in the days following Mrs Muliaga's death it became apparent that Mercury Energy was not com-

1 This case has been published with express permission of the ANZSOG Case Program: www.casestudies.anzsog.edu.au. The author acknowledges the assistance of Janet Tyson of the ANZSOG Case Program in the preparation of this case.

© HEC Montréal. Reproduced with the permission of the HEC Montréal Case Centre.

All rights reserved for all countries. Any translation or alteration in any form whatsoever is prohibited.

The *International Journal of Case Studies in Management* is published on-line (www.hec.ca/revuedecas/en), ISSN 1911-2599.

This case is intended to be used as the framework for an educational discussion and does not imply any judgement on the administrative situation presented. Deposited under number 9 40 2011 038 with the HEC Montréal Case Centre, 3000, chemin de la Côte-Sainte-Catherine, Montréal (Québec) Canada H3T 2A7.

pliant with government guidelines on disconnections involving low income consumers. The guidelines, created by the national regulator, the Electricity Commission, were voluntary rather than compulsory as part of a government approach which preferred self-regulation by companies to "heavy-handed" regulation by government. The focus of the case is the social responsibilities of both Mercury Energy and the government. Mercury Energy undertook many community initiatives as part of its commitments to corporate social responsibility (CSR), but this case shines the spotlight on its less publicised activities. To explore this issue, the case focuses on the actions of Mercury Energy in the period leading up to, and following, Mrs Muliaga's death. It also focuses on the role played by the Electricity Commission, both before and following Mrs Muliaga's death and raises questions around whether it acted responsibly in deciding against regulation.

Folole Muliaga, a 45-year-old Samoan woman, and her son Ietitaia were in their Mangere Bridge, Auckland home on the morning of May 29, 2007.[2] Mrs. Muliaga was in the dining room and Ietitaia was seated at the computer in the living room. At around 10:25 a.m., Ietitaia saw a man walk to the rear of the house and knock on the door, which he answered. "Good morning, I'm from Mercury Energy and Mercury Energy is disconnecting your power for arrears," said the man, an employee of VirCom Energy Management Services (hereafter VirCom), which was contracted to perform Mercury Energy's disconnections.[3] He handed Ietitaia a disconnection notice which he took to his mother, who told him to invite the man in to speak with her. By the time Ietitaia went outside again to do this, the contractor had cut the power supply to the house. Ietitaia asked him to come inside, and the man followed him to the dining room, stepping over a tube running from a machine in Mrs. Muliaga's bedroom to the prongs attached to her nose.

Folole Muliaga was not a well woman. Since migrating to New Zealand in 2000 with her husband Lopaavea and four children in search of a better life, her health had deteriorated. A trained school teacher, she first received treatment at Auckland's Middlemore Hospital on April 5, 2007 for breathing difficulties associated with her weight, which had risen to 212 kilograms. She was diagnosed with obesity hyperventilation syndrome, an illness that prevented her from breathing adequately to remove carbon dioxide from her body. Mrs. Muliaga was treated with drugs and a ventilator and by the time of her discharge from hospital on

---

2   The events described in this section are based on the findings of Coroner Gordon Matenga released in September 2008 on the inquest into the death of Folole Muliaga.
3   The name of the contractor was permanently suppressed by the coroner because of possible threats to his own safety and that of his family.

May 11, 2007, her weight had fallen to 184 kilograms. She was given two machines to continue oxygen treatment at home.

Eighteen days later, the contractor, a trained electrical installer, was led by Ietitaia into the dining room where his mother was seated. The contractor explained that he had disconnected the power on instruction from her power company, Mercury Energy, as the account was NZ$168.40 (US$87) in arrears. Mrs. Muliaga asked, "So how do I get my power on?" to which the contractor replied, "You either pay or ring Mercury Energy." Ietitaia did not hear all of the conversation, but heard his mother say "Please give us a chance," to which the contractor replied "I'm just doing my job." The contractor could see the plastic tubes coming from Mrs. Muliaga's nose, but he did not know what they were for and did not feel it was his business to ask about them. He did not see any oxygen machines or any tubes on the floor. He also did not hear the alarm that was triggered when power supply to the oxygen machine was cut.

Once the contractor left the house, Mrs. Muliaga's health deteriorated rapidly. She took some pills, but Ietitaia and his brother Ruatesi, who had arrived home, were concerned. She asked Ietitaia to play a song on the guitar but halfway through the song she was struggling to breathe. Ietitaia went to the dining room to call an ambulance but their phone was disconnected. He returned to find his mother unconscious and Ruatesi attempting resuscitation. Ietitaia went to the neighbours' house and an ambulance was called. Two ambulance staff arrived and continued attempts to resuscitate her but it was too late. Folole Muliaga was dead.

The 'blame game' begins

Mercury Energy was the third largest energy retailer in New Zealand, providing electricity and gas services to 315,000 residential and business customers throughout New Zealand. It was a profitable business – between 2003 and 2007, its earnings nearly doubled to more than NZ$300 million, though its return on shareholders' equity fell by more than half during this time, to less than 6% (see Appendix 1). Mercury Energy had a strong presence in Auckland, with more than 50 years of history supplying customers in the region. The Auckland region is ethnically diverse—of the population of 1.2 million, 15% identified as Pacific people (for example, Samoans, Tongans, Fijians), 19% Asian and 11% Māori.[4] Mercury Energy attributed its strong market position to "industry-leading levels

---

4   2006 Census of Populations and Dwellings. Available at http://www.stats.govt.nz/Census/
    2006CensusHomePage/QuickStats/quickstats-about-a-subject/nzs-population-and-dwellings
    .aspx. Māori are the indigenous people of New Zealand.

of service and customer-friendly initiatives and products."[5] Mercury Energy was active in community initiatives to support the company's goal of "the natural evolution of partnerships which genuinely benefit those local to its facilities and customers, bringing together the Company and surrounding communities so that the needs of each are mutually understood."[6] For example, in 2007, Mercury Energy insulated free of charge the homes of 50 patients of Auckland's Starship Children's Hospital who were suffering from respiratory illnesses, to make their houses warmer and drier.

The day following Mrs. Muliaga's death, news reports began to surface in New Zealand. These were soon picked up by international news outlets, including the BBC and CNN, their attention drawn by the apparent death of a woman over a $168.40 electricity bill. "Lopaavea Muliaga's wife died for the sake of less than £70," reported the BBC.[7] Politicians from New Zealand's government and opposition parties were quick to start pointing the finger of blame. Prime Minister Helen Clark accused Mercury Energy of a "hard-nosed commercial attitude"[8] and said it was unbelievable the contractor had gone ahead with the disconnection even though he saw a tube coming out of Mrs. Muliaga's nose. Ms. Clark said it was intolerable that such heartlessness on the part of a company and a contractor had conveyed a poor and inaccurate image of New Zealand around the world.[9] Former State-Owned Enterprises Minister Richard Prebble said it was ironic Prime Minister Clark was attacking Mercury Energy, given that her government owned it.[10]

Pressure intensified on Mercury Energy when it emerged that the company had refused to reconnect the Muliagas' power later on the day of her death, even when told that Mrs. Muliaga had died.[11] Mercury Energy initially insisted it had done nothing wrong. Doug Heffernan, chief executive of Mercury Energy's parent company, Mighty River Power, said the company did not know of Mrs. Muliaga's medical condition. While the family had made two recent payments and the date for final payment on the outstanding amount of $168.40 was not until June 13, the family was using more power than the amount of the repayments, meaning they were getting further into debt, he said. Mercury Energy's general manager James Moulder said he felt sure the power supplier was not to blame.

5   Available at http://www.mightyriverpower.co.nz/AboutUs/MercuryEnergy/. Downloaded January 5, 2009.
6   Mighty River Power Limited, Annual Report 2007, p. 28.
7   "NZ Police Probe Power Cut Death," *BBC*, May 30, 2007. Available at http://news.bbc.co.uk/2/hi/asia-pacific/6703395.stm.
8   Dan Eaton, "Power-Cut Tragedy: The Facts," *The Press*, June 6, 2007.
9   "New Zealand Embarrassed and Devastated Over Fatal Disconnect—PM," *Radio New Zealand Newswire*, June 1, 2007.
10 Richard Prebble, "Look to Government Over Mercury Culture," *New Zealand Herald*, June 14, 2007.
11 "Lights Out at Call Centre," *Waikato Times*, June 6, 2007.

"Throughout the 6–7 week process of disconnecting the home, and on the day in question, we were not alerted that there was a person resident dependent on a medical device reliant on electricity," he said.[12]

In the days after Mrs. Muliaga's death, Mercury Energy softened its stance as further details of the case were revealed. Senior management visited the family's home to offer their condolences and a $10,000 cheque to cover funeral expenses.[13] They had been coached by members of their staff in the Samoan custom of *ifoga,* where the wrongdoer appears before the wronged. Dressed in traditional Samoan lava-lavas wrapped around their suits, they were left standing outside the house for more than two hours before being invited in by the family. Inside, the group sat cross-legged on mats in the living room surrounded by Muliaga family members, their eyes lowered as they were addressed by a Samoan high chief. Mr. Heffernan told the family: "I hope the pain will pass and that you will be able to get strength from the memories you have of your wife, your mother," while Mr. Moulder assured the gathering that the company's condolences were sincere. "We are deeply remorseful . . . Thank you very much for receiving us."[14] Mrs. Muliaga's nephew Brenden Sheehan said the family accepted the executives' show of remorse as "human beings," but "as managers of companies, they should be sacked."[15]

The question of who was most to blame for Mrs. Muliaga's death became the subject of intense public debate, with several national media outlets running polls. One poll, taken before it became public that the Muliaga family had sought help from Mercury Energy about their power bill weeks before her death, found that 40% of New Zealanders believed the Muliaga family was most to blame.[16] It was argued that Mrs. Muliaga was responsible for letting her health deteriorate to the point it had and that her sons should have done more to seek medical attention once they saw her condition worsen after the power was disconnected. In the poll, 22% said Mercury Energy was most to blame because it ordered the disconnection, while 5% blamed the health system for failing to provide adequate care for Mrs. Muliaga. While the public debated whether the Muliaga family or Mercury Energy were most to blame, sections of the media also raised the possibility that the regulatory structure of New Zealand's electricity sector might also have been a key contributor to the tragedy. According to an editorial in New Zealand's largest newspaper, "the contractor who pulled the plug in Mangere Bridge was the last link in a very long chain of policy-setting and decision-making that stretches back to Wellington and, through both Labour and National administrators, to 1984."[17]

12   "Mercury and Family Disagree Over Power Cut Death," *New Zealand Herald*, May 30, 2007.
13   "Fine Mats, Tears and Forgiveness," *New Zealand Herald*, June 2, 2007.
14   "Power Bosses Kept Waiting," *The Dominion Post*, Edition 2, Page 3, June 2, 2007.
15   "Fine Mats, Tears And Forgiveness," *New Zealand Herald*, June 2, 2007.
16   "It's More the Fault of the Family: Poll," *New Zealand Herald*, June 26, 2007.
17   "Muliaga Death Still a Tangle of Unanswered Questions," *New Zealand Herald*, June 10, 2007.

New Zealand's electricity industry reforms since 1984

Prior to 1984, electricity generation and transmission had been the responsibility of the Ministry of Energy, a government department, which was also responsible for policy advice and regulatory functions. The Ministry of Energy operated New Zealand's hydro-electricity network and its gas and coal-fired stations, as well as maintaining the transmission system that distributed electricity to local power boards and councils, which sold it to consumers.

In 1984, the newly elected Labour government faced a foreign-exchange crisis that provided the catalyst for a series of wide-ranging neo-liberal economic reforms that transformed New Zealand from one of the most regulated economies in the OECD to arguably the least regulated. Treasury, the department that advised the government on economic policy, argued the Ministry of Energy was over-staffed and inefficient and suggested a number of market reforms for the sector.[18]

In 1987, the Electricity Corporation of New Zealand (ECNZ) was set up as a company under the State-Owned Enterprises Act to own and operate New Zealand's generating stations and the transmission system. Policy and regulatory activities were separated out and largely retained within the Ministry of Energy. Section 4 of the State-Owned Enterprises Act 1986 stated that:

> [1] The principal objective of every State Enterprise shall be to operate as a successful business and, to this end, to be—
>
> [a] As profitable and efficient as comparable businesses that are not owned by the Crown;
>
> [b] A good employer; and
>
> [c] An organisation that exhibits the sense of social responsibility by having regard to the interests of the community in which it operates and by endeavouring to accommodate or encourage these when able to do so.

An Electricity Task Force comprising members from government departments, ECNZ and local suppliers was established in 1987 to advise the government on the structure and regulatory environment for the industry. Among a series of recommendations made in 1989 was the development of a "light-handed" regulatory regime that involved the use of the existing competition policy regime (the Commerce Act 1986) to deal with anti-competitive behaviour, together with extensive information disclosure and the threat of further regulation if dominant market players abused their position as a natural monopoly. "Light-handed" regulation was seen as preferable to "heavy-handed" regulation, such as price controls, which were considered complex, costly to administer and not

---

18   "Lights Out," *The Dominion Post Weekend*, December 6, 2008, p. 7.

always capable of producing the desired result. By maintaining a light-handed approach, regulations could be kept to a minimum, with additional measures introduced to overcome any weaknesses in the regulatory framework that arose over time.[19]

In 1989, the Ministry of Energy was abolished, with its policy, regulatory and other non-commercial roles transferred to the Ministry of Commerce. The national government elected in 1990 continued to reform the electricity industry by introducing a range of competitive incentives in an attempt to improve efficiency and effectiveness. Wholesale and retail markets for electricity were created, so that instead of having to buy electricity from one state-owned monopoly, wholesale customers now had a choice of power suppliers. In the competitive retail market, consumers were given the choice of a range of electricity retailers. In 1998, ECNZ was split into four different generation companies—Meridian, Genesis, Mighty River and Contact, the last of which was privatized.

In 1999, the newly elected Labour government inherited an electricity industry that was largely self-regulating, with market participants subject to few legislative and government restrictions. While it was Labour that had begun the neo-liberal reforms in 1984, its electoral success in 1999 was based on a pledge to curb the excesses of the free market, especially in the provision of essential services, such as electricity. The following year, the government announced a ministerial inquiry into the electricity industry, with the inquiry panel subsequently supporting the continuation of a light-handed regulatory approach. Government stated that it favoured industry solutions where possible, but signalled its intention to regulate if the industry failed to self-regulate responsibly. In late 2000, it announced a new governance structure for the industry, including a self-governance board. However, by 2003, industry participants had failed to reach agreement on self-governance arrangements, prompting the government to establish an Electricity Commission (EC) to take over governance of the industry.

While the electricity reforms since 1984 had their supporters as well as critics, there was agreement that, for whatever reason, the reforms had largely failed to benefit domestic consumers. In the mid 1990s, electricity prices fell for residential, commercial and industrial users, but these gains did not last for residential customers. Between 2000 and 2007, real consumer prices (adjusted for inflation) increased nearly 40%, with the difference between industrial and commercial prices continuing to increase.[20]

---

19   Ministry of Economic Development, "Light-Handed Regulation of New Zealand's Electricity and Gas Industries," June 7, 2006. Available at www.med.govt.nz.

20   "Lights Out," *The Dominion Post Weekend*, December 6, 2008, p. 7.

The Electricity Commission and its guidelines for low-income customers

The EC, funded by a levy on electricity companies, was responsible for over-seeing the governance and operations of New Zealand's electricity market. The EC's principal objective was to ensure that electricity was produced and deliv-ered to all classes of consumers in an efficient, fair, reliable and environmen-tally sustainable manner. Consistent with New Zealand's light-handed regulatory approach, the EC had extensive powers to regulate but was expected to use "its power of persuasion and promotion, and provision of information and model arrangements to achieve its objectives rather than recommending regulations and rules."[21] The Commission was governed by an executive chair and four other members appointed by the Minister of Energy.

In July 2005, the EC announced it was considering implementing a set of guide-lines to assist low-income domestic consumers to ensure that minimal discon-nections occurred, and to establish standards for these disconnections. It was hoped that by introducing guidelines, all parties would benefit—retailers' bad debts would be reduced as well as the costs that resulted from enforcing them, social agencies would reduce the money they were advancing to customers struggling to pay their bills and consumers would benefit from a continuous supply of electricity. The EC's preferred approach was "a series of guidelines that electricity retailers should be encouraged to implement . . . rather than regulation."[22] The EC noted that all retailers had initiatives in place for dealing with low-income customers, but some made more strenuous efforts than others before making a disconnection.

The proposed guidelines drew formal submissions from, among others, Con-tact Energy and Mighty River Power. Contact Energy was concerned that the guidelines would become de facto regulations. While accepting that electricity retailers, such as themselves, had a role to play, they argued that "electricity retailers are first and foremost businesses (as are retailers of other life essen-tials such as food and clothing)" and additional costs caused by more strin-gent processes related to disconnection would have to be passed on to other customers.[23]

Mighty River Power, parent company of Mercury Energy, supported the objec-tives of the guidelines but said that retailers already had disconnection processes and the EC had failed to demonstrate there was a problem with them. Mighty

---

21 Electricity Commission profile. Available at http://www.electricitycommission.govt.nz/aboutcommission/comprofile.
22 Electricity Commission, "Consultation Paper: Guidelines to Assist Low Income Domestic Consumers," June 2005, p. 5.
23 Contact Energy, Submission to Electricity Commission on Guidelines to Assist Low Income Domestic Consumers, August 8, 2005, p. 1.

River Power said that while disconnection was considered a "last resort,"[24] the ability to disconnect was needed to ensure bad debts did not get too big and to provide an incentive for bad debtors to pay their bills. Any actions which delayed disconnection would:

> distort the current prioritisation process by sending a very clear signal to low income and vulnerable individuals that electricity should be the last obligation that they should be concerned about.[25]

Both Contact Energy and Mighty River Power preferred guidelines to regulations, but this view was not shared by all who made submissions to the EC. Wellington resident Jim Delahunty argued for "an absolute right of heat and light"[26] and said that State Owned Enterprises should not be allowed to disconnect consumers. With regard to the proposed guidelines, Mr. Delahunty concluded that "trying to make private or public capitalists into Mr. Nice Guys is a waste of time."[27]

Grey Power, a lobby group for those aged 50+, also favoured regulations, saying electricity retailers might ignore guidelines they found difficult or costly to implement. The only way for the EC to ensure low-income consumers would be protected, they argued, was to regulate.[28]

Findings of the coroner's inquest into the death of Folole Muliaga

Two weeks after Folole Muliaga's death, police announced there was no evidence to justify any charges against either Mercury Energy or their contractors, VirCom, and they referred the case to the coroner. The inquest was conducted by Coroner Gordon Matenga in May 2008, and his report, released in September 2008, concluded that Mrs. Muliaga died of an arrhythmia caused by morbid obesity and that "the cessation of oxygen therapy and stress arising from the fact

---

24 Mighty River Power, Submission to Electricity Commission on Guidelines to Assist Low Income Domestic Consumers, August 8, 2005, p. 14.
25 Mighty River Power, Submission to Electricity Commission on Guidelines to Assist Low Income Domestic Consumers, August 8, 2005, p. 5.
26 Jim Delahunty, Submission to Electricity Commission on Guidelines to Assist Low Income Domestic Consumers, August 1, 2005, p. 1.
27 Ibid.
28 Grey Power Federation of New Zealand, Submission to Electricity Commission on Guidelines to Assist Low Income Domestic Consumers, 2005.

of the disconnection (as opposed to the way in which the power was disconnected) have contributed to her death."[29]

The VirCom contractor escaped blame, with the coroner accepting that he
knew nothing of Mrs. Muliaga's medical condition, the oxygen machine or the
need for power to keep it operating. The coroner accepted that had the contractor been aware of the situation, he would have followed the standard procedure
and telephoned Mercury Energy to advise them that the power should not be
cut off. The contractor had given two examples when he had done this in the
past, one case involving children with intellectual disabilities and the other a
newborn child.

The coroner also made a series of findings regarding the medical treatment
Mrs. Muliaga received from her local health provider, Counties Manukau District Health Board. He was concerned about communication between medical
staff and Mrs. Muliaga and her family, and investigated the extent to which she
and her family knew the seriousness of her condition. The coroner concluded
that her children did not know how sick she was and that they did not know
doctors felt resuscitation should not be attempted if she went into cardiac
arrest. Counties Manukau District Health Board did not follow its own policy
when the decision about the non-resuscitation order was made, since no discussion was held with Mrs. Muliaga or her family. A series of recommendations
for improving the health board's communication processes were included in
the coroner's report.

The remainder of the coroner's report concerned the actions of Mercury
Energy. The coroner found that Mercury Energy sent a warning notice to the
Muliaga household on April 23, 2007, while Mrs. Muliaga was in hospital. Her
husband, Lopaavea, called Mercury Energy on May 1 to attempt to pay off the
bill at $50 per week. He said his wife, who was the account holder,[30] was in hos-
pital. The Mercury Energy employee who took the call advised Mr. Muliaga that
because of New Zealand's privacy laws she could not discuss the account with
him. She said Mrs. Muliaga would have to call back and that the overdue amount
would need to be paid in full. The coroner concluded that Mercury Energy's systems had failed, since the call-taker should have referred the call to her manager,
which she did not. Once aware of Mrs. Muliaga's health issues, further enquiries
should have been made to assess whether the Muliaga family was a vulnerable
customer. No such enquiries were made.

Critical to the coroner's investigation were Mercury Energy's actions leading
up to the disconnection being ordered, in relation to the EC's guidelines concerning low-income consumers. The guidelines involved a two-step process: first,
the electricity retailer would inform its customers on how to identify themselves

29 Coroner Gordon Matenga, "Findings of the Inquest into the Death of Folole Muliaga," Office
    of the Coroner, September 19, 2008, p. 33.
30 Until her hospitalization, Mrs. Muliaga was the sole income earner for her family, working
    as a teacher.

as a low-income domestic consumer who would face hardship if the electricity was disconnected. The onus was then on vulnerable customers to follow the process. At the time of Mrs. Muliaga's death, Mercury Energy did have a "Do Not Disconnect List" that included 59 customers with medical conditions, but she was not on the list. Mercury Energy accepted they had not fully complied with the guidelines. While they did assist vulnerable customers who identified themselves, they did not provide information on the process of self-identifying as a vulnerable customer. The coroner concluded that:

> It is perhaps no surprise that the Muliaga family did not advise Mer-
> cury Energy of Mrs. Muliaga's medical condition. There is no evidence
> before me that the Muliaga family was aware that help was available
> to them.[31]

The coroner concluded by congratulating Mercury Energy for acknowledging that their previous practices were not compliant with the 2005 guidelines and for voluntarily making changes to their disconnection practices in the weeks following Mrs. Muliaga's death. The changes include treating all customers as vulnerable to ensure no one is missed and producing information brochures in six different languages (including Samoan). In addition, it was now routine procedure to ask customers calling Mercury Energy whether anyone in the household was either vulnerable or medically dependent on electricity.

EC's revised guidelines following the death

In June 2007, as a direct result of the death of Folole Muliaga, the Electricity Commission issued a revised set of guidelines for assisting low-income consumers, which included enhanced processes concerning disconnections. Whereas the 2005 guidelines were "advisory, in line with its objective to encourage rather than regulate,"[32] the 2007 guidelines stated that "retailers must report annually on their level of compliance with the guidelines, and where the guidelines have been deviated from, provide reasons for each type of deviation."[33] This compliance information would be publicly available on the Commission's website.

---

31   Coroner Gordon Matenga, "Findings of the Inquest into the Death of Folole Muliaga," Office of the Coroner, September 19, 2008, p. 16.

32   Electricity Commission, "Guidelines on Arrangements to Assist Low Income Domestic Consumers," June 2005, p. 3.

33   Electricity Commission, "Guidelines on Arrangements to Assist Low Income Domestic Consumers," July 2007, p. 3.

Despite the tougher stance it had taken, the EC stopped short of imposing regulations. Consistent with the "light-handed" regulatory approach taken since 1984, the Commission's 2007 guidelines threatened regulation in the event that electricity retailers did not respond satisfactorily to the guidelines.

Some commentators, including Sue Bradford, Member of Parliament for the Green Party, believed the guidelines did not go far enough:

> In this case it appears that the threat of regulation is considered to be more important than the possible consequence of not doing something more regulatory, leading to the consequence of possible further tragic circumstances.
>
> Effectively, the companies are being slapped on the wrist and told: "Don't do it again," when we have already had codes of responsibility and codes of practice for them that should have stopped them from doing this, but did not.[34]

---

34 Sue Bradford, "Urgent Debate: Mercury Energy," June 12, 2007. Available at http://www.greens.org.nz/speeches/urgent-debate-mercury-energy.

Appendix 1: Financial data for Mighty River Power, owners of Mercury Energy[35]

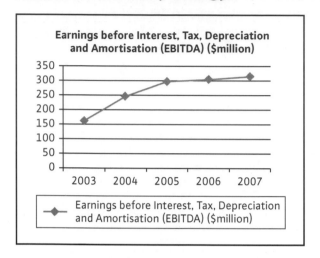

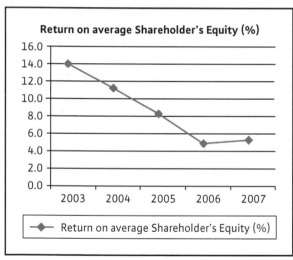

35   Mighty River Power Limited, Annual Report, 2007.

Appendix 2: Timeline

1987	
	Electricity Corporation of New Zealand (ECNZ) is established as a state-owned corporation to own and operate New Zealand's generating stations and the transmission system.
1989	
	An Electricity Task Force recommends the establishment of a "light-handed" regulatory regime, which seeks to minimize regulation of the industry.
1998	
	ECNZ is split into four different generation companies—Meridian, Genesis, Mighty River and Contact, the last of which was privatized.
2000	
	Following public criticism of the market-reforms, the government warns it will regulate if the industry cannot self-regulate responsibly.
2003	
	The government establishes an Electricity Commission (EC) to take over governance of the industry. The EC is given powers to regulate but is expected to regulate as a last resort.
2005	
July	EC announces it will develop guidelines to assist low-income domestic consumers to minimize disconnections and to establish standards for these disconnections.
August	Mighty River Power, parent company of Mercury Energy, says the ability to disconnect is needed to provide an incentive for bad debtors to pay their bills.
	Grey Power, a lobby group for those aged 50+, says electricity retailers might ignore voluntary guidelines they found difficult or costly to implement. They believe regulation is needed.
2007	
April 23	Mercury Energy sends a warning notice to the Muliaga household for an overdue account. Mrs. Muliaga, the account holder, is in hospital for treatment of breathing difficulties associated with her obesity.
May 1	Her husband, Lopaavea, calls Mercury Energy, seeking to pay off the bill at $50 per week. He is told only the account holder can make such arrangements. The call-taker is made aware of Mrs. Muliaga's health issues but fails to refer the call to her manager to have the family assessed as a vulnerable customer.
	Mercury Energy is not compliant with the EC guidelines for vulnerable customers. They have not informed vulnerable customers that help is available to them. Mrs. Muliaga is not on the "Do Not Disconnect" list and there is no evidence the family is aware of its existence.

continued

May 29	A contractor disconnects power from the Muliaga home for an overdue bill of NZ$168. Mrs. Muliaga dies shortly after.
May 30	Doug Heffernan, chief executive of Mercury Energy's parent company, Mighty River Power, says the company did not know of Mrs. Muliaga's medical condition.
June 2	Mercury Energy softens its stance as details of the call made by Mr. Muliaga on May 1 are revealed. Senior management visit the family's home to offer their condolences and a $10,000 cheque to cover funeral expenses.
June 14	Police announce there is no evidence to justify any charges against either Mercury Energy or their contractors.
	Mercury Energy changes their disconnection practices to ensure vulnerable customers are not missed.
	The EC revises its voluntary guidelines for assisting low-income consumers, putting in place stricter processes for disconnections. It stops short of imposing regulations.
2008	
September	The coroner finds that the disconnection of power contributed to Mrs. Muliaga's death. He accepts that had the contractor been aware of the situation, he would have not gone ahead with the disconnection. He congratulates Mercury Energy for voluntarily changing their disconnection practices following Mrs. Muliaga's death.

About the author

Todd Bridgman is a Seni or lecturer in the School of Management, Victoria University of Wellington, New Zealand, where he teaches organisational behaviour. He completed his PhD at the University of Cambridge and held research fellowships at Judge Business School and Wolfson College, University of Cambridge. His research interests are located within critical management studies; in 2009 he edited, with Mats Alvesson and Hugh Willmott, *The Oxford Handbook of Critical Management Studies* (Oxford University Press).

Teaching notes for this case are available from Greenleaf Publishing. These are free of charge and available only to teaching staff. They can be requested by going to:
www.greenleaf-publishing.com/darkside2notes

4

San Rafael[1]

Emmanuel Raufflet[2]
Department of Management, HEC Montreal, Canada

San Rafael is a village located within the municipality of Tlalmanalco, 40 km southeast of Mexico City, in the foothills of the Iztaccihuatl volcano in Mexico. San Rafael gave its name to an early corporation that dominated not only the region but also the pulp and paper industry in Mexico for most of the 20th century.

This case examines the political, economic, cultural and organizational factors that affected the relationship between the village of San Rafael and the eponymous corporation, the local major employer throughout three eras covering a century of operations.

---

1   A first version of this case study was shortlisted in the 2010 Dark Side Case Writing Competition organized by the Critical Management Studies Division of the Academy of Management (AOM).

© HEC Montréal. Reproduced with the permission of the HEC Montréal Case Centre.

All rights reserved for all countries. Any translation or alteration in any form whatsoever is prohibited.

The *International Journal of Case Studies in Management* is published on-line (www.hec .ca/revuedecas/en), ISSN 1911-2599.

This case is intended to be used as the framework for an educational discussion and does not imply any judgement on the administrative situation presented. Deposited under number 9 40 2011 038 with the HEC Montréal Case Centre, 3000, chemin de la Côte-Sainte-Catherine, Montréal (Québec) Canada H3T 2A7.

2   The author dedicates this case study to Dr. Fernando de la Macorra (1930–2008) for his exemplary commitment to the Sierra Nevada's sustainability and cultural conservation, as well for sharing with the author his passion and knowledge of the region.

First era (1893–1936)

Founded in 1893, endowed with modern imported equipment and abundant natural resources and protected by high import tariff barriers, the San Rafael factory soon became the leading pulp and paper producer in Mexico. Growing from 120 workers in 1900 to 500 in 1910, and more than 1,000 in the early 1930s, San Rafael, the main producer of newsprint, enjoyed a monopoly until the 1930s (Espejel, 1993).

Compared to its competitors, the San Rafael factory represented an industrial powerhouse and marked a key investment and technological breakthrough in the Mexican industrial landscape. Its Swiss-made machinery, driven by 15 water-powered turbines, had a capacity of 12 tons a day—about three times that of its national competitors combined (Garcia Luna, 1998). It built 16 km of underground canals in the mountain to secure its water and hydro-power supply, acquired the San Rafael–Mexico City railway company and established control of local haciendas to access land and forests (Huerta Gonzalez, 1994). It further strengthened its position in 1904 by acquiring El Progreso Industrial, a smaller but modern plant located close to Mexico City (Haber, 1989: 97).

At the local level, haciendas were the cornerstone of social and economic local life at the time.

High land concentration had led most farmers to work and live as labourers (*peones*) on the haciendas (Huerta Gonzalez, 1994: 284). For instance, in 1891, only 8% of the farmers in Tlalmanalco owned land. Although labourers and their families were provided a subsistence livelihood, including housing (*caserío*), a salary and credit in hard times, they were tied to the hacienda through debts to rural stores (*tiendas de raya*). These stores, the only sources of basic items and staple foods, sold their products at steep prices, and labourers and their families were not allowed to leave if they had a debt (Araya Perez, 1997).

Labour practices and relations with the local community

The San Rafael company gradually took over the hacienda's pivotal role in local social and economic life. First, the de la Macorra family soon became emblematic of the factory management. Born in Spain and trained as a forestry engineer, Don José de la Macorra was the director-general of the company between 1897 and 1936. His son Don Fernando replaced him from 1936 until his retirement in 1968. Various relatives also occupied managerial positions in the company. As in the traditional hacendado, the family lived in the *casco* (main residence) of the Hacienda de Zavaleta, located close to the factory. Second, the company referred to labour contracts as *convenio de servidumbre* ("servant's agreements"), which required that workers be loyal, with no restrictions on the firm's ability to hire or fire workers according to industrial needs (Huerta Gonzalez, 1994: 476). Many landless farmers had little choice but to work in the factory to earn their livelihood. They gradually built their houses on the firm's land with no guarantee of a continuous work relation with San Rafael. On the other hand, the director-general led initiatives to alleviate the difficulties of workers' lives. He started and financially supported mutual solidarity funds (*mutualidades*) and charities for workers' families in an effort to support ill and elderly workers and their families. The director-general, as protector and honorary president of these funds, had the right to access information and could veto decisions. In a letter written in 1922, José de la Macorra, the director-general, stated his motivations for launching initiatives such as:

> the mutual fund, the consumers' co-operative, and other initiatives in the cafeterias (*comedores*) and in the market place. I launched these initiatives with much willingness to please and much pleasure so as to do good around me in the big family (José de la Macorra, cited in Huerta Gonzalez, 1994: 477).

In San Rafael, the influence of the director-general went beyond the sphere of labour and social protection or welfare. He also presided over the celebrations sponsored by the factory and used the local social sphere to demonstrate his initiatives and generosity. An ex-worker provides an example:

> [In the 1920s] for patriotic holidays, they used to build a tent up there by the factory. On September 15 [National holiday], that year, the tent collapsed under heavy rain. Don José got soaked. The same night, he stood up and said: "I promise that next year we will have a celebration hall." And that was it. 1 peso a week was taken away from the workers' wages and the following year the celebration hall was ready. Don José then inaugurated it.

A challenge for management was to transform workmanship from that of farmers to that of industrial workers. All the workers had previously been farmers and maintained their links with agricultural activities, which were central to their traditional livelihood and way of life. Often illiterate, they cultivated a piece of land, raised animals, worked seasons in the factory and returned to the fields to sustain their households. This other income was a guarantee for times when work at the factory was insufficient. There was a permanent tension between paternalism and rigour in manager–worker relations. While managers were invited to the family gatherings and celebrations of workers, such as baptisms or communions, they had to remain the main enforcers of rigour and discipline in the workplace (Espejel, 1993). Managers in charge of the modern organization of labour in the factory expected workers to be loyal and "disciplined, silent, methodical, less violent and nothing spontaneous, in other terms, to become factory workers" (Espejel, 1993: 503).

A new group: managers and technicians

The educational level in the region was low: most local residents were illiterate, as educational facilities were non-existent. As a result of this low regional educational level, skilled and technical labour was very scarce. The management of the company had to import these skilled workers and engineers from other parts of the country and from Europe. Recruitment and retention of highly skilled workers were constant concerns for management. For example, European engineers supervised the construction of the hydraulic system in 1890–1894, and Swiss and German engineers installed the manufacturing facilities (Lenz, 1990). Some of them later established Loreto y Pena Pobre, San Rafael's main competitor at the time. Company reports from the 1920s also repeatedly mention that José de la Macorra, the director-general, traveled to Europe to visit plants and recruit pulp and paper engineers. The firm constantly sought to retain these experts by offering them competitive working conditions and providing them with some of the features of urban life, such as quality housing, leisure and entertainment opportunities. These technicians were *personal de confianza;* they had stable labour contracts and were provided with special housing whose level of comfort and sophistication was unrivaled in the whole region. In 1900, management authorized the construction of 25 houses for single men, mainly engineers (Huerta Gonzalez, 1994: 290). In 1904, the *casino cosmopolita*—an accommodation and entertainment centre for bachelors—was built (Arango Miranda, 1997: 50). Overall, due to the educational and training gap between illiterate or poorly trained locals and the group of skilled workers and engineers, no local is reported to have had a managerial or senior technical position in the company for the first three decades (interview with an ex-worker).

Company–community relations

Before the factory was built, forests and water were goods that belonged to the community, under the jurisdiction of the municipality. However, various presidential decrees (1893, 1897) and company–government agreements (1897) bypassed these communal rights and accorded usufruct of the forest and water to the factory. Local residents contested the 1893 presidential decree that had given an exclusive concession for water and timber to the factory; however, the influence of the factory largely prevailed over the interests of the small, mainly rural group, and their protest was in vain. Local farmers quickly lost any rights to use local natural resources (Huerta Gonzalez, 1994).

The 1910–1919 Mexican revolution affected the factory in various ways. Communities were hard hit by epidemics, causing local populations to decrease. Causes of the revolution in Mexico included increasing inequalities between an elite and the population who lived in very precarious conditions. The San Rafael installations and forests were damaged by the Zapatistas' four-year occupation of the region, affecting the supply of raw materials. In the 1920s, the factory was forced to recruit from more distant areas. It took from 1920 to 1921 for "normal" working conditions to return.

The 1917 Mexican Constitution gave workers the right to strike and to unionize and established an eight-hour working day. These rights were, however, ignored by the management of San Rafael, and were not enforced. In the 1920s and 1930s, San Rafael gradually built a model village, "whose climate of modernity contrasted with the mainly rural landscape of the region" (Espejel, 1993). In 1923, it established the San Rafael Sportsclub, which later became one of the country's leading sports associations. It also opened the Tienda Grande, a uniquely modern shopping centre, in 1928; the Casino Obrero, a social club for workers, in 1929; a school for adults, and a dispensary for workers and their families in the 1930s. A company document (San Rafael, 1931: 96) depicted the village as:

> It is a veritable city in constant growth. It has its own market, stores for the sale of groceries, clothing, shoes and other utilities and essential household goods; a barber shop; a complete installation of steam, Russian, Turkish, shower and tub baths; and free medical, pharmaceutical and nursing attention, all of which conformed to the prescriptions of hygiene. Workers have their own chapel, casino, billiard room and dance hall, with pianolas, phonographs and radio; a library well stocked with books of all descriptions, magazines, and periodicals; a musical section that maintains the *Orquesta tipica* de San Rafael, composed of 50 professors, workers from the mills, which gives concerts periodically; and a large, well-decorated celebration hall especially built for theatre performances, gymnastics and movies, public meetings, banquets, etc., with a capacity for more than 3,000 people.

Labour relations were depicted in the same document (p. 97) as follows:

> The company works in this manner and lives without strikes or conflicts in complete accord with its employees and workers, contributing to the community through its stimulation and educational solicitude. The company established a suggestions contest, which is celebrated annually, with each idea or procedure for the improvement of the different phases of work being awarded with a prize.

Second era (1936–1970)

As mentioned previously, the 1917 Constitution had established workers' rights to strike, to unionize and to work eight hours a day. In 1922, a group of workers created the first trade union to enforce these rights and went on strike. A former worker, who was 17 in 1922 (active in the company from 1920 to 1951), remembers:

> When I started, salaries were so miserable. Then we got all together and went on strike to demand an increase of 75%. And after four months, we obtained it. We also obtained school supplies for schools,

housing for workers. We obtained all this because we were from the Revolutionary Trade Union.

The corporate annual report conveys management's reaction to the list of claims presented by workers during the 1922:

> In October, workers presented a list of demands while the director-general José de la Macorra was in Europe. A fair and satisfactory solution was found. Our company has accepted, as it always does, the workers' justified demands and has rejected the unjustified ones.

In 1923, one year after this first strike, the firm recognized the local section of the CROM (Central Revolucionaria de los Obreros Mexicanos), a management-controlled union, as the workers' only representative.

A second strike broke out 13 years later, in 1936. The trade union made the following statement in a letter to the President of the Republic, Lazaro Cardenas:

> The undesirable Spaniard José de la Macorra has exploited and humiliated more than 3,500 Mexican workers over more than 30 years. Due to its location in the foothills of the mountains, it has always been difficult to have the federal authorities intervene in the factories and enforce constitutional rights (The strike committee—Excerpts from the letter to the President of the Republic, Làzaro Cardenas, p. 42-43).

This letter laid out the workers' expectations, namely the alignment of working conditions with the rights promulgated by the Constitution 19 years before, and a call to the national government to counter the power of the dominant local family. The strike lasted four months. Some trade union leaders were killed in conflicts between two competing trade unions. President Làzaro Cardenas sent his personal secretary to mediate. Eventually, management accepted most of the workers' grievances.

As a result, as a founding section of the CTM (Confederation of Mexican Workers), the local section of the trade union emerged as the counterweight to the firm's management.[3] This union, independent from management, negotiated a new contract that recognized the workers' rights as established by the 1917 Constitution and laid the groundwork for later annual negotiations which led to the addition of further clauses.

An era of prosperity

At the time, with 3,000 workers, the San Rafael company was the largest paper producer in Mexico and among the leaders in Latin America. It also gradually

---

3 Founded in 1933 and led by Fidel Velazquez until his death in 1997, the CTM was the dominant confederation of Mexican Trade Unions and the labour pillar of the PRI (Partido Revolucionario Institucional), which dominated the national political system.

became a Mexican-owned firm, as Mexican industrialists acquired equity from foreign investors. By 1950, it was a fully-owned Mexican company.

To the extent that it provided workers with above-average salaries and housing, sponsoring sports, cultural activities, and patriotic and religious celebrations, the factory represented a "privileged enclave," a "model village" with benefits for workers and their families, including housing: between 1936 and 1970, around 860 houses were built by the company (Arango Miranda, 1997). An internal department of the company took care of their maintenance:

> If the light bulb in our house was broken, we just had to call the factory and it was repaired the following day. For free. San Rafael took care of everything (Ex-worker).
>
> We [at San Rafael] were a model village. We used to have the best patriotic celebrations in the whole Republic [Mexico]. We had sports clubs, cultural associations ... We realized how lucky we were when we went to other villages. San Rafael was clean, tidy, and wealthy. People were educated. Everybody depended directly or indirectly on the factory (Resident, San Rafael).

A number of indicators confirmed the positive effects of the factory on the development of the village of San Rafael compared to the rest of the region. For instance, in 1950, the literacy rate in San Rafael was 64%, compared to 50% in the rest of the state of Mexico; the common diet in a San Rafael family offered more variety than the average diet in the rest of the state (Arango Miranda, 1997). The factory provided lifetime, secure employment to workers based on the collective work contract:

> I started working at 16. As a son and brother of workers, I had priority— almost the right—to get a job there. The factory used to come to the local secondary schools to recruit us before graduation. Money at the factory was good. Working there solved all the economic problems of raising a family (Former secretary-general, trade union).

A new player: the trade union

If daily and interpersonal interactions between workers and managers are remembered as being generally convivial, yearly negotiations over the company-wide labour contract were moments of tension between the representatives of the factory and leaders of the trade union. Annual management–union negotiations centred on pay issues and working conditions—conversations never dealt with the position of the company in its markets or with production issues. A former secretary-general of the trade union describes the pressure from the community before negotiations with management:

Workers had told me: "We have elected you to defend our interests and don't sign the agreement easily." And a leader who would make the mistake of signing would be retaliated against back here in San Rafael. ... You know, we live in a village and everybody knows everybody. He and his family would be shunned. He would be seen as a traitor, ruthless and vile.

The firm, the trade union and the municipality of Tlalmanalco

The municipality paled in comparison to two institutions—the factory as provider of material life and the trade union as supplier of labour and link with the corporatist national system:

> The company provided everything and we did not take into account the municipality and we were not even interested in [knowing] who the mayor was. We had everything. The factory was the mother and father of the village and it is also thanks to the village that the factory grew. They provided the money and we provided the labour (Former trade union secretary-general, San Rafael).

While the factory sponsored local life, the trade union leadership oriented the affairs of the municipality. Of the 14 men who served as mayors between 1935 and 1970, eight were union members, some of them former secretary-generals. The affiliation with the CTM meant closer ties with the national corporatist regime. Being a predominantly industrial municipality, Tlalmanalco was part of the industrial part of the country in the national division of political power between the industrial, agricultural and urban parts of the corporatist regime. As a consequence, the CTM appointed the PRI municipal candidate invariably elected from 1936 until 1991. A former trade union secretary-general remembers:

> Once with Don Fidel Velasquez, they [my companions from the factory] spoke on my behalf. They mentioned to him that, on the strength of my past experience and my responsibilities as a secretary-general, they wanted to nominate me for the [municipal] presidency, and that they wanted to see whether Don Fidel would support me. The only thing Don Fidel told me was:
> - And you, what do you say?
> - Well, in certain ways I feel tired because of the work I have done and I would like to, but ...
> - Do you want it or not?
> - Well, if I can count on your support and on my companions' support, let's go for it.
> - Prepare your documents. We will see, we will submit your application to the party (PRI).

A few months later, being the only candidate in the municipal elections, he was elected mayor of Tlalmanalco.

The generation change in the leadership of the factory also brought a new style of leadership. Under the new contract, Fernando de la Macorra's role was mainly that of a mediator and sponsor of local life, as he had personal ties to most of the members of the local community. A former trade union leader (1955–1983) explains:

> Look, as I would tell you, in San Rafael, there was a mentality of protection. It was like a mother factory ... They gave us everything. Don Fernando would arrive and his word was law ... If you had a personal problem, you would ask for a meeting with him, you would explain your problem and he would provide the solution.

On his retirement in 1968, he was praised by the municipal authorities as "a great contributor to the welfare of the municipality," and by the trade union as a "model director-general." His proximity to the community is illustrated as follows:

> Don Fernando helped the people a great deal. He used to live with the people, he used to go to the fiestas with the people. He knew people's needs and for that reason the people miss him and we genuinely love him (Worker [1940–1985], former trade union leader [1955–1958]).

Under the reassuring presence of the director-general, these golden years were an era of sustained economic growth and model labour relations.

Third era (1970–1991)

In the 1970s, life in the community was determined by the pace of daily work, annual negotiations and celebrations. However, the world was changing, both internationally and nationally. At the international level, a trend towards market concentration was changing the shape of the world's paper industry. Several small- and medium-sized companies, predominantly active in national markets, were acquired or merged into a few conglomerates based in countries well endowed with natural resources—especially Scandinavia, the U.S., Canada, and Australia (Arango Miranda, 1997: 64). At the national level, built on an inwardly oriented import-substitution economic strategy, the Mexican model of "conservative modernization" that had brought 30 years of unprecedented economic growth showed increasing signs of fatigue in the 1970s. Paradoxically, despite decades of industrialization, the Mexican economy still relied on oil for 75% of its exports (Haber, 1989). This reliance on raw materials revealed the problems of the Mexican industrial structure. As a whole, industry depended heavily on government subsidies and protection, had a very limited capacity for technology and innovative development and produced relatively high-cost products through inflexible and aging production methods (Haber, 1989: 46). The gradual devaluation of the Mexican peso against the U.S. dollar revealed these difficulties, further exacerbating the problems facing Mexican companies. In 1970, the U.S. dollar was worth 12 pesos; in 1977, it was worth 22.69 pesos; and in 1982, after a major devaluation, 1,405 pesos.

San Rafael: compounding problems

In the 1970s, the San Rafael company was a study in contrasts between the apparent strengths of a perpetual industrial powerhouse and increasing internal and external vulnerabilities. San Rafael continued to employ around 2,700 workers; it was the principal benefactor of the village and an unchallenged regional employer. It produced around 10% of the paper consumed in Mexico and offered a wide array of quality paper distributed by retailers. In 1973, President Echeverria praised the company as "a model and the mother of all Mexican pulp and paper companies" and even considered nationalizing it (Arango Miranda, 1997). However, its eroding market position and bleak financial situation seriously threatened its future. San Rafael's production had not grown at the same pace as the Mexican market. For instance, Atenquique, one of its competitors, increased its production from 30,000 tons a year to 120,000 by the end of the 1970s, the average growth of the paper sector. San Rafael, on the other hand, only increased its production two-fold (Arango Miranda, 1997). Also, in the 1940–1970 period, 35 new companies entered the Mexican pulp and paper market and new products were launched, such as tissue and new cardboards. It became increasingly obvious that most of the economic value was created by these new products, which relied on the internal capacity of firms to innovate.

Equipped with old machinery and hampered by an old and expensive labour contract, San Rafael had limited ability to react to these changes. The gradual deterioration of its finances exacerbated this inertia. It had become a Mexican-owned company. However, it turned out to be a poor investment, since returns were much lower than the industry average. The company's debt had also increased during this high-growth period. In 1970, the Nacional Financiera, its main creditor and a state-owned financial institution, finally bought the financially bankrupt company. These changes in ownership and control equally hampered the company's capacity for restructuring. The director-generals appointed by the Nacional Financiera changed frequently. As explained by a San Rafael worker (1971–1991):

> They did not know the pulp and paper industry. They were bankers appointed by the banks. Almost every year, there was a new director-general.

In 1981, San Rafael was purchased by Crisoba, a subsidiary of Scott Paper and one of its main competitors. A difference in product strategy between the two companies further limited San Rafael. While Crisoba, as a Scott company, focused on tissue papers, San Rafael specialized in quality papers for writing. Crisoba Scott pursued a product strategy that was detrimental to San Rafael and restricted reinvestment in the plant and equipment.

Decline in workers' morale

The 1970s were a crossroads for management, with limited financial reinvestment and frequent changes in managerial and leadership positions. On the workers' side, informants reported a gradual decline in morale and increased sabotage, strikes and absenteeism covered up by colleagues and the trade union. A former worker described the declining situation (1971–1991):

> This is when the decline started. There are many things that contributed to this. First, we the workers were lazy and others who were on sick leave and social security would agree. Then, many managers used to take machinery out. They said it was old and they would build their own little plant around here. And there were various other factors. Management was never concerned about the future and they believed that the factory would last forever.

A newly hired engineer remembers one of his first days on the job in the factory in 1988 or 1989:

> They were craftsmen … They had long lunches together in the afternoon, even with *pulque* [local alcoholic beverage] and beer. Once, this happened in 1988 or 1989, they even cooked a turkey here in the plant between the two machines and spent the afternoon eating it. Everybody knew everybody. There were many parties. Social life was great. Since the ones supposed to watch were friends of the ones being watched, everybody was able to leave [work] whenever they wanted. But their teammates would make up for the job in their absence.

The trade union endorsed this eroding commitment of workers to the company. As a former trade union leader put it:

> I was a leader and, well, I learned that what we did was harmful to the company, but as a trade union leader, I had to support absentee workers. We didn't have much of a choice, one had to deal with these people and support them. If not, I would lose face, my job, and my family would be ostracized.

Reduced managerial and labour commitment further deteriorated trade union–management relations. Mutual trust and commitment, probably the prevailing characteristic of the relationship before 1970, gradually eroded. A former trade union leader mentions:

> In the 1980s, management always gave us numbers in the red. We did not believe them, partially because we did not trust them, but also because none of us knew anything about accounting and finance. We did not know for sure whether the numbers were really in the red. Every year they told us that the factory was losing money ... We did not trust them any more ... It was logical that the trade union leaders did not accept the deals proposed by the company.

Relations were rigid, as illustrated by the trade union leader's reaction to the announcement of a restructuring in the early 1980s. Management announced that 250 workers were to be fired, as production was slowing down:

> We replied: "We don't agree with this restructuring and we will go on strike." Then, we spread the news among the people. We told them about the situation: No we don't agree with the plan. We come first and if the company goes bankrupt, well, they have to compensate us first. The law and the contract say so. We have priority. So we have to conquer it and the banks will find a way to get their money back. And we went on strike for 41 days and fortunately we reached an agreement.

In June 1991, management announced the closing of the factory. The motives invoked included:

> ... lack of investment, extreme obsolescence of the machinery and the equipment, the disposal of polluting emissions into rivers and the atmosphere, ... and countless problems of various nature ... All these problems have become so persistent that our company is in a poor competitive situation ... For these reasons, the board of directors has decided to close the plant on June 9, 1991. All collective labour relations will be terminated as of this date (Cited in Barreto Flores, 1998: 52).

In September 1991, the company opened again with about one-fourth of the personnel. The new labour contract was aligned with national federal labour laws. The company discontinued its sponsorship of community activities. The polluting cellulose plant was closed and the San Rafael-Crisoba plant stopped using local lumber. A wall was erected, physically and symbolically separating the factory from the village. In 1995, as Crisoba was bought by Kimberly-Clark, the San Rafael plant then became part of Kimberly Clark de México, the leading pulp and paper producer in the country. As of 2009, the San Rafael plant had around 400 workers.

Post mortem: San Rafael at the crossroads of its history

San Rafael's location as a hub between Mexico City and the mountainous areas, previously a source of comparative advantage in the industrial era, has become a liability as pressures from the urban area threaten the local balance. Mexico City's population comprises around 20 million and is sprawling into what used to be rural areas. Uncontrolled urban sprawl from the metropolis disrupts the sense of localness as two trends threaten to gradually transform San Rafael into a bedroom community. First, since 1991, the local economy is depressed and about 50% of the local workforce commutes daily to the metropolitan area (Noyola Rocha, 1999). Second, many residents from the metropolitan area are settling in Tlalmanalco, as land there is more affordable than in more densely populated areas of the metropolis (UAM, 2000). As a result, the population of Tlalmanalco grew from 29,000 in 1980, to 43,000 in 2000 and to 70,810 in 2007. For most local residents, the company is gone, the enclave is increasingly becoming part of the metropolitan area and locals feel a sense of powerlessness faced with these new threats.

References

Anaya Pérez, Marco Antonio (1998). *Rebelión y revolución en Chalco – Amecameca (1821-1921)*, Vol. 2, U.A. Chapingo, México, Instituto Nacional de Estudios Históricos de la Revolución Mexicana.

Arango Miranda, Azucena (1997). *Industria y espacio en San Rafael, México: Formación, desarrollo y desenclave*, Tesis de Licenciatura en Geografía, UNAM, México, DF.

Barreto Flores, Salvador (1998). *El movimiento campesino en la región Iztaccihuatl-Popocatépetl y la explotación forestal por la fábrica de papel San Rafael (1986-1992)*, Tesina, Facultad de Ciencias Políticas y Sociales, UNAM, México, México.

CDI (Club Deportivo Internacional) (1938), *A la fábrica de papel de San Rafael!* 16 p.

Espejel, Laura (1993). "San Rafael, una enclave," in *Entre lagos y volcanes: Chalco Amecameca, pasado y presente*, Alejandro Tortolero (Ed.), Vol. 1 and 2, Toluca, México, El Colegio Mexiquense.

Garcia Luna, Margarita (1998). *Los orígenes de la industria en el Estado de México (1830-1930)*, Toluca, México, Gobierno del Estado de México.

Haber, Stephen (1989). *Industrialization and Underdevelopment*, University of Texas Press.

Huerta Gonzalez (1994). Transformacion del paisaje, recursos naturales e industrializacion, el caso de la fabrica de San Rafael, estado de México, 1890–1934, in *Tierra, Agua y bosques: Historia y Medio Ambiente en México Central*, Alejandro Tortolero Villasenor, coord., coleccion Ecologia, Coed. Centro Francès de Estudios Mexicanos y Centroamericanos y Centro de Investigaciones Dr. José Maria Luis Mora, Potrillo Ed.

Lenz, Hans (1990). *Historia del papel en México y cosas relacionadas*, México, Porrua Ed.

Noyola Rocha, Jaime (1999), *Monografía de Tlalmanalco*, Estado de México.

San Rafael (1931). *A la fabrica de papel de San Rafael*, 16 p.

UAM (2000). *Atlas de los recursos naturales de Tlalmanalco*, México City, UAM.

About the author

 **Emmanuel Raufflet** (PhD McGill) teaches management, corporate social responsibility and sustainable development at HEC Montreal. He has written articles and books on corporate social responsibility and sustainable development He serves as chair at the NACRA (North American Case Research Association) of the Business and Society/Business Ethics Track. He has published numerous books and articles.

Teaching notes for this case are available from Greenleaf Publishing. These are free of charge and available only to teaching staff. They can be requested by going to:
www.greenleaf-publishing.com/darkside2notes

Section B
Human rights and business

5

Kraft Foods Argentina
The H1N1 disparity

Susan Myrden
Maine Business School, University of Maine

Kathy Sanderson
Faculty of Business Administration, Lakehead University

In July of 2009, an announcement was made by the Argentinean government, expressing their concern about the severity of the H1N1 outbreak. This announcement caused much unrest with the workers in a Kraft Foods factory, located in the suburbs of Argentina. When management ignored the requests of both the government and the employees for basic improvements in the conditions around the plant to protect the workers, the employees took action against the company by way of a protest. This incident resulted in 160 people being fired (including all of the non-official union members), ultimately causing a more severe retaliation which led to a work stoppage in the factory. Days later, the workers were removed by the police with force, injuring many. Since the incident, Kraft has been forced to re-instate many of the fired workers but is still in legal battles regarding the rest of the workers.

The case highlights a series of incidents that involved workers' rights at this international factory of a multinational U.S. company. It highlights the power and influence that exists within organizations and shows how each of the key stakeholder groups use this power in order to influence change. It highlights how leadership styles and barriers to communication can impact the overall health of an organization. It illustrates the differences in business practices within developing countries when they are heavily reliant on outside investments and host countries, how the espoused and enacted values differ significantly, and how the treatment of employees creates new and significant risks for individuals, families and communities who are already marginalized and oppressed.

Introduction: the snapshot

It was October 28th, 2010, and a number of the Kraft-Terrabusi workers, both past and present, sat around a table, contemplating what they had witnessed over the past months and wondering where to go from here. The workers were not happy with the way things had unfolded. "They can't get away with this ... we have to do something," commented Eduardo, a former Kraft worker. "It's crazy to think that asking for basic health necessities could get so many people fired ... they can't walk in here and bully us around—we are people too with families to support!" "You are absolutely right! Just because a few of us got our jobs back doesn't mean they can silence us," said Carlos, "it's just not right—we have to do something!"

It had been almost four months since Kraft had fired 160 people from their plant just north of Buenos Aires, Argentina, after workers created a work stoppage inside the plant after being refused basic health necessities in the wake of the H1N1 virus.

Kraft Foods: the company

Kraft, which opened its doors back in 1903, is the largest food manufacturer in the U.S. and the second largest in the world, next to Nestlé S.A. At that time, James L. Kraft opened a cheese distributor in Chicago, Illinois, where its head-quarters still exist today.

Kraft has grown to become one of the largest food companies joining forces with Nabisco Foods in 2000. The company produces in more than 70 countries, and distributes in more than 160, earning over $48 billion in annual sales in 2009. It employs approximately 97,000 people worldwide located in more than 180 pro-cessing and manufacturing facilities. Kraft's activities are still concentrated within the North American domestic market; however, additional areas of importance are Europe, South America, and Australia. The development of its Asian and east-ern European markets have been seen as insufficient to date. Kraft Foods' multi-national strategy utilizes relatively independent regional or local company units. Among these elements are cost cuts and the optimization of existing locations (e.g., through application of technical progress in the transnational framework or optimization of capacities and consolidation on a regional and global scale). In addition, advantages are sought through cheaper raw materials and the use of pro-duction sources in free trade areas. In all, Kraft's impact is strong and far reaching.

Kraft Foods: the commitment

As a global employer, Kraft has identified what they term as key 'Responsibili-ties' to all of their stakeholders. These standards of behavior apply to all of their plants and businesses, and include clear statements on the treatment of employees, safety and a detailed code of conduct. The Kraft Foods Responsibility Report (Kraft 2010) and Code of Conduct (Kraft 2009b) states that Kraft is committed to the following:

Working to build a better world

- Through actions large and small, global and local, Kraft is doing what's right and holding themselves accountable.

- A world where ethics and profit are not mutually exclusive. And where everyone is treated fairly.

A great place to work

- Keeping workers safe. Safety is a top priority.

- Safety and health improvement are both an individual and team responsibility.

- Each of us must be dedicated to conducting all activities with the highest concern for employee safety and health.

- Accordingly, Kraft is committed to: meeting or exceeding all applicable safety and health regulations; continuously improving the safety of our work environment by investing in our people and our facilities; creating and maintaining a world-class safety culture to achieve an accident-free work environment.

Sustaining a legacy of trust

Ensuring people feel safe to speak up: Under our Speaking Up policy, Kraft expects employees to ask questions and raise concerns about business practices when they see something they think might be wrong. There may be times when employees are not comfortable speaking with their supervisors, compliance officers or human resources contacts, or simply wish to remain anonymous. Kraft has established a toll-free telephone helpline ... so that its employees can confidentially and, if they wish, anonymously report instances of suspected wrongdoing or ask questions about compliance matters.

Code of Conduct

The ten rules described below reflect Kraft's values, particularly the most essential one—trust. Trust means that others can rely on us to speak truthfully, to honor commitments, and to treat people fairly.

Rule 1:   Make food that is safe to eat

Rule 2:   Market responsibly

Rule 3:   Treat people fairly

Rule 4:   Respect the free market

Rule 5:   Compete fairly

Rule 6:   Respect the environment

Rule 7:   Deal honestly with the government

Rule 8:   Keep honest books and records

Rule 9:   Never trade on inside information

Rule 10:   Give Kraft Foods your complete business loyalty

- Ignoring problems only makes them worse, and damages trust. We all must play by the same rules, and we want to know our colleagues honor the same values. When problems come up, we'll carefully look into all the facts and circumstances, from all perspectives. We will conduct all investigations fairly.

- Maybe you're worried about retaliation. Kraft Foods won't tolerate that. Anyone who retaliates against someone for raising a concern in good faith will face discipline, which may include termination. If you report a violation, Kraft Foods will fully support you, because it's fair and it's vital to our business.

Kraft Foods: Argentina

U.S. activity in foreign markets has been both extensive and influential, creating, in some cases, substantial dependence on the host companies. For instance, U.S. investments in Argentina have generated over 155,000 jobs to Argentinean workers alone.

In 1994 Nabisco Foods, a subsidiary of Kraft Foods since 2000, purchased Terrabusi, the nation's largest cookie/cracker manufacturer. Kraft's entrance had meant great things for the small town and at the time, the Pacheco Plant employed 8,000 workers (although by 2009, that number had fallen by over half to only 2,700 employees) making it an important employer in the municipality of Tigre, where it is located. The company covers nearly 50% of the U.S.'s cookie market, making Kraft's plant in the working class suburb of Pacheco one of the most important outside of the United States.

In many countries, like Argentina, Kraft quietly buys out local labels and markets the brand under the same name. Consolidation of market power throughout the food industry has been the trend.

Two thousand and nine impacted many companies with the bleak state of the economy. Fortunate for Kraft, it is one company that has managed to do well in spite of the downturn. With skyrocketing food prices, many consumers are turning to more economical, processed food. However, Argentina on the whole is being impacted by the economy. Companies are being forced to reduce their costs. In its pursuit to recoup these costs, which would provide additional safeguarding against the economic crisis, word was spreading that Kraft was looking to restructure, altering its shift structure by employing two 12-hour shifts, replacing its current arrangement of three 8-hour shifts and dismissing the redundant workers. A Kraft worker who was quoted in a local Argentinean newspaper noted:

> [The Company] wanted to get rid of the workers who put themselves at the front of the struggle in order to implement the American production system of 12 hour shifts, which is already in place in the Kraft plant in San Luis (a western province of Argentina) to get rid of a whole shift (West, 2009).

Noted one worker,

> They wanted to quiet us so they could begin applying the 12-hour American work shift, employing agency laborers that rotate every six months, increasing production without increasing salary or work force, freezing salaries and all the measures that these types of companies apply.

As a result of this and numerous similar issues the workers decided to stand up for the collective and demand what they felt they were entitled.

Conflict at Kraft Foods Argentina: the employees' fears

It was July of 2009 and coupled with the turmoil created about possible restructuring, there was a rumbling amongst the workers after news of the H1N1 virus epidemic had made its way around the country. The threat of the virus created much unrest with the workers as they feared for their own health as well as the health of their family members. An announcement from the Health Ministry had just been made on a local news channel, which detailed guidelines for workplaces around the country to deal with the outbreak. It included such measures as providing antibacterial soap, alcohol gel and paper towels to its workers in order to increase the level of hygiene throughout the workplace. The announcement also encouraged companies to grant leave to women who were pregnant, as these people were much more susceptible to contracting the virus. In response, schools, public spaces and workplaces were shut down throughout the country to prevent the virus from spreading. However, when Kraft was asked to enforce the guidelines, they refused.

"We have rights! It's not too much to ask for basic things that will keep us safe!" demanded Christiano, a member on the factory's Internal Commission, elected to represent the interests of the workers (the Pacheco Plant has had 11 Internal Commission delegates and 19 representatives—referred to as "Congresales").

"You have all that you need," commented Benito, a factory manager, "one thing we will do in order to protect you is to shut down the [company] daycare center—we'll give the women 200 pesos (70 dollars) to find their own private child care."

After weeks of persistent requests, the workers proceeded to strike, briefly preventing managers from leaving the building, to demand proper health measures at the company's factory. One worker reflected:

> A few years ago (2004) the Kraft Foods company bought out the most important food production factory in Argentina, where we produce goods for local consumption as well as for neighboring countries. The buyout was through a business deal, which allowed Kraft to purchase the company at a very low price.
>
> Since the multinational took over the company, working conditions have become more than bad. In the midst of a world pandemic caused by the H1N1 virus, children and government employees were excused from duties in order to prevent the spread of the disease. The mothers working at the Kraft factory didn't have anyone to watch over their children. Furthermore, there are horrible hygiene conditions and security in the factory, much less in the factory's daycare center; there wasn't even a bottle of disinfectant for the hands of the 3,000 employees. When we had our first case of H1N1 within the factory, we had to go on strike so that they would give us the days off.

As a result of the strike, in August 2009 the Company elected to fire 160 of the workers, including the majority of its elected Internal Commission delegates, violating Argentinean law. The union demanded their jobs be reinstated, but Kraft refused.

It was no secret that Kraft had its own plan to restructure the plant, similar to that of its other plant in a western province in Argentina, where it made many of its workers redundant in a quest to save money. "When the conflict started over health measures for the swine flu (H1N1), Kraft already had a plan to fire the union delegates in order to make cut backs, adding to poverty and unemployment throughout the region" noted Sandra, a member of the human rights organization, Mothers of Plaza de Mayo.

In response to Kraft's actions, eighty workers showed up at the factory and took over the plant in protest, placing the operation at a standstill. Outside the plant, the majority of the remaining workers (2,700 in total) participated in numerous protests to show their solidarity to the occupying workers. Eduardo recalled: "The conflict started during the H1N1 epidemic. We were demanding improvements like paper towels, toilet paper, alcohol gel, and other health measures. Because we made our demands, they fired 160 workers."

Eduardo was a 45-year-old employee of the Pacheco plant that had been there even before Kraft had taken over. He was a native to Argentina and had a wife and four children. He was elected to the Internal Commission just over a year ago but had fought for the rights of the workers since the beginning. He had been around for a long time and knew the impact that a big company like Kraft could have on the workers of this small town if they weren't protected. Eduardo was one of the 160 fired as a result of the events that had developed over the past few months.

The scene outside the plant was that of support from not only the factory's employees, but also people who were not affiliated with the organization. Around the country thousands of students, union activists, human rights groups and other groups organized actions of solidarity. Marches of thousands of supporters could be seen for miles. Some supporters could be spotted with their fists in the air chanting "unity of the workers" at the top of their lungs even as the police had them sitting in the dust and surrounded by dogs. The media were present as the events unfolded, making front page news in every major newspaper, in addition to being filmed live by the major news channels. Inside the plant the workers were camping out peacefully to demand their jobs. Although, outside and unaware of what was happening inside, representatives from Kraft were singing a different tune. "They are inside the plant forcing the other employees from leaving against their free will," commented a company spokesperson.

"Inside and outside, the plant had been militarized," shouted Carlos. "Look at that place! It resembles a prison, not a factory. Barbed wired borders the gates, guards walk the perimeter with attack dogs, and police patrol on horseback and the union members are barred from entering."

The Company's most direct violation of Argentina's labor code has been to prohibit union delegates from entering the plant. According to the law, companies must allow even suspended delegates to fulfill their roles inside the plant.

Following failed negotiations between the Labor Ministry, Kraft, and union delegates, late on September 25, 2009, police surrounded and entered the plant and attacked protesters. They beat the activists and opened fire with rubber bullets and tear gas and forcibly removed the workers so that Kraft could resume plant operations. They arrested 65 people and injured 12, including workers and their family members.

Eduardo, who was one of the workers that went into the factory to protest, witnessed, first hand, the police attack on September 25th and noted:

> The assault was televised live, and millions of Argentineans witnessed levels of violent repression not seen since the 70's and 80's military

dictatorship or the December 2001 rebellion, which removed the government in the wake of a major economic collapse. Here in Argentina the economic crisis is getting worse. Many companies need to "restructure" and cut labor costs to maintain profits. Kraft, and other multinationals that have the [Union Industrial Argentina's] support, are seeking to restructure personnel. This is why the government allows violent repression against workers. They want the workers to carry the burden of the economic crisis.

Conflict at Kraft Foods Argentina: the company line

Days after the events had occurred, Simon, an executive who had been brought down to Buenos Aires from Kraft's head office in Chicago to assess the circumstances, could be seen in front of a news camera commenting on the situation:

> On Friday, September 25th, over two weeks after the occupation of the Pacheco facility, provincial Buenos Aires Police acting under a court order from the Judge of Warranties No. 2 of San Isidro, upon request of the Talar de Pacheco Criminal Prosecutor, evicted the group of workers occupying the plant. I would like to be clear that the eviction was not carried out by or under the direction of Kraft Foods; and Kraft regrets that this unfortunate event took place (Kraft, 2009a).

He went on to say, "we are incredibly troubled by what happened at the plant over the past few weeks, but we feel that the situation was unwarranted as [Kraft] hadn't violated any laws."

"Kraft Foods´ sanitation and hygiene standards are well above those that can be found in other industries," noted Roger, a manager at the Pacheco plant.

> Our food production processes include hand washing stations and the use of hairnets and smocks to ensure proper sanitary conditions inside production facilities. Shortly after we were made aware of the guidelines issued by the Healthy Ministry, The Company took a number of measures to rectify the situation including reinforcement of sanitation practices at the plants and in open spaces and common areas, initiated an employee information campaign, outlining safeguards to prevent flu contamination, and assigned new cafeteria shifts to minimize crowds and personal contact (Kraft, 2009a).

"We're dumbfounded by all of this," stated Simon. "We felt as though the demands of the delegates of the Internal Commission to completely close the Pacheco facility and provide thirty days of paid leave for all production employees in addition to the daycare remaining open were unreasonable."

In order to convey the impeccable work conditions that the plant provided, Simon went on to say,

> The Pacheco facilities include five acres of park land, with a soccer field, volleyball and tennis courts, and two running paths. These, as well as an outdoor barbecue space and recreational room, can be used by any employee free of charge, including for personal or family use. There is also a gym, for which Kraft Foods offers subsidized membership. The salary level of production employees at Pacheco is well above the average for the industry in Argentina. Kraft Foods currently compensates production employees at Pacheco between 15 and 20 percent above amounts required by the current "Convenio" (the Agreement reached between a company and its labor union). The Pacheco facility also offers several additional benefits. There is a cafeteria where all employees are provided breakfast, lunch or dinner free of charge. Kraft Foods also provides a daycare center for all employee children four years or younger without charge. Kraft Foods has been ranked as employer of choice in Argentina. As part of its commitment to corporate social responsibility, Kraft Foods is one of the main donators to the Food Bank Foundation in Argentina (Kraft, 2009a).

Managers that represent the company maintain that the dismissal of the workers had nothing to do with unionization. "We released the workers because of an incident that transpired on July 3, 2009, when 200 employees surrounded the administrative building at the Pacheco location for three hours, preventing employees and managers inside from leaving the premises with threats and physical force," commented a representative. "We felt that we could specifically identify those involved in criminal acts." According to Kraft, on August 18, these workers were dismissed "with fair cause" under Argentine labor law.[1]

Conflict at Kraft Foods Argentina: human rights?

As human rights advocates around the world celebrate International Human Rights Day, the International Labor Rights Forum (ILRF) had released a report identifying the "Worst Companies of 2009 for the Right to Associate," which included a list of the four worst multinational corporations on the basis of union organizing, a list that afforded Kraft Foods centre stage (ILRF 2009).

Despite the labor rights protections in the United Declaration of Human Rights (UDHR), United Nations (UN) and the International Labor Organization (ILO) declarations and national labor laws, workers continue to see their rights

---

1   Article 242 of Ley de Contrato de Trabajo: http://www.infoleg.gov.ar/infolegInternet/anexos/25000-29999/25552/texact.htm.

thwarted on a daily basis. "In the midst of these *selective firings* they sacked our union leaders, the factory committee and our union delegates. We know that the Kraft Foods plant in Chicago doesn't have a union and we're sure that this is what these factory owners want to do, even in violation of the Argentine laws," reflected one union delegate (West, 2009).

As the global economic crisis spreads, many labor advocates fear that companies are using the crisis as a pretext for cracking down on unionized workers and instituting employment schemes that reduce the number of workers guaranteed union protections.

Intimidation, mistreatment and violence against trade unionists continue to be common tactics of major multinational corporations, who protect their profit at the expense of workers' fundamental human rights. In the incident that occurred at the Pacheco plant, 12 individuals were injured.

Kraft was one of four companies that made the International Labor Forum Rights list with violations in not only Argentina, but also China, Honduras and the United Kingdom. With respect to Argentina, in particular, the Americas Program of the Center for International Policy issued a report revealing that a large number of workers were terminated by Kraft Foods in Argentina in retaliation to worker protests (Trigona, 2009). The workers had decided to take a stand against Kraft's exploitive practices and degrading conditions. Kraft Foods was not a stranger to this type of activity. "Kraft has a history of getting rid of the organized workers and union organizers that are not under their control," notes a representative from the campaign to boycott Kraft in the United States (Trigona, 2009). For instance, Colombia's Food Union, Sinaltrainal, has reported persecution of union members at Kraft factories in that country. "The plant managers that have passed through this company over the last six years have had rising careers, climbing through various posts and seeking promotion by strictly applying the company's anti-union policies and using coercive measures against the workers," noted Philip, a Sinaltrainal Union worker (Trigona, 2009).

In fact, Kraft closed five factories in South America after the acquisition of Nabisco brands. Since 2003, the company has fired hundreds of workers, cutting personnel by 37%. When firings weren't enough to stave off union activity, the company has resorted to direct threats, as in the case of a group of 30 workers who were locked inside a lunch room and told to sign letters of resignation. Similar to Argentina, in Columbia, Kraft has also used the police to forcefully remove protesting workers from factories (Trigona, 2009).

Conflict at Kraft Foods Argentina: uncertain future

Despite a government order to rehire the delegates and negotiate on further rehiring, Kraft refused. The campaign to get the 160 workers back resulted in two months of militant action in solidarity with the fired workers.

"Kraft is a North American multinational that has the money to finance repression and pay fines to the Labor Ministry when they violate Argentina's labor laws," commented Eduardo. The corporation has violated the Obligatory Conciliation period ordered by the Labor Ministry, which would enforce the temporary rehiring of all fired workers until both sides of the conflict reached an agreement. Kraft even called for the U.S. Embassy to take its side in the costly labor conflict.

Bama Athreya, Executive Director of the International Labor Rights Forum, said: "As we celebrate International Human Rights Day and the Universal Declaration of Human Rights, consumers and labor rights advocates globally can support the human rights of workers by letting these companies know that they need to respect the right to organize" (Athreya, 2009).

Although Kraft claimed to have addressed the request of the Internal Division, the Americas Program Report gives reasons to be suspicious of the sincerity of Kraft's claims. Workers claim that plans to restructure and let go part of the factory's employees were already in the works. If implemented, the restructuring would eliminate a shift by employing two 12-hour shifts, replacing its current arrangement of three 8-hour shifts and dismissing the surplus workers. Therefore, the protest would have provided an opportunity for Kraft to dismiss union members and jump start the restructuring while disingenuously placing the responsibility on the workers.

The U.S. embassy issued a statement demanding protection of private property and a permanent solution to the conflict at Kraft. The Embassy had followed the conflict based on their interest in promoting U.S. investments in Argentina which have helped generate jobs for over 150,000 Argentine workers. The workers struggle has shown the extent to which capitalist governments will go.

Conflict at Kraft Foods Argentina: back on track?

Kraft has now partially retreated. The company first agreed to rehire 30 of the workers (excluding the Internal Commission), but later agreed to hire back an additional 20 in order to comply with the decrees of the courts. Since then, the company has rehired 70 of the 160 terminated employees, promised not to close any shift and to maintain all existing jobs, allowed the delegates to enter the plant and do their union work, and agreed to discuss the situations, one by one. Forty-five workers have not been rehired, while the remaining 45 agreed to leave in exchange for large buyouts. The company calls this an act of "good faith," rather than "responding to legal and consumer pressure by backtracking on its infringement of workers' freedom of association."

Although production has resumed and some have returned to work, others have been left out in the cold. "I am happy to see that some of the workers are back at work. They are refreshing their forces and having assemblies in the factory to discuss the next steps. Elections for union delegates will be held in November of 2009. Union members are expected to show the company, through a vote, that they support the Commission's leadership. This is different to management's opinion that the conflict was caused by a small group of troublemakers," comments Eduardo. "However, I'm not sure what's going to happen to me—or those like me. There are very few jobs in this region, but I have to find a way to take care of my family."

Review questions

1. What do you think has motivated the workers to take action? Why do you think this has occurred at this point in time?

2. What counterproductive work behaviors are the employees engaging in? Do you think these actions are helping or hindering their efforts to change the work environment?

3. What forms of power and influence have the employees attempted to utilize? What impacts, positive, negative and neutral, do you think this strategy has produced?

4. What forms of power and influence has management and government attempted to utilize? What impact, if any, do you think this has had on the employees?

5. Identify the unethical behaviors of the employees and the management. What impact do you think these actions had on the relationship between the two parties?

6. If you were a manger in this plant, what type of leadership style would you adopt? How do you think this style would affect the labor/management relations?

7. At what point do you think the communication between employees and management broke down. Identify the factors that contributed to the breakdown. What actions of employees and management do you think are directly attributable to this breakdown?

8. What impact do you think the structure of the organization is having on the current labor issue? Identify the ways that the structure is impacting both communication and leadership considerations.

9. Compare the espoused and enacted values of the company. In what areas does this case illustrate congruence and in what areas does it illustrate divergence?

References

Athreya, B. (2009). *Worst companies for union organizing highlighted for international human rights day*. Washington, D.C.: ILRF.

Bureau of Western Hemisphere Affairs. (2010). Argentina. Retrieved February 1, 2011, from http://www.state.gov/r/pa/ei/bgn/26516.htm.

Colquitt, J. A., LePine, J. A., Wesson, M. J., and Gellatly, I. R. (2010). *Organizational behaviour* (Canadian edition). Toronto: McGraw-Hill Ryerson.

Geare, A. J. (1972). The problem of industrial unrest: Theories into the causes of local strikes in a New Zealand meat freezing works. *Journal of Industrial Relations*, 14, 13-22.

Hebdon, R., and Brown, T. C. (2008). *Industrial Relations in Canada*. Toronto: Nelson.

ILRF. (2009). *Working for Scrooge: Worst companies of 2009 for the right to associate*. Washington, D.C.: ILRF.

Kraft. (2009a, October 13). Kraft foods response to concerns alleging Kraft Argentina fired union workers for organizing protests and about alleged collaboration with violent police behavior. *Business and Human Rights Resource Centre*, from http://www.business-humanrights.org/Documents/Kraft-response-re-labour-rights-concerns-in-Argentina-13-Oct-2009.pdf .

Kraft. (2009b). *Our Way of Doing Business: The Kraft Foods Code of Conduct*.

Kraft. (2010). *Working to build a better world: The Kraft Foods Responsibility Report*.

Kraft Foods. (2009). Company Fact Sheet. from http://www.kraftfoodscompany.com/assets/pdf/kraft_foods_fact_sheet.pdf.

McShane, S., and Steen, S. (2009). *Canadian Organizational Behaviour* (7 ed.). Toronto: McGraw Hill Ryerson Limited.

Sniderman, P. R., Bulmash, J., Nelson, D. L., and Quick, J. C. (2010). *Managing organizational behaviour in Canada* (2 ed.). Toronto: Nelson Education Ltd.

Trigona, M. (2009). Kraft firings feed protests. Available at http://www.zcommunications.org/zsearch/contents_list/1467.

UNDP. (2000). *Human development report 2000*. New York: Oxford University Press.

West, T. (2009). The struggle at Kraft-Terrabusi in Argentina. *League for the Fifth International*. Retrieved from http://www.fifthinternational.org/print/content/struggle-kraft-terrabusi-argentina.

Ximenez, D. (2009, October 30). Kraft foods workers in Argentina occupy factory. Labor Notes. Retrieved from http://labornotes.org/node/2545.

About the authors

 **Susan Myrden** is an Assistant Professor of Marketing at the University of Maine located in Orono, Maine. A native of St. John's, Newfoundland, Canada, she completed her B.Comm. (Co-op) at Memorial University of Newfoundland and her MBA degree from the University of North Carolina at Greensboro. She received her PhD from Saint Mary's University in Halifax, Nova Scotia in 2013 where her dissertation research focused on the relationship between leadership and service quality. After holding a faculty appointment at Memorial University of Newfoundland since 2005, she has recently joined the faculty at the Maine Business School where she teaches courses in introductory marketing and advanced courses in services marketing and international marketing at the undergraduate level.

Kathy Sanderson is a Sessional Lecturer in the Faculty of Business Administration at Lakehead University in Thunder Bay, ON. She teaches undergraduate courses in Organizational Behaviour, Organizational Change, and Human Resources Planning. Kathy obtained her BAdmin and MMgt from Lakehead University, and is currently a PhD (Candidate) with St. Mary's University in Halifax, NS. Her research focuses on workplace ostracism. Kathy is also the Executive Director of Crossroads Centre, an Alcohol and Drug Recovery Home, located in Thunder Bay.

Teaching notes for this case are available from Greenleaf Publishing. These are free of charge and available only to teaching staff. They can be requested by going to:
www.greenleaf–publishing.com/darkside2notes

6

When clothes for children are made by children

Guillaume Delalieux
Sciences Po Lille, France

The rat race for low prices in the clothing industry has encouraged companies to relocate outside Europe, in South East Asia. Created in 1996 DISTRI (not its real name) decided to have its clothes manufactured in South East Asia, where costs are low, emulating thereby the majority of its competitors. This low cost supply chain allowed the firm to pursue a strong growth strategy: in 1996 DISTRI had five stores in France. Ten years later DISTRI had more than 500 stores (two-thirds abroad) with sales over €400 million and had more than 3,000 employees on its payroll. By reducing the costs of production to such a low level, distributors were able to spend a lot of money in marketing and advertising while keeping selling prices low.

In 2002, in the wake of the Collectif ESE event, a journalist asked the founder of DISTRI why his company was working with Burmese suppliers. At a loss to give an answer the founder went on to join an industry association with a program of social auditing, and asked his wife to benchmark the CSR practices of his competitors. This benchmark was then used by employees of the firm in a CSR project, with CSR associations being consulted, which led to the creation of a firm foundation for children in countries where DISTRI was selling clothes. The founder of the firm took part in numerous events where he talked about the CSR values of the firm and the positive impact of its presence in Burma.

DISTRI[1] and the clothing industry

Clothing industry overview

The first wave of relocations took place in the late 1980s in southern Europe (Spain and Portugal), then in North Africa and finally in China and South East Asia. Since the end of the MFA (Multi Fibre Arrangement) at the beginning of the 21st century, the proportion of the South East Asian countries in the output of the textile industry has increased dramatically.

Labor-intensive industry with low social and environmental standards and poor quality products

The production conditions (social and environmental standards) in those countries are widely criticized by international organizations, trade unions and NGOs. China, which accounts for more than half of world textile production, is the main target of NGOs and trade unions. The latter accuse China of not respecting the fundamental ILO standards as regards working conditions and the environment. Even though there is no official labor regulation in China, the main principles that regulate working relations between employers and employees were settled by the labor regulations passed in 1995. China is accused of basing its economic development on the exploitation of its own working population (the Mingong), by artificially maintaining a yuan low exchange rate and by controlling its trade unions.

Regarding ILO standards, the working conditions in these countries located in Southeast Asia are very bad, very close to modern slavery in many cases. The huge number of people who are willing to work (reserve army) tend to keep wages at too low a level for one or two workers to provide for a whole family, thus forcing children to work.

As a result of this low cost policy, the clothes produced have become of such poor quality that it is impossible to recycle them. Associations specialized in the recycling of clothes such as Emmaüs in France have called into question the fact that they are forced to pay for the burning of the clothes people bring them.[2] Associations, but also some politicians, have rejected this business model, which leads to the externalization of jobs to foreign countries where social and environmental standards are low and quality of products poor. Even though people are under the impression that they are buying cheap clothes, in fact they are paying a high price through local taxes for the recycling of the cheap clothes and also through social benefits like the RMI[3] or unemployment benefits given to people who lost their jobs in the process.

---

1   The real name of the company has been removed here since we guaranteed anonymity to interviewed people during our research.
2   Taxe emmaüs was created in 2006 by the French governement: less than €0,01 is levied on each piece of cloth sold in order to finance the recycling of the clothes.
3   Revenu Minimum d'Insertion: a monthly payment given to any French resident (for at least 5 years) over 25 with no income at all.

Denunciation campaign

The French distribution sector, in the same way as the textile industry, has been the target of much criticism and public denunciation since 1995, in particular from a social activist organization which includes trade unions and NGOs under the name "Collectif Ethique sur etiquette" (ESE).[4] These denunciations were intended to force distributors to admit their responsibility in the poor social and environmental conditions[5] under which their suppliers found themselves. Before these campaigns took place, distributors were used to putting forward the lack of a legal connection between themselves and their suppliers to deny responsibility. The campaigns launched by ESE in 1995 in France got some of the distributors to take a different approach. They eventually agreed to collaborate with the social movement organization (SMO) ESE in developing programs of social auditing.

Recently, new business models for the textile industry have re-emerged in France and in many other countries. These business models are based on the idea of fair trade: textile industry workers are paid decent wages (determined by NGOs and associations or ILO standards) and accordingly clothes are sold at a higher price. So far, this tendency has not had an impact on the traditional business model of the clothing industry. The market share of fair trade is so small compared to the total amount of "unfair" trade that the impact is not noticeable.

DISTRI overview

Distri was created in 1996 by the manager of another clothing brand for adults, who decided to quit his job at the company he worked for and create his own clothing firm for kids. However, the name of the brand only appeared in 2001. In 1996, the founder of the firm decided to continue to have its clothes manufactured in South East Asia, where costs of production were low, emulating thereby the majority of its competitors. This low cost supply chain allowed the firm to pursue a strong growth strategy: in 1996 Distri had five stores in France. Ten years later DISTRI had more than 500 stores (two-thirds abroad) with sales over €400 millions with more than 3,000 employees in its stores. These low prices of manufacturing made it possible for distributors to spend a lot of money in marketing and communication while keeping low selling prices.

---

4   Collectif ESE: created in 1995 by Pascal Errard at the behest of Artisan du Monde, a fair trade association. More than 53 organizations (trade unions, NGOs, consumer associations) were members of the collective in 1996. ESE is the French branch of the European Clean Clothes Campaign created by trade unions and NGOs at the beginning of the 1990s with the support of members of the Clinton administration and based on the model of FLA (Interview with a member of a European trade union).

5   The culture of cotton is one of the most polluting in the world: a big water consumer; cotton crops use a quarter of insecticides in the world and 10% of the world pesticides. The ennoblement uses a lot of chemical products which are very toxic for both manufacturers and consumers. Clothes transport contributes to global warming.

The Burmese episode

In spite of the continuous claims of the promoter of the company that "The commitment to CSR has always been crucial to DISTRI, CSR is in DISTRI's DNA" (Interview with the promoter, February, 2005), in 2002 a journalist[6] asked the founder of the firm why his company was making clothes in Burma. The name of the company appeared on the Burma list. At first, the founder was at a loss to answer this question, which he apparently had not anticipated. And yet scandals of this kind had already occurred many times before: Nike for instance in the US had been struggling for years with trade unions and human rights association denouncing the working conditions of its suppliers (Boje, 1998). In France, the SMO ESE attacked the French distribution sector in 1996 for the same reasons.

As a result the founder's wife decided to leave her job and was appointed head of the CSR project, in the purest tradition of what might be called in France "dame patronnesse."[7] His wife benchmarked competitors CSR practices and became involved in a network of philanthropic and sustainable trade associations. She recommended that a philanthropic foundation be created. The foundation came into being a year later: its main purpose was to finance philanthropic projects in the countries where the firm was commercially established. The financing of the foundation was ensured by using a percentage of the profits made by the firm. This in turn enabled the company to pay less tax. At the beginning of 2005, a nursery was created at DISTRI, in partnership with the social services of the city where the head of the company was established.

Two years later, the HR Director assumed responsibility for the project and started to collaborate with a local philanthropic association named Alliances (see description below). Yet his poor knowledge of CSR problems forced him to hire a person in charge of CSR in 2006.

As an ex-consultant in sustainable development, this person knew exactly what firms expected from CSR projects. His prior job as a consultant in sustainable development consisted in promoting the positive impact of sustainable development practices for firms, what consultants generally call win–win situations. Now he found himself in the opposite position: his task was to convince the members of the firm's board that consultants' talk of win–win situations rested on firm ground and that the company might really benefit from opting for sustainable practices. He knew he would have to clarify these issues before he made his first recommendations to the founder and the HR director of the firm.

The person in charge of the CSR project had to face several problems: how were they to produce low cost items (i.e. the basis of the firm business model)

---

6 What is interesting here is that the founder never mentioned this event. The CSR project of DISTRI was officially developed on a voluntary basis. We were even told that CSR values were in the DNA of the firm. We discovered by chance on the Internet several journal articles mentioning this event.

7 A long-standing tradition in wealthy upper-class French families emphasizing a division of work between a paternalistic figure embracing the world of work and a wife indulging in charity.

and sustain a CSR friendly image at the same time? How could the firm continue to work with countries where working conditions were poor and at the same time promote a CSR brand image?

Could the firm increase selling prices? What were the costs of adopting CSR practices? How much would it cost to comply with NGOs demands (fair trade etc.)?

How would the firm benefit from carrying out such a policy? What were the expectations of the consumers on these subjects? What was the additional cost consumers were prepared to pay for such items?

Having made the decision to stay in South East Asia and China, the person in charge of CSR decided to look for an international NGO capable of monitoring the existing supply chain of DISTRI and to vouch for it. A meeting with a member of YAMANA (see description below), a French NGO, the French equivalent of the Fair Labor Association (FLA), took place in late 2006.

Alliances overview

At first glance, Alliances looks like a BONGO.[8] Created in 1994 by a former top manager of a bank, with the support of an employers' union, the aim of the association was to encourage CSR practices by local firms by promoting local CSR practices. The association strategy consisted in campaigning and winning the consent of top managers on issues related to CSR and on the opportunities it could offer them. The commitment of organizational elites (Zald, Morrill and Rao, 2005: 273) to the goal of the association was obtained by resorting to arguments based on the win–win principle, which assumes the mutuality of business and environmental or social interests (Levy and Egan, 2003).

Alliances regularly organizes gatherings during which a varied range of topics are broached (setting up businesses, ethical purchases, diversity within the company). The managers of companies and outside contributors were invited to these gatherings. These meetings give these "experts" the opportunity to discuss ideas and set up networks.

Alliances had five employees in 2006 and many voluntary workers. In addition to the annual event promoting the CSR practices of local firms, an employee of the association offered his service to evaluate CSR practices of firms members of the association and, if necessary, to help them develop their CSR policy.

In 2006, the budget of the association amounted to about €600,000 (half of it state-funded and half of it private-funded). Many founders of the top family local businesses, including DISTRI, belong to the founding members of the association. Some of the top executives of DISTRI regularly attended the lunches organized by the association partnership to discuss sets of CSR issues (diversity, etc.). An employee of Alliances evaluated the CSR policy of DISTRI in 2004. The results emphasized the lack of environmental commitments of the firm. The

8 Business Owned Non Governmental Organization.

study did not mention the problem of the working conditions, which from the very beginning were not considered to be part of relevant CSR issues.

YAMANA overview

YAMANA, a development NGO, was created in 1998. In 2006, its budget amounted to €700,000, mainly derived from public funding. In 2006, Yamana had eight employees. The goal of YAMANA is to try to improve the living conditions of people who live in the poorest Asian countries, and more particularly to improve the working conditions in the textile industry. Accordingly, Yamana launched in 2006 a label of social and environmental certification. The objective of the label is to certify the practices of all the actors that intervene throughout the textile production process as abiding by fair trade principles. This NGO belongs to the category of "participative" NGOs, seeking to gather as many actors as possible (trade unions, employees, various experts, human rights and environmental NGOs) to devise an approach of CSR. Today more than thirty companies, textile purchasers, local authorities and consumers' associations are members of Yamana and support its certification program. This monitoring of the whole production process, which is close to the idea of "product stewardship" (capacity to keep track of the product throughout the production process according to the various components that compose it) requires cooperation between all the components of the production process.

DISTRI and the building of CSR practice

A critical analysis of DISTRI's business model

In 2002, the name of DISTRI appeared on the list of the Burma Campaign, an NGO listing companies having commercial and financial relations with Burma.[9] Journalists were quick to ask DISTRI promoter about the presence of his firm in Burma. At first he did not say anything. Then came the official statement: "We refuse to abandon the population of Myanmar and prefer to stay so that we can go on helping them."[10] "The workers of Burma do not have to suffer from the consequences of our withdrawal: we cannot let them down."[11]

9   Burma is governed by a military junta which has been sustaining the dictatorship in the country since 1989. NGOs are unanimous in denouncing the violations of human rights in the country. Forced labor is a common practice, which makes it possible for the country to be almost the only one to compete with China as regards the costs of production.

10 Words of the founder of DISTR found on the website of the Institut Montaigne a French BONGO with more than 200 firms members, April 4, 2004.

11 In answer to a journalist for justifying the presence of his firm in Burma (http://www .novethic.fr/).

The controversy about DISTRI's presence in Burma clearly has to be put in the wider institutional and historical context of the firm. This controversy stemmed from the broader initiative the Collectif ESE.

The DISTRI promoter was clearly shocked by this episode at a period when he was still working for one of the biggest French retailer of the clothing industry. The negative impression he got of the organization clearly reduced the possibilities of working with them: "The measures recommended by this SMO are completely foolish. We do not need that sort of advice, especially coming from people who are jealous of our success as businessmen" (Promoter of DISTRI, Interview October 2005).

For the promoter, it is crucial to keep control of the processes of the company, especially regarding CSR issues: "Power within the company is essential, what is important is to keep control on what occurs within the company" (Founder of DISTRI, October 2005).

The reaction of DISTRI

Accordingly, in 2002 and some time after the Burmese episode, DISTRI joined the retail industry association ICS[12] and its program of social audits. One of the people in charge of the logistic department at DISTRI took part in the development of the internal code of conduct, by adapting the ICS code to the firm's needs. According to the logistics manager, half of the DISTRI suppliers had been audited at the end of 2006. Most suppliers were located in South East Asia: half in China, a third in India and the rest of them in Bangladesh. The inability of social audits in terms of raising working standards should come as no surprise. Trade Unions and NGOs have been straightforward in pointing out the inability of the so-called social auditing made by big auditing companies. Even some of the members of the ICS working for other retailers were, off the record, critical of them:

> The audits of the ICS are not unexpected as companies are warned in advance. As a rule factories are cleaned up before the visits of the auditors, and yet there are still so many nonconformities that the list of the corrective actions to implement is long. Furthermore these audits do not allow for a real improvement of working conditions, if that was what we really wanted to achieve, the factories would need to have a vested interest in the outcomes of the audit (a member of ICS, former social auditor, November 2005).

12 Initiative Clause Sociale, an association gathering French textile retailers to counter the Coll. ESE An industry association created in 1998 after several trade unions, NGOs and consumers associations denounced the poor working conditions of the suppliers of the French retail industry. Social audits were being conducted by big companies.

Nevertheless, according to the DISTRI CSR manager, a former consultant on sustainable development who was hired in 2006, the social auditing program of ICS was fully satisfying: "Our program of social and environmental auditing is really sufficient" (Interview, Responsible for CSR DISTRI, October 2006).

The role of Alliances and Yamana in the CSR project

Alliances and the CSR project

The DISTRI promoter is also a founding member of the association Alliances. As a member of this association, DISTRI received in 2004 a free audit on its CSR policies by an employee of the association specialized in auditing the CSR policies of companies. In addition, several of the DISTRI main managers regularly took part in meetings organized by Alliances, in order to share experiences and suggest better practices.

The results of this CSR audit, based on an adaptation of the tool developed by CSR Europe,[13] whose outcomes were communicated to the steering committee in 2005, concluded that the environmental section of DISTI CSR policy was not sufficient.

> Most of the time frightening the managers (boycott, denunciation campaign) is counter-productive. It is very difficult to collaborate effectively with a company which was the butt of attacks by NGOs, trade unions and other associations, even if they were justified. It is not the method we favor here at Alliances: we try to convince managers that it is in their best interest to adopt good CSR policies. Change within organizations is much more efficient once top managers are convinced and once they agree (a member of Alliances, Interview, March 2006).

One of the actions taken by Alliances was to propose the DISTRI employees a training course about "fair purchases," which resulted from the collaboration of the association with many distributors. This training course included the visit of some of the suppliers, as well as books on the purchase function. Textile purchasers want to buy products at the lowest cost possible but it creates paradoxes. As a matter of fact they have to consider cost and CSR when choosing the retailers they are going to work with. The two people (one was in charge of the logistics department, the other of the purchasing department) we interviewed after the training course told us that they were happy with the training, that it allowed them to have a better understanding of the CSR issues at stake in their firm. Asked about the presence of DISTRI in Burma they admitted they had first felt unconfortable with the fact that some of the suppliers resorted to child labor but eventually answered that child labor was better than child prostitution.

---

13   An industrial (BONGO) CSR European association.

Yamana and the CSR project

Yamana is well established in the textile industry of the professional clothing and as a result, it succeeded in mobilizing many actors (purchasing, users, producers). Yet the sector of kids and adult clothes is more difficult to reach and influence.

> The distributors and their federation addressed a very cold welcome when we launched our program. We already tried to contact them but it was quite difficult. They had already launched their own program (ICS) and do not see what the point of our program really was and what we could bring them (a member of Yamana, interview, November 2005).

The distributors do not want to relinquish their model of low cost supplies which enables them to save money for marketing and distribution expenses.

Facing the economic model which dominated the textile industry, Yamana tried to impose a model close to fair trade, a model which would rely on ILO standards from a social point of view and French standards from the environmental point of view. Yamana standards are devised not only by the members of the NGO but also by a group of independent experts who are hired by the members of Yamana. Those experts may belong to textile federations, trade unions, consulting companies, or be environment and health specialists. The target Yamana tries to reach is to undermine the low cost supply model. For instance they include on the label certification the overall amount of money paid to the various suppliers throughout the process of production.

All in all the founders of DISTRI and Yamana met once. For the founder of DISTRI, higher wages are not the solution: "Economics is best left to business-men! NGOs activists don't understand a thing!" (Interview, November 2005) The members of Yamana did not share his views.

> Progress it is not merely measured in working conditions in the supplying countries in Asia, but also in salary increases, in the reduction of the chemical substances used and in a better environment for the workers, because there is no need to have extinguishers in all the factories if the immediate environment of the workers is polluted by other factories, if for example there is no wastewater treatment plant. If possible, and on a case-by-case basis, it is necessary that the factory be able to work and take part in the development of such local infrastructures" (a member of Yamana, interview, March 2006).
>
> ... Even if we cannot say it too loud, we need those NGOs that blow the whistle on the bad practices of some firms. They prompt some companies which are afraid of bad publicity to come closer to us (a member of Yamana, interview, March 2006).

A meeting was organized at the end of 2006 between one member of Yamana and the manager, who had just been hired and was in charge of CSR issues at

DISTRI. The DISTRI manager, just before the meeting, told us how important to him was the environmental dimension that Yamana could bring to its company: "The ICS social audits are really sufficient, we just have some work to do as far as the environment goes, the rest is OK" (DISTRI CSR manager, interview, October 2006).The social audits carried out by the ICS are considered to be sufficient by DISTRI, although they are much criticized, even by social auditors.

Beside the Yamana advantages on the environment side, DISTRI decided not to work with Yamana. "They have no credibility. We don't get enough in compensation for working with them. They are hardly known internationally and so they would not improve our image" (DISTRI CSR manager, interview, October 2006). Nevertheless, collaboration between Yamana and DISTRI has not been completely rejected. Distri is merely waiting for Yamana to really make it worth their while.

Bibliography

Bartley, T., 2003. Certifying forests and factories: States, social movements, and the rise of private regulation in the apparel and forest products fields, *Politics and Society* 31.3: 433-464.

Bartley, T., 2007. How Foundations Shape Social Movements: The Construction of an Organizational Field and the Rise of Forest Certification, *Social Problems* 54.3: 229-255.

Boje D. M., 1998, Nike, Greek goddess of victory or cruelty? Women's stories of Asian factory life, *Journal of Organizational Change Management* 11.6: D 0953-4814.

Grillo R.D. 1997, Discourses of development: the view from anthropology, in R.D. Grillo and R.L. Stirrat (eds) *Discourses of development: anthropological perspectives*. Oxford: Berg.

Khan, F. R., Munir, K. A. and Willmott, H., July 2007. A dark side of institutional entrepreneurship: Soccer balls, child labour and postcolonial impoverishment, *Organization Studies* 28.7: 1055-1077.

Lehman, G., 1999, Disclosing new worlds: a role for social and environmental accounting and auditing, *Accounting, Organizations and Society* 24: 217-241.

Levy D.L. 2008, Political Contestation in Global Production Networks, *Academy of Management Review*, 33.4.

Levy D.L. and Egan, D. 2003, A Neo-Gramscian Approach to Corporate Political Strategy: Conflict and Accommodation in the Climate Change Negotiations, *Journal of Management Studies* 40.4: 803-829.

Parker, M., 2003. Introduction: Ethics, politics and organizing *Organization* 10.2: 187-203.

Rao H., Morrill, C. and Zald, M. N. 2000, Power plays: how social movements and collective action create new organizational forms, *Research in Organizational Behaviour*, 22: 239-282.

Taylor V. and Van Dyke, N. 2004, Tactical repertoires of social movement, in *The Blackwell companion to social movement*, Ed by David Snow, Sarah O. Soule, Hanspeter Kriesi, Blackwell Publishing: 262-296.

Zald, M. N., Morrill, C. and Rao, H. 2005, The impact of social movements on organizations: environment and responses in *Social Movements and Organization Theory*, Ed. G. F. Davis, D. McAdam, W. R. Scott and M. N. Zald, Cambridge University Press.

About the author

 **Guillaume Delalieux** (Dr. Bus. Adm.) is an Associate Professor at Sciences Po Lille in France. His dissertation dealt on the limited influence that CSR tools promoted by neoliberal public policies of Western governments can have on multinational corporations' practices with a case study of a French nongovernmental organization's private mechanism of certification in the textile industry. His main research interests are focused on the organizational manifestations of neoliberalism such as New Public Management reforms of administration or nongovernmental organizations' increased activity. His research has been published in French journals such as *Politique et Management Public* and *Mondes en Développement* and books dealing with the third sector for Emerald Publishing.

Teaching notes for this case are available from Greenleaf Publishing. These are free of charge and available only to teaching staff. They can be requested by going to:

www.greenleaf-publishing.com/darkside2notes

7

The Bhopal Gas tragedy
Revisited after twenty-five years[1]

Debapratim Purkayastha
IBS Hyderabad, India

Hadiya Faheem
IBS Hyderabad, India

December 3rd, 2009 marked the 25th anniversary of the world's worst ever industrial disaster—the gas leak that occurred at Union Carbide India Ltd (UCIL)'s pesticide plant in Bhopal (Madhya Pradesh, India). The tragedy that instantly killed more than 3,000 people and left thousands injured and affected for life, occurred when water entered Methyl Isocyanate (MIC) storage tank No. 610 of the plant on December 3rd, 1984. MIC is one of the deadliest gases produced in the chemical industry and is known to react violently when it comes into contact with water or metal dust. Though the plant was soon closed down, the after-effects of the accident left an estimated 25,000 people dead and around 600,000 people affected due to gas-related disorders. What compounded the tragedy was that the victims failed to get adequate compensation and, a quarter of a century later, toxic chemicals lay in the vicinity and the survivors were fully exposed to it.

After the disaster, the U.S.-based Union Carbide Corporation (UCC), the parent company of UCIL, stuck to its argument that the incident had occurred due to an act of

1 This case was a Finalist in the 2010 Dark Side Case Competition organized by CMS Division of Academy of Management. It was written by Hadiya Faheem, under the direction of Debapratim Purkayastha, IBS Hyderabad. It was compiled from published sources, and is intended to be used as a basis for class discussion rather than to illustrate either effective or ineffective handling of a management situation. © 2010, IBS Center for Management Research.

sabotage by a disgruntled worker, downplayed the health effects of MIC and discredited the victims and activists fighting for justice. In 2001, after UCC merged with the U.S.-based Dow Chemical Company (Dow), Dow too refused to take responsibility for the incident. The victims' struggle against UCC, and then Dow, have been recognized as the world's longest-running struggle against corporate excesses.

> Twenty-five years is a long time to wait for Dow and Union Carbide to right this devastating wrong, and it's even longer when the tragedy keeps on giving. Because site contamination has still not been adequately contained, nor cleaned up, the poisons continue to pollute the groundwater that more than 30,000 people rely on for drinking water. Again, how is it that a corporation gets away with this?[2] (Tonya Hennessey, Project Director, CorpWatch,[3] in December 2009).
>
> Bhopal is not just an incident of industrial disaster and human suffering from the last century. It is very much an issue of the present century of corporate accountability, peoples' rights, and government responsibility. The lack of mandatory laws and norms governing multinationals, legal complexities, and government failures are serious obstacles in ensuring justice for the people of Bhopal, and for the victims of corporate complicity in crimes against environment, peoples' lives, and safety[4] (Amnesty International,[5] in November 2009).

25 years on ... new victims are born everyday

December 3, 2009, marked the 25th anniversary of the world's worst-ever industrial disaster—the deadly gas leak at the Bhopal-based[6] pesticide plant of Union Carbide India Limited (UCIL). Tragedy struck on December 3, 1984, after water entered the Methyl Isocyanate (MIC) storage tank No. 610 at the plant. MIC is one of the deadliest gases produced in the chemical industry and is known to

---

2   Tonya Hennessey, "25 Years and Still Fighting for Justice: When Will Dow Chemical Clean Up its Poisonous Legacy in Bhopal," www.corpwatch.org, December 14, 2009.

3   CorpWatch is non-profit investigative research and journalism formed with the stated aim "to expose corporate malfeasance and to advocate for multinational corporate accountability and transparency."

4   "Disaster, Corporate Responsibility and Peoples' Rights," http://kafila.org, November 30, 2009.

5   Amnesty International, founded in London in 1961, is an international non-governmental organization (NGO) formed with the stated mission "to conduct research and generate action to prevent and end grave abuses of human rights and to demand justice for those whose rights have been violated."

6   Bhopal is the capital of the central Indian state, Madhya Pradesh.

react violently when it comes into contact with water or metal dust. What followed was a catastrophe that killed more than 3,000 people immediately and left thousands of people injured or affected for life. While the incident was horrendous in itself, what made it even worse was that its effects continued to be felt down the years by people living in the environs of the plant. In the months, years, and decades that followed the disaster, thousands of survivors and their next generations suffered from ill health and multiple symptoms while their livelihood and future were severely affected. By the end of 2009, it was estimated that 25,000 had died and around 600,000 people were affected due to gas-related disorders.[7]

Though the plant was shut down soon after the incident, the toxic remains at the plant left it in a state to create even more havoc with each passing day. It was reported that after a heavy rainfall, the heavy metals and solvents had seeped into the groundwater resources, contaminating them. The residents used this water for drinking, cooking, and washing and this had led to physical disabilities and stunted growth in children. Despite this, the people residing in the surroundings of the plant could not abandon the site and move to safer places as the compensation due to them was delayed for many years. This was because Union Carbide Corporation (UCC), the parent company of UCIL, allegedly evaded responsibility for the disaster and engaged in lengthy litigation. Subsequently, some victims did get a paltry amount as compensation but many more did not get even this. Even as the victims continued to suffer, some experts and people around the world were disgusted to see that the company responsible for the disaster refused to be held accountable. "Since the gas disaster of 1984, Union Carbide Corporation (now part of Dow Chemicals) has played a cat-and-mouse game of corporate restructuring in a bid to conceal liability from Indian courts,"[8] said Eurig Scandrette, a lecturer in sociology at the U.K.'s Queen Margaret University. The Indian government too drew a lot of flak from critics who felt that it was siding with the multinational corporation.

Despite protests from activists and survivors, UCC consistently refused to take any liability for the clean-up of the site, saying the plant had been sold to The Dow Chemical Company (Dow) in 2001. It also pointed out it had paid a "heavy" one-time compensation of US$470 million. Dow too contended that the matter had been resolved and added that the company had insulated itself from UCC's Bhopal liabilities by virtue of how it had structured the acquisition.[9]

The fact that UCC and then Dow had been able to "evade" the real costs of compensation and clean-up, was viewed by critics as an example of a multinational

7   "Bhopal Victims Protest Yoga Care Denial in Hospitals," www.thaindian.com, January 13, 2010; "Bhopal Marks 25 Years Since Gas Leak Devastation," http://news.bbc.co.uk/1/hi/world/south_asia/8392206.stm, December 3, 2009.

8   Eurig Scandrett, "The Demand for Corporate Accountability," http://infochangeindia.org, September 2009.

9   Jack Doyle, *Trespass Against Us, Dow Chemical and the Toxic Century*, Monroe, ME, Common Courage Press, 2004.

corporation's power and impunity. As the after-effects of the world's worst industrial disaster threatened to affect the next generations in Bhopal, victims and social activists intensified their efforts to make Dow realize that it was also the company's responsibility to clean up the mess and provide at least some relief to the victims. But industry observers wondered whether Dow would ever look beyond the concerns of its shareholders and address this issue. People also wondered how the regulators had failed to bring the perpetrators to book even after 25 long years, and whether there were any mechanisms to hold a powerful multinational company accountable when things go wrong, especially overseas.

Background note

The history of Union Carbide Corporation (UCC) dates back to 1917 when four U.S. companies—Union Carbide Co., Linde Air Products Co., National Carbon Co., Inc., and Prest-O-Lite Co., Inc. producing batteries and arc lamps for street lighting and headlamps for cars—were merged to form UCC. UCC manufactured industrial gases such as nitrogen, oxygen, methane, ethylene, and propane, used in the petroleum industry as well as chemical substances like ammonia and urea used in the manufacture of fertilizers.

In the 1950s, UCC along with other companies worked on creating a pesticide that would eradicate parasites since the fodder crops and plantations in the U.S. were being destroyed by pests. UCC developed "Experimental Insecticide Seven Seven," which came to be known as "Sevin," Sevin was manufactured through the reaction of phosgene gas with monomethylamine gas. The two gases reacted to form a new molecule called MIC. MIC was known to be one of the most dangerous compounds ever formulated in the chemical industry. It was reported that animals which had been exposed to MIC vapors during experiments had faced a sudden death. It was also noted that when MIC came into contact with water or metal dust, it led to an uncontrollable violent reaction, resulting in the formation of a fatal cloud in the atmosphere. To prevent any hazard, MIC had to be stored permanently at zero degrees Celsius. Hence, provisions were made to store the MIC in drums or tanks.

UCC began its operations in India by setting up an assembly plant for batteries at Kolkata in 1924. The company carried out its operations in India through its subsidiary Union Carbide India Limited (UCIL). UCC held 50.9 percent of the stock in UCIL. The remaining 49.1 percent was held by several Indian investors. At that time, foreign companies had to limit their stake in any Indian subsidiary to 40 percent. However, the Government of India (GoI) waived this restriction in the case of UCC due to the company's export potential and sophisticated technology. The government and the citizens of India were happy with UCC not only for the huge technology transfer, but also because it offered employment to many. At one point in time UCIL employed more than 10,000 people, who earned an average of US$250, which was considered an excellent salary by Indian standards then.[10]

Under an agreement with the GoI in 1966, UCIL was permitted to import 1,200 tons of Sevin from UCC. It was decided that within five years, UCC would build a plant in India to produce Sevin. In 1969, UCC set up its pesticide plant in Bhopal and the GoI granted UCIL a license to manufacture 5,000 tons of Sevin per year. Eduardo Munoz (Munoz), an Argentinean agronomic engineer who worked at UCC, was entrusted with the responsibility of making the project a success. Munoz felt that to develop Sevin, a huge amount of MIC would be required. As he was not in favor of storing such large quantities, he suggested an option like batch production. This would make it unnecessary to store huge quantities of Sevin. But the UCC officials turned down the suggestion. Munoz also raised his voice against locating the plant at the proposed site saying it was too close to where people resided. However, officials from UCC again overruled him, contending that it was the right place for setting up the plant. The proposal was, however, against the rules of the municipal planning regulations which said that no industrial undertaking likely to emit toxic gases could be set up on a site where the prevailing wind might carry effluents into densely populated areas. At the Kali Grounds in Bhopal where the plant was set up, the wind usually blew from north to south, toward the densely populated parts of the old town. Under such circumstances, the application should have been rejected. But the UCC officials did not mention that their proposed plant would be making pesticides out of the most toxic gases available in the chemical industry.

In 1979, the UCIL plant at Bhopal was inaugurated. When the Bhopal plant was opened, it was considered to be world-class.[11] It was welcomed by the government as well as the residents as people found jobs opportunities that were well-paid and with high social status.[12] Initially, the plant did not have the capacity to produce MIC for manufacturing Sevin and hence the insecticide was imported from the parent company. In May 1980, the Bhopal plant produced its first gallon of MIC and it was stored in three huge tanks. Warren Anderson (Anderson), the new CEO of UCC, visited Bhopal especially for this event.

By 1984, UCIL had 9,000 employees. It operated 14 plants and was organized into five divisions. In the same year, it was reported that UCIL had annual sales of US$200 million.[13]

---

10   John Riddle, *Bhopal*, (Infobase Publishing, 2002).

11   Dominique Lapierre and Javier Moro, *It was Five Past Midnight in Bhopal* (Scribner, 2002).

12   Ingrid Eckerman, *The Bhopal Saga: Causes and Consequences of the World's Largest Industrial Disaster*, (Universities Press, 2005).

13   Paul Shrivastava, "5 Long-term Recovery from the Bhopal Crisis," www.unu.edu/unupress/unupbooks/uu21le/uu21le0c.htm.

Negligent management practices at UCIL?

In 1980, trouble started brewing at the Bhopal plant with several incidents of death and injury being reported. For instance, in December 1981, a plant operator was killed due to a phosgene gas leak and two others were injured. In view of these accidents, UCC sent three American engineers to conduct an audit at the UCIL plant. These engineers were entrusted with the task of evaluating the site to see whether it met all the safety standards laid down by UCC. The audit team noted that the plant had leaking valves and 61 hazards were reported. Of these, 30 were major and 11 had occurred in the MIC/phosgene unit.[14]

The report submitted to UCC revealed that plant was not maintaining safety standards. It described the surroundings of the site as being "strewn with oily old drums, used piping, pools of used oil, and chemical waste likely to cause fire." It criticized the carelessness of the workers in some areas. The equipment was damaged, circuits were corroded, there were no automatic sprinklers in the phosgene and MIC production zones. Besides, there was a risk of explosion in the gas evacuation flares. The report also found that there were leaks of MIC, phosgene, and chloroform; the pipes and sealed joints were ruptured, the earth wire was missing on one of the three MIC tanks; and there was poor adjustment of certain devices where excessive pressure could lead to water entering the circuits. The engineers also raised concerns over the inadequate training offered to the staff, substandard instruction methods, and poor maintenance reports.

The local daily newspapers also criticized the poor management at the UCIL plant. In October 1982, an incident occurred at the UCIL plant when MIC leaked from an open valve, critically affecting four workers and causing breathlessness and eye irritation to people residing in the surrounding areas. This should have served as a signal to the management that all was not well with the plant. However, the management chose to turn a blind eye to the incident, experts said.

In the early 1980s, Warren Woomer (Woomer) was appointed as the managing director (MD) of the pesticide plant at Bhopal. According to analysts, the appointment of Woomer indicated that UCC aimed to exercise some control over the UCIL management. After the retirement of Woomer, Jagannathan Mukund (Mukund) was appointed as the new MD in 1982. In 1983, Mukund came under pressure from the top management at UCC to cut costs at the UCIL plant. As part of the cost-cutting measures, Mukund asked two hundred technicians and skilled workers to resign. In the MIC unit, manpower was cut by half in each shift. In the control room, only one person was retained to single-handedly manage 70 dials, counters, and gauges, which relayed the pressure and temperature of the tanks containing MIC.

In December 1982, the issue of the danger posed by the UCIL plant was raised in the Madhya Pradesh (MP) Assembly. However, T S Viyogi, labor minister in

---

14 S. Muralidhar, "Unsettling Truths, Untold Tales," www.ielrc.org, 2004/5.

the Arjun Singh[15] government, said that a lot of investment had already been made and hence the site could not be shifted. Moreover, he put to rest all apprehensions saying that there was no danger to the Bhopal plant.

In 1983, Mukund ordered the shutting down of the principal safety systems in the plant. The justification for this was apparently that since the plant was no longer active, these systems were not needed. Analysts pointed out that Mukund had failed to pay attention to the fact that sixty tons of MIC were stored in the tanks. Interrupting the refrigeration of these tanks might possibly have saved a few hundred rupees worth of electricity a day, but it violated a fundamental rule laid down by UCC's chemists, which stipulated that MIC must, in all circumstances, be stored at a temperature close to zero degrees Celsius. In order to save a few hundred Kg of coal, the flame that burned day and night at the top of the flare tower was also extinguished. The flame was supposed to burn off any toxic gases emitted into the atmosphere in the event of an accident. Other essential equipment, such as the scrubber cylinder used to decontaminate any gas leaks, was subsequently deactivated.

Industry observers said that the situation prevailing at UCIL at that point served as a signal to several well-trained and skilled engineers to look out for some other safe and suitable employment. By 1983, between one-half and two-thirds of the skilled engineers working on the MIC project had left.

Some experts were of the view that the top management of UCC was no longer interested in carrying out the operations at UCIL and so was neglecting the plant. Moreover, the UCIL plant was incurring losses since it did not produce MIC in the quantities it was licensed to manufacture. Therefore, UCC planned to shut down the Bhopal plant and put it up for sale. However, when no one came forward to buy the plant in India, UCC decided to dismantle the UCIL plant and shift it to another country. Industry observers opined that the financial losses coupled with plans to dismantle the Bhopal plant had aggravated the negligent management practices at UCIL.

That fateful night

At around 9:30 pm on December 2, 1984, a large quantity of water entered storage tank 610 containing more than 40 tons of MIC (Refer to Exhibit 1 for chronology of events after the disaster). When water mixed with MIC, it triggered an exothermic reaction, producing a lot of heat. This led to a sudden increase in the pressure and temperature in the tank. As a result, the safety valve of the tank burst with such force that the concrete coating around the tank also broke. The reaction of MIC with hydrogen cyanide and other products led to an explosion at around 12:30 am. The safety systems that could have helped tackle the

15 Arjun Singh was the then Chief Minister of Madhya Pradesh.

situation were inoperative. It was alleged that nearly 20 to 30 tons of MIC were released within an hour of the leak starting. Senior officials at the plant were aware of the fatal build-up in the tank at least an hour before the leak started. However, they informed the neighborhood communities to move out of the vicinity of the plant only after nearly an hour after the gases started leaking. By then, the toxic gases had already spread to an area of 40 square kilometers, killing thousands of people. The tragedy assumed such massive proportions that the law, administration, and healthcare services proved woefully inadequate to tackle it.

It was reported that several people had died due to multiple organ failure after breathing in the highly toxic gases. According to unofficial estimates, the death toll had crossed 10,000 in the next 72 hours.[16] Instead of evacuating people from the site, government trucks were reportedly used to carry away dead bodies to bring the death count down. Over 500,000 residents, who came into contact with the deadly vapors complained about eye irritation, acute breathlessness, and vomiting. The poisonous cloud hung over the ground for more than four hours. Thousands of people poured into hospitals complaining about burning in their eyes and lungs and the doctors called up the plant medical officer to know what they were supposed to do. They were informed that the gas was like tear gas.

UCC's take on the tragedy

When informed about the incident, Mukund's first reaction was, "The gas leak just can't be from my plant. The plant is shut down. Our technology just can't go wrong, we just can't have such leaks."[17] However, later UCC said that the gas was not that fatal. The GoI sued UCC for a compensation of US$3 billion. But UCC blamed the GoI for the disaster and filed a countersuit against the GoI and the state government of MP. The central and the state governments were charged with "contributory" responsibility for the gas leakage. UCC alleged that the government had failed to take necessary precautions that could have prevented a disaster though they were aware of the toxicity of MIC.

According to UCC, "No analysis of Union Carbide's reaction to the Bhopal tragedy is possible without recognizing the considerable emphasis the company and its affiliates had placed on safe operations."[18] Jackson Browning (Browning), Vice President responsible for the Health, Safety, and Environmental Pro-

---

16 "Bhopal Victims Protest Yoga Care Denial in Hospitals," www.thaindian.com, January 13, 2010.
17 "India—Health and Safety at Work," www.itulip.com, December 6, 2007.
18 Pratima Ungarala, "Bhopal Gas Tragedy: An Analysis," www.hu.mtu.edu, May 19, 1998.

grams at UCC, wrote a document titled, *Union Carbide: Disaster at Bhopal*. In the document, under two segments titled, "First Steps at Control" and "Contingency Planning and Experience Help," UCC listed all the things it had done after the tragedy. The first vital decision taken was shutting down the UCC plant making the MIC in the U.S. This was followed by setting up of the task force headed by Anderson and dispatching medical and technical teams to the tragedy site "within 24 hours" (Refer to Box I for some measures taken by UCC). At a news conference in December 1984, Anderson accepted moral responsibility for the disaster and announced that he would travel once to India to offer relief to the gas victims. He also proposed to offer US$1 million immediate aid. UCIL also announced US$840,000 for the victims.

UCC defended its position saying that it had a stake of just 50.9 percent in UCIL. The company also said that all the employees at UCIL were Indians and that the last American employee had left two years before the disaster took place. It argued that the daily operations at UCIL were independent of the parent company and hence it was not responsible for the gas leak.

Box 1 Measures taken by UCC

- UCC offered nearly US$2 million in aid to the Prime Minister's Relief Fund immediately after the disaster was reported
- It provided medical equipment and supplies
- It shared all its information on the toxicity of MIC with the government
- It funded the presence of Indian medical experts at conferences conducted on research and treatment of gas victims
- It offered a US$2.2 million grant to Arizona State University for setting up a vocational-technical center in Bhopal
- It offered an additional US$5 million to the Indian Red Cross[19]
- It established a charitable trust for Bhopal hospital with an initial funding of nearly US$20 million
- It offered US$90 million to the charitable trust as directed by the court order.

Adapted from "The Incident, Response, and Settlement," www.unioncarbide .com, 2001–2009.

Contrary to what the document said, analysts felt that UCC had not approved any emergency plan at UCIL. This was highlighted by the fact that when the tragedy struck at the Bhopal plant and people started pouring into the hospitals complaining about several illnesses, the hospital staff had no idea of what had happened or how to treat the victims. Some investigators also pointed out there were considerable differences between the safety measures in the UCC plant in the U.S. and that at Bhopal. They also did not buy UCC's claim that the company

---

19 Founded in 1920, the Indian Red Cross is a Delhi-based voluntary humanitarian organization.

did not have control over UCIL. Some investigations revealed that UCC had considerable authority over its affiliate. Only some of the daily activities such as staffing and maintenance were left to the Indian officials, but all major decisions including the annual budget were approved by UCC.

The sabotage theory

It was reported that nearly 500 experiments had been conducted on the residue of tank 610 by UCC, the government, and other independent organizations. However, a study carried out by Arthur D Little,[20] paid for by UCC, had an interesting story to narrate. It reported that water could have been deliberately added to the tank that led to a massive chemical reaction since all the safety systems were in place and were operational enough to control the flow of water to the tank. In March 1985, UCC issued its research report in which it concluded that water had entered the MIC tank. In the same year, UCC announced that "an act of sabotage" by a Sikh terrorist had led to the disaster. Later, it laid the blame on a "discontented worker" at the UCIL plant.

Other investigators attributed several different causes for the disaster. It was alleged that some portion of the safety equipment had been obsolete for four months and the rest of the equipment had failed. Industrial safety experts argued that the disaster could have been prevented and blamed UCC and UCIL for their negligent management practices. The investigations also revealed that the non-availability of information about MIC had led to a delay in the detoxification measures. This prompted the Indian Council for Medical Research[21] (ICMR) to carry out extensive studies on toxicology and other related analyses. The toxicology project revealed that there were several chemical constituents including 9 to 10 unidentified compounds and MIC, the toxicity of which was not known.

Some experts opined that UCC had aired the "sabotage" theory only to avoid paying huge sums as compensation to the Bhopal gas victims. This was supported by the fact that UCC had failed to provide any evidence supporting its theory. Moreover, UCC never revealed the name of the guilty worker.

---

20 Arthur D Little is a global management consulting firm.
21 The Indian Council for Medical Research is a New Delhi-based organization responsible for the coordination, formulation, and promotion of biomedical research.

Settlement made by UCC

After a few months of the disaster, the GoI appointed itself as the exclusive representative of the victims for any legal dealings with UCC related to compensation. It filed a lawsuit to claim damages and compensation against UCC with the United States District Court for the Southern District of New York. In addition to this, the GoI was entrusted with the responsibility of registering the claims of all the gas victims in Bhopal. Industry experts, however, believed that this task had not been carried out with any seriousness over the next ten years.

In May 1986, Judge John K. Keenan (Keenan) passed a ruling that said that India was the appropriate forum to deal with the compensation litigation for the Bhopal plant as opposed to the U.S. In the first pre-trial hearing of the case, Keenan asked UCC as "a matter of fundamental human decency" to offer US$5–10 million as an interim relief payment. UCC approved US$5 million interim relief to the victims provided a suitable plan of accounting and distribution of funds was formulated.[22] For nearly eight months, UCC and GoI negotiated the conditions and terms of reference for using the interim relief. In November 1986, UCC and the GoI agreed that the money would be channeled through the American Red Cross[23] to the Indian Red Cross. Even one year after the tragedy had struck, no one, including officials of the MP state government responsible for the relief of victims, had any idea what the Red Cross would do with the money.

On December 17, 1987, a Judge at the Bhopal District Court passed an order that required UCC to pay Rs.3.5 billion as interim relief. UCC refused to accept the order and challenged it in the MP high court (at Jabalpur) on the grounds that the trial judge was not authorized to pass the order under any provisions of the Indian Civil Penal Code. Upholding the district court's decision, Justice S. K. Seth (Seth) of the High Court reduced the interim compensation to Rs.2.5 billion, on April 4, 1988.[24] UCC appealed to the Supreme Court of India against the High Court order saying, "No court that we know of in India or elsewhere in the world has previously ordered interim compensation where there is no proof of damages or where liability is strongly contested."[25]

On February 14, 1989, the Supreme Court of India passed an order directing UCC to pay up US$470 million in "full and final settlement" of all claims, rights, and liabilities arising out of the disaster. The Supreme Court ruled that the US$470 million settlement was "just, equitable, and reasonable." It also ordered

22 "Chronology," www.unioncarbide.com, June 2009.
23 Founded in 1881, the American Red Cross is an organization that offers disaster relief, emergency assistance, and education in the US.
24 "Bhopal Timeline—The Chronology of Disaster," www.indiatogether.org, February 1, 2010.
25 An independent investigation carried out by Arther D. Little, Inc., on behalf of UCC, showed that the Bhopal incident was caused by a disgruntled employee who introduced a large volume of water by connecting a water hose directly to the tank.

the GoI to purchase a medical insurance policy covering 100,000 patients who might later develop symptoms.[26] The GoI was also instructed to make up for any shortfall of funds if required. Besides, the central government was entrusted with the responsibility of addressing the ongoing concerns of the gas victims. The state government took up the responsibility of cleaning up the site.

Ten days after the decision was announced, UCC and UCIL paid the amount to the GoI. Subsequently, the GoI agreed to drop all the criminal lawsuits against UCC. Experts felt that the compensation was the largest ever in India and was US$120 million more than the plaintiff's lawyers had said was fair in the U.S. courts.[27] The court concluded that the compensation was far greater than any company would pay under the Indian law. In November 1990, the Reserve Bank of India[28] (RBI) stated that the compensation with interest was nearly double of what was estimated to compensate the gas victims.

Critics, however, felt that the settlement amount of US$470 million was meager for a disaster which had left thousands of people dead and around 600,000 injured. It was estimated that the compensation amounted to Rs.10,000 per victim if divided equally among all victims. The fact that the compensation paid by UCC was low was highlighted when a report by *The Times of India*[29] stated that around US$40,000 had been spent on rehabilitating sea otters affected by the Alaska oil spill.[30] In 1991, the GoI agreed to reopen the criminal cases against UCC after it experienced violent protests from survivors for letting the culprits off so easily. There were also allegations that a significant part of the compensation had been siphoned off by corrupt officials, politicians, and middlemen.[31]

On September 9, 1993, UCC sold its stake in UCIL to the McLeod Russell India Ltd[32] (Eveready Industries).[33] Though UCC washed its hands of the disaster, the survivors lobbied with the government to take some action against the company.

In 1996, William H. Joyce (Joyce), chief executive of UCC, said that the company had paid the compensation and had no intention of doing anything further

---

26 "The Incident, Response, and Settlement," www.unioncarbide.com, 2001–2009.
27 Ibid.
28 The Reserve Bank of India (RBI) is the Central Bank and the supreme monetary authority of the country. Its basic functions are to regulate the issue of bank notes, to keep reserves for securing the monetary stability of the country and to operate the currency and credit system of the country.
29 *The Times of India* is a daily English-language newspaper.
30 ExxonMobile Corporation (then Exxon), an oil and gas company, was involved in a major disaster in 1989, when one of its tankers met with an accident and spilled 11 million gallons of oil in Prince William Sound in Alaska.
31 Praful Bidwai, "Cleaning Up after Bhopal Gas Tragedy—Not Begun," www.ipsnews.net, September 10, 2007.
32 McLeod Russell India Ltd. was later renamed as Eveready Industries India Limited.
33 Earlier in December. 1986, the company had sold its worldwide Agricultural Products business to the French chemical and pharmaceuticals company, Rhone Poulenc, for US$585 million. The deal included Rhone-Poulenc's purchase of UCC's chemical plant in Institute, West Virginia.

for the victims. In 1998, the MP state government, which had leased the location to UCIL, took over the plant and assumed all accountability for the site, including the completion of any additional remediation.

The tragedy continues

Having paid the US$470 million compensation, UCC maintained that it did not have any more liability for the tragic incident. However, survivors of Bhopal gas tragedy argued that UCC and Anderson should be brought to justice. Both UCC and Anderson were accused of manslaughter, grievous assault, poisoning and killing of animals, and other serious offences. Anderson, who was charged with culpable homicide not amounting to murder by the local court, did not even have to face the courts, as he was released on bail on December 7, 1984, and refused to come back to India to face trial. Several attempts to call upon Anderson to answer their allegations were unsuccessful. Some observers felt that if Anderson was a fugitive, it could be difficult for the victims to hold UCC accountable. This was because the organization no longer existed as Dow had purchased it for US$10.3 billion in 2001 (Refer to Exhibit 2 for a brief note on Dow).

Several activists' groups and forums also felt that UCC and its parent company Dow could not get away from its responsibility after paying just a meager compensation. It was pointed out that the disaster continued to impact the lives of the survivors. They accused UCC of offering inadequate medical relief and compensation to the victims. The victims said that after the Bhopal plant was shut down, hardly any cleaning of the site was done. Several toxins and chemicals were left in the surrounding areas and children playing near the plant came into direct contact with them. Several studies had also found that the groundwater near the plant area contained toxic heavy metals and organic chemicals.

In March 1985, an NGO carried out a study on people living in the vicinity of the plant. The study revealed that 50 percent to 70 percent of the non-hospitalized population in the exposed areas of Bhopal had one or more symptoms of MIC poisoning. In October 1989, an epidemiological study sponsored by Jawaharlal Nehru University, New Delhi, confirmed that 70 percent to 80 percent of the people living in the severely affected communities and 40 percent to 50 percent of the people living in the mildly affected communities continued to suffer from illnesses related to MIC exposure even five years after the disaster.

In 1994, studies conducted by the National Environmental Engineering Research Institute[34] (NEERI) reported that the plant had high concentrations of semi-volatiles such as Sevin, Lindane, and Temik at depths of at least 60 cm from

---

34   National Environmental Engineering Research Institute is an environmental research organization. It seeks to provide innovative and effective solutions to environmental problems.

the ground.[35] In November 2002, an analysis by Greenpeace[36] research laboratories reported that the soil and the stockpiles from the solar evaporation pond contained hazardous materials like carbaryl and benzene hexachloride in every sample. These ponds were used to store wastewater containing highly concentrated inorganic chemicals at the plant. After heavy rainfall, these solvents and heavy metals contaminated the groundwater and the water that was used by the residents for consumption. Though municipal tankers provided potable water, the residents had to rely on the contaminated groundwater sources as the supply was inadequate. The British Broadcasting Corporation[37] (BBC) in its visit to Bhopal reported, "It [samples of water collected from the areas near the plant] had levels of contamination 500 times higher than the maximum limits recommended by the World Health Organization."[38] The BBC's sample of water from an in-use hand pump near the plant, contained nearly 1,000 times WHO's recommended maximum amount of carbon tetrachloride, a pollutant known to cause cancer and liver damage.[39]

Activists said that this poisoned environment had led to huge casualties since the disaster. The survivors had been left with compromised lung function and eyesight and their immune system had also been affected. People living near the site complained of aches and pains, rashes, fevers, eruption of boils and other skin complaints, headaches, nausea, lack of appetite, dizziness, constant exhaustion, etc. Contaminants such as lead, mercury, and organochlorines were found in the milk of nursing mothers living near the plant. There were an unusually high number of children born with birth defects such as cleft lips, missing palates, twisted limbs, etc. and stunted growth. There was also an unusually high incidence of children born with a mental handicap. Women suffered from excessive uterine discharge, chaotic menstrual cycles, and miscarriages. The number of women suffering from cervical cancers was also higher than normal. According to activists, the government had suppressed the finding of the medical studies that were initiated in 1985 but discontinued abruptly in 1994.[40]

The economic effect of the disaster on the lives of the survivors was also huge as the survivors, who were mostly poor, lost their livelihood or earning members. Many of them were left with a reduced capacity to work due to disability or illnesses. The plight of the women was even worse as they had to suffer the stigma of being a "gas survivor," which hampered their chances of marriage. Some of them were also deserted by their husbands as these women were often ill and unable to work.

---

35 K. Rajani Priya, "Cleaning up Bhopal Cost-effectively," www.indiatogether.org, December 2004.
36 Founded in 1971, Greenpeace is a Netherlands-based non-governmental environmental organization.
37 The British Broadcasting Corporation (BBC) is one of the leading broadcasting networks in the world.
38 Ibid.
39 "Bhopal Marks 25 Years since Gas Leak Devastation," http://news.bbc.co.uk/1/hi/world/south_asia/8392206.stm, December 3, 2009.
40 "Worst Industrial Disaster Still Haunts India," www.msnbc.msn.com, December 2, 2009.

These allegations regarding the continuing health problems were strongly opposed by UCC. The company underplayed the health effects of MIC claiming that "... severe injury to the lung is limited to a small percentage of the population and there is no serious residual eye disease."[41] It also claimed that medical studies had shown that one-time exposure to MIC did not cause cancer, birth defects, etc. Browning, in his report, not only downplayed the health effects of MIC, but also claimed that UCC was being victimized despite the company bringing the benefits of industrialization to India. He wrote:

> Whatever our contributions to national industrialization goals, the current political arguments expediently recast us as an archetypal multinational villain, exploiting India's people and resources. As legal actions proceeded in the United States, it became evident to us that this caricature was designed to gain access to Union Carbide's financial resources.[42]

UCC also claimed that the site had been cleaned after the disaster. It contended that the Environmental Impact Assessment ratings for the Bhopal plant revealed favorable ratings in terms of carbon monoxide emissions and wastewater disposal. UCC also maintained that the gas leak did not contribute to contamination of soil and groundwater. The company referred to the 1997 report issued by NEERI, which said that there was contamination of soil only in three areas used for chemical treatment and disposal within the plant premises. It also pointed out that the local water-wells were not affected by the disposal. However, the study did not reveal water contamination outside the plant site, UCC contended. The company also pointed to a 1998 study by the Madhya Pradesh Pollution Control Board, which found some level of contamination in water but not due to the plant. It was found to be due to the drainage water and other sources of environmental pollution. UCC also maintained that it was not liable for the site clean-up since it had sold its shares to Eveready Industries and the land was held in custody by the state government of MP. UCC further claimed that

> activist groups and non-governmental organizations (NGOs) have protested against and repeatedly blocked remediation attempts by those who offered to help raise funds for clean up or to conduct pro-bono remediation. It's surprising that the very people who claim to have dedicated their lives to helping the people of Bhopal continue to block efforts to clean up the site.[43]

---

41 Barbara Dinham and Satinath Sarangi, "The Bhopal Gas Tragedy 1984 to?: The Evasion of Corporate Responsibility," *Environment&Urbanization*, Vol. 14, No. 1, April 2002.
42 Jackson B. Browning, "Union Carbide: Disaster at Bhopal," in Jack A. Gottschalk, *Crisis Response: Inside Stories on Managing Image under Siege* (Gail Research Incorporated, 1993).
43 "The Bhopal Plant," www.bhopal.com/plant.htm.

Longest-running struggle against corporate crime and government neglect

Following the disaster, a number of experienced activists from around the world and the country converged on Bhopal to support the relief effort, but it soon became a grassroots struggle based on independent trade unions, neighborhood committees, and pensioners' rights campaign. The target of their protest was the government, UCC, and—since 2001—Dow. They wanted the government to press Dow to pay compensation to take care of all the healthcare and economic needs of the survivors and their children, clean up the site, and ensure that Anderson and other authorized representatives of UCC were brought to justice.

In 1992, the local court in Bhopal declared Anderson a fugitive as he had gone into hiding. In July 2002, Greenpeace and the *Daily Mirror* traced his whereabouts.[44] Though a proclaimed offender in India, he was leading a luxurious life in a palatial home in Bridgehampton in Long Island near New York. These activists believed that the criminal trial of Anderson was very important to ensure corporate accountability.[45] Industry observers said that the U.S. government was lobbied by representatives of the U.S. industry to not allow the extradition of Anderson.[46]

While the Indian government was accused of not being serious about the extradition of Anderson, Dow was also accused of harboring a fugitive. Critics also charged that Dow was trying to evade its responsibility. They claimed that by acquiring UCC's assets, Dow had assumed responsibility for UCC's liabilities.[47] Dow also drew criticism for adopting a combative stance against the activists and some of its remarks on the issue were viewed as insensitive. For instance, in July 2002, Kathy Hunt, Public Affairs specialist at Dow, said that "$500 is plenty good for an Indian."[48] The company had also reportedly tried to crack down on activist groups threatening them with lawsuits. Dow also maintained it could not be subjected to the jurisdiction by an Indian court since it was an American company.

Since no action was being taken to address their grievances, the survivors and activists carried out various novel ways of protests such as hunger strikes, demonstrations, etc. Some activists also kept the companies engaged in litigation both in India and the U.S. The struggle also received support from activists and student groups in other countries. In 2003, as Bhopal entered its twentieth year after the

44   Nityanand Jayaraman, "At Long Last, an Extradition Request," www.indiatogether.org, July 2003.

45   Ibid.

46   Suchandana Gupta, "Bhopal Gas Tragedy: Slow Poisoning Continues," http://southasia.one world.net, December 2, 2009.

47   Dow Chemical Company, http://www.greenpeace.org/usa/campaigns/toxics/justice-for-bhopal/dow-chemical-company.

48   Mariam Khan, "Students Rally for Justice in India Tragedy," www.thelantern.com, November 29, 2009.

disaster, several victims confronted Dow in Mumbai and The Netherlands with hand-delivered samples of poisonous wastes. Several protestors lay down on Mumbai's Marine Drive in a bid to recreate the disaster site. Some carried out processions carrying a torch in their hands with banners that read, "Remember Bhopal" and "Dow—you have the blood of Bhopal on your hands."[49]

The protests were carried out at a Dow shareholder meeting in Michigan. At the meeting, an activist raised a question asking how Dow had accepted UCC's asbestos liabilities in the U.S. while it continued to ignore its responsibilities in Bhopal. To this, Dow's CEO told the shareholders that the company had addressed the asbestos liabilities because it was the subject of an ongoing litigation, while no such litigation existed in the case of Bhopal.[50]

This was followed by a 12-day hunger strike. Students from 25 colleges and universities from several countries worldwide organized rallies demanding that Dow fulfill the demands of the Bhopal gas victims. The activists claimed that the GoI was not championing the cause of the victims, as they were concerned that any action taken against Dow would hamper foreign investment in the country.[51] The protests gained support from activists in the U.S. who pressurized Dow to clean up the Bhopal site. In April 2003, the survivors went to the Appeals Court to pray for a relook at the decision taken by Keenan related to clean-up of the toxic wastes around the site. They also demanded that UCC compensate people affected by consuming contaminated water. In light of these protests, the GoI filed an extradition request with the U.S. State department in July 2003.

Faced with continuing protests, analysts felt that Dow's image had taken a beating. *Forbes* magazine attributed the decline in Dow's stock prices in the first two years following the acquisition of UCC to the "Indian-bred tort litigation" and "ruckus" created by demonstrations against it. Activists claimed that Dow was putting its reputation at risk by continuing to ignore the plight of the victims.[52] According to Jack Doyle, author of *Trespass Against Us: Dow Chemical & The Toxic Century*,

> Dow obviously knew about the potential downside at Carbide when it first calculated the acquisition, and no doubt believed it could minimize those through a combination of good lawyering, lobbying, and creative public relations. But Dow may have miscalculated... With Union Carbide, Dow just might have gotten more than it bargained for.[53]

The struggle for justice by the survivors drew support from various quarters. In 2004, two survivors, Rasheeda Bee (Bee) and Champa Devi (Devi) were

49 Tarun Jain, "Bhopal: A New Momentum," www.indiatogether.org, December 2003.
50 Nityanand Jayaraman, "Bhopal Goes to Dow Chemical," www.indiatogether.org, May 2003.
51 "Bhopal Gas Tragedy Victims End Fast," www.rediff.com, May 13, 2003.
52 "Recognition for Bhopal Campaigners," http://indiatogether.org, April 2004.
53 Jack Doyle, *Trespass Against Us, Dow Chemical and the Toxic Century*, Monroe, ME, Common Courage Press, 2004.

recognized with the Goldman Prize[54] for their relentless efforts for justice. Devi and Bee felt that the award would give a boost to the campaign they were carrying out against Dow. Bee added,

> This award affirms our struggle and makes the issues we are raising credible. It brings out the truth in our campaign. Dow has been trying to portray us as a fringe group with unreasonable demands. This award nails that lie, and shows that our campaign and demands are based in truth.[55]

In 2004, in response to the lawsuit filed by the survivors in the U.S. court in 1999, the U.S. Second Circuit Court of Appeals in New York said that the New York District Court should take into account claims made by the survivors against UCC. The court set June 20, 2004, as the deadline for receipt of the letter. Though the state government issued a letter, the central government refused to issue any letter to the U.S. court. The law ministry opined that all the issues related to the disaster had been dealt with in the Gas Leak Settlement in 1989. On June 23, 2004, the GoI finally agreed to issue a letter to the U.S. court.

The GoI sent a No Objection Certificate to the New York District Court for cleaning up of the site. This led to the opening of the legal liability case and affixed responsibility on Dow for the clean-up of the site. However, UCC contended that Dow was not responsible for the clean-up since it had acquired shares of UCIL in 2001 much after the settlement was made. The GoI estimated that the costs of the site clean would be around Rs.1 billion.[56]

Faced with continuous criticisms from survivors and activists, UCC and Dow kept pointing out to studies such as the one conducted by the National Institute of Occupational Health (NIOH), Ahmedabad, that reportedly found that the pesticide levels in people residing near the plant site were comparable to those in people of other countries and that other volatile organic compounds were below the level of detection of the instrument.

As the struggle for justice continued, it also received support from some U.S. Congressmen. In 2006, U.S. Congressman Frank Pallone, of New Jersey, stated,

> It's outrageous that over twenty years have passed and that the CEOs of Union Carbide and its successor Dow Chemical still have yet to be brought to justice... In Bhopal, some of the world's poorest people are being mistreated by one the world's richest corporations. As Union Carbide's successor company, Dow Chemical is now responsible for the disaster.[57]

---

54 The Goldman Environmental Prize is a prize given annually to grassroots environmental activists.

55 Tarun Jain, "Recognition for Bhopal Campaigners," www.indiatogether.com, April 2004.

56 K. Rajani Priya, "Cleaning up Bhopal Cost-effectively," www.indiatogether.org, December 2004.

57 http://bhopal.org/index.php?id=104.

He said that there was support in the Congress for the victims and that U.S. multinational corporations should not be allowed to get away with such excesses in other countries that they operated in.

In late 2007, Dow agreed to partially bear the expense for cleaning up the site in return for freeing itself from the liabilities it inherited from the acquisition of UCC in 2001. However, Dow continued to lobby hard with the GoI officials in a bid to obtain a ruling in its favor. The company was accused of holding out the lure of large-scale investments in India if it was let off the hook. Critics observed that powerful Indian industrialists were lobbying with the Indian government on Dow's behalf saying that resolving this issue in Dow's favor "would send a strong positive signal to U.S. investors."[58] "Evidently, all manner of entrenched interests are at work to help Dow duck its legal liability and obligation to clean up the site ... It's truly appalling that the Indian government is bowing to their pressure ... [This showed] utter servility on the part of the government toward the U.S. and giant transnational corporations, a phenomenon that has been in evidence ever since 1984,"[59] said Nityanandan Jayaraman.[60]

In late-2007, the Indian government sought US$22 million from Dow as an advance for cleaning up the site.[61] But Dow did not pay up, saying that the government asking it to deposit US$22 million was "inappropriate."[62]

Two decades and a half later...

On July 31, 2009, a few months before the 25th anniversary of the disaster, the Chief Judicial Magistrate of Bhopal court re-issued a warrant for the arrest of Anderson. However, no action was taken. On November 29, 2009, the survivors of the Bhopal gas tragedy staged violent protests and burned effigies of Anderson, demanding his arrest. The victims demanded that the government get Anderson extradited or have him face trial in an American court. The victims also demanded pension for widows of victims who had lost their lives. They insisted that the government provide them with pure water to drink and remove the toxic wastes lying in the surrounding areas of the plant.

---

58 Nityanand Jayaraman, "Union Carbide Must Clean Bhopal Mess—Residents," www.corp watch.org, September 1, 2006.

59 Praful Bidwai, "Cleaning Up After Bhopal Gas Tragedy—Not Begun," www.ipsnews.net, September 10, 2007.

60 Nityanand Jayaraman is an independent journalist and researcher investigating and reporting on corporate abuses of environment and human rights. He is a long-time volunteer with the International Campaign for Justice in Bhopal.

61 "Bhopal Gas Tragedy Victims to 'Expose' Central, State Governments," http://blog.taragana .com, *November 26, 2009.*

62 Manjeet Kripalani, "Dow Chemical: Liable for Bhopal?" www.businessweek.com, May 28, 2008.

However, UCC defended Anderson as it stuck to its sabotage argument. "Overwhelming evidence has established that the Bhopal gas release was caused by an act of employee sabotage that could not have been foreseen or prevented by the plant's management. The release had terrible consequences, but it makes no sense to continue to attempt to criminalize a tragedy that no one could have foreseen,"[63] said Tomm F. Sprick (Sprick), UCC's spokesman. Sprick also argued that the UCC did not have any role in the operations of the plant and pointed out that it had given substantial monetary and medical aid to the victims following the disaster.

In November 2009, the associations formed by the victims launched a campaign to expose people in the government favoring Dow. As part of the campaign, the leaders organized a buffet and invited government officials to partake of several "delicacies" prepared using the groundwater and chemicals from the disaster site. On December 3, 2009, its 25th anniversary, the survivors of the Bhopal gas disaster marched to the disaster site holding placards bearing slogans such as "Hang Anderson and give us clean potable water" and "Foreign companies leave India" to reiterate their commitment to carrying on their fight against UCC, Dow, and the government. They took a pledge that they would continue their fight against injustice. In addition to their regular demands, the activists urged Dow to admit that it was wrong and to deposit the US$22 million asked for by the GoI to clean up the site. Activists and student bodies in other countries too showed their solidarity with the victims. For instance, hundreds of students in New York City joined protests around the world demanding accountability from Dow and the GoI. Several hundred students from Parsons the New School for Design lay down in formation to spell the word "DOW" while other participants held up placards spelling out "Clean Up Bhopal" in the background.[64]

Meanwhile, a December 2009 report by the Center for Science and Environment[65] (CSE) revealed that the "groundwater in areas even 3 km away from the factory site contains almost 40 times more pesticides than normal Indian standards." "Continuous intake of this groundwater can have drastic effects on the human body ... This is like slow poisoning,"[66] CSE's director and activist Sunita Narain claimed. However, this claim was refuted by Union minister for environment and forests, Jairam Ramesh, who said, "I held the toxic waste in my hand. I am still alive and not coughing. It's 25 years after the gas tragedy. Let us move ahead."[67] Babulal Gaur, the state minister for gas relief and rehabilitation, too

63   "Company Defends Chief in Bhopal Disaster," www.nytimes.com, August 3, 2009.
64   "NYC New School Students Die en Masse to Protest Dow's Criminal Neglect in Bhopal," http://theyesmen.org, December 3, 2009.
65   The Center for Science and Environment (CSE) is an independent, non-governmental organization with the stated aim of increasing public awareness about science, technology, environment, and development. CSE was established in 1980 and is based in New Delhi.
66   Suchandana Gupta, "Bhopal Gas Tragedy: Slow Poisoning Continues," http://southasia.one world.net, December 2, 2009.
67   Ibid.

insisted that the plant site had no toxic contamination and dismissed allegations that the defects in new-born children were related to the catastrophe. He added that the diseases in children were a result of living in slums. These denials were made despite the fact that inspections by several committees had found around 44,000 kg of tarry residues and 25,000 kg of alpha naphthol lying in the open since 1984. Several studies had also unveiled that groundwater, vegetables, and soil had traces of toxic chemicals in them. Activists claimed that UCIL had been routinely burying huge amounts of poisonous waste on its premises since 1969.[68]

Despite several efforts made by the Bhopal gas survivors and activists, the victims continued to suffer. Sadhna Karnik Pradhan, an activist, said, "Even 25 years after the biggest industrial disaster of the era, the second and third generation of Bhopal gas victims are suffering from life-threatening and crippling diseases and are forced to drink polluted water and live in a polluted atmosphere."[69] Activists claimed that the survivors were still suffering from serious health problems. On an average, 6,000 gas-affected patients visited hospitals in Bhopal each day.[70] They claimed that mothers exposed to the gas as children, were still giving birth to children with birth defects. The average number of brain damaged and malformed babies born in Bhopal was 10 times more than the national average.[71] A 2009 report by the Gas Tragedy Relief Department had said that the morbidity rate was 20 percent among the Bhopal gas victims as opposed to 5 percent rate among unaffected citizens.[72]

Several activists pointed out that only 105,000 people had received compensation as fixed by the government. This implied that several injured people had still not been compensated. N. D. Jayaprakash of Bhopal Gas Peedit Sangharsh Sahayog Samiti (BGPSSS)[73] opined that it was a massive fraud since the number of gas-affected victims was arbitrarily fixed by the government at 105,000. This included the 3,000 who were reported to be dead. He reported that around 20,000 people had died and nearly 570,000 were injured. Of the Rs.7.13 billion compensation amount nearly Rs.1.13 billion was used for loss of livestock and properties, according to the activists.[74]

Some observers were appalled at the fact that even 25 years after the disaster, the victims continued to suffer from the after-effects of the gas leak and that no one had been punished. They noted how people affected by the disaster were

---

68 Subodh Varma, "Bhopal Gas Tragedy: Endless Nightmare," http://timesofindia.indiatimes .com, December 3, 2009.
69 "Force US to Own up Bhopal, Urge Gas Victims' Kids," www.in.com, December 18, 2009.
70 Subodh Varma, "Bhopal Gas Tragedy: Endless Nightmare," http://timesofindia.indiatimes .com, December 3, 2009.
71 "Bhopal: The Victims are Still Being Born," http://www.independent.co.uk, November 29, 2009.
72 Subodh Varma, "Bhopal Gas Tragedy: Endless Nightmare," www.timesofindia.com, December 3, 2009.
73 BGPSSS is one of the NGOs working for survivors of the disaster.
74 Ibid.

still waiting for adequate compensation and even the full facts of the leak and its impact had not been properly investigated. Activists said that it was UCC's greed that had led to the disaster and that UCC had then diverted the blame by making the outrageous claim that the disaster had been due to an act of sabotage and sticking to it.[75] They were also very critical of the Indian government and its courts. "In every form of civilized society, it is the judicial system that decides whether an accused has a case to answer. India's courts have decided that Union Carbide and its new owner, Dow, do—but the company sticks two fingers up,"[76] said Tim Edwards, a trustee of the Bhopal Medical Appeal.

Critics felt that the situation in Bhopal only went to show how multinational corporations had amassed disproportionate power and influence in the global stage. It showed contemporary capitalism in the worst light as the corporations refused to be held accountable for their crimes. They noted that the Indian government was also not leaning on the company too hard, as it feared a backlash from foreign investors who had become more important players in the Indian economy following liberalization.[77] Activists alleged that rather than siding with them, the GoI was siding with Dow. They pointed out that though the U.S. Securities & Exchange Commission had fined Dow US$325,000 for having paid US$200,000 in bribes to Indian officials over a 6-year period,[78] the GoI had not taken any action against the company.[79]

Critics also alleged that Dow, which claimed to be a good corporate citizen with high standards of environmental stewardship, had spent millions of dollars in marketing, public relations (PR), and contributions to lobby groups to ensure that it was not subjected to stringent regulation and did not have to pay the real costs of the suffering it had caused.[80] Bee said, "If Dow were a truly responsible company, it would have settled the Bhopal issue the day they acquired Union Carbide."[81] Critics alleged[82] that Dow's much touted water sustainability initiative in India was nothing but a business agenda.[83] According to Tonya

---

75 "20 Years After Bhopal," http://dow.radicaldesigns.org, December 2004.

76 "Bhopal: The Victims are Still Being Born," www.independent.co.uk, November 29, 2009.

77 Deepro Sen, "Bhopal Gas Tragedy," www.goforthelaw.com/articles/fromlawstu/article80 .htm.

78 Dow bribed officials to register Dursban in India. The product was banned for home use in the U.S. because it had caused permanent injury or even death to dozens of children.

79 "Dow is Fined $325,000 by the US SEC for Bribing Indian Officials over 6 Years," http://dow .radicaldesigns.org, February 13, 2007.

80 "Driving Dangerously: The Truth about DOW," http://dow.radicaldesigns.org/downloads/ Driving_Dangerously_The_Truth_About_Dow.pdf.

81 "20 Years after Bhopal," http://dow.radicaldesigns.org, December 2004.

82 Nityanand Jayaraman, "Bhopal: Generations of Poison," www.corpwatch.org, December 2, 2009.

83 Critics claimed that these reverse osmosis plants were aimed at generating a replacement market for Dow's membranes. They claimed that the water plants set up in 2006 and 2007 had since become non-functional.

Hennessey, Dow's CSR initiative "Dow's Global Water Initiatives, which doesn't have a project in Bhopal—is a classic greenwash of its public image."[84]

Can accountability be fixed?

Dow continued to maintain that it did not have any liability since UCC had settled the matter by paying a one-time compensation of US$470 million. Its spokesman Scott Wheeler (Wheeler) said that Dow had "never owned or operated the Bhopal plant site and Dow did not inherit any liabilities of Union Carbide Corp."[85] Dow added that the responsibility of the plant now rested with the state government and hence it was not responsible for the safety of the citizens and clean-up of the site. In a statement, Dow said that the compensation "resolved all existing and future claims. [The company] did all it could to help the victims and their families."[86] Reacting to criticisms that Dow was engaged in intense lobbying with the government, Wheeler said,

> Attempts to attach any liability to Dow are misplaced... like all global companies, it is common for Dow leaders to meet with government leaders and officials wherever we do business and have plans to grow. It is also common for companies to discuss challenges and opportunities related to investment.[87]

Experts noted that the movement started by the survivors and activists in 1984 had, over the last two and a half decades, become a grassroots struggle that was recognized as the world's longest running struggle against corporate excesses. Not only had it not allowed the attention of the world community to shift from UCC and Dow, but it had also succeeded in generating support from various quarters. In mid-2009, the victims also received support from the U.S. Congress, which asked Dow to address issues related to soil and water contamination and provide relief to the victims.[88] Some international supporters of the Bhopal gas survivors called for adequate steps to clean up the site.[89]

With the GoI being increasingly viewed as siding with Dow, the various organizations that had sprung up to demand justice for the victims of the world's

---

84   Tonya Hennessey, "25 Years and Still Fighting for Justice: When Will Dow Chemical Clean Up its Poisonous Legacy in Bhopal," www.corpwatch.org, December 14, 2009.
85   Manjeet Kripalani, "Dow Chemical: Liable for Bhopal?" www.businessweek.com, May 28, 2008.
86   Randeep Ramesh, "Bhopal Marks 25th Anniversary of Union Carbide Gas Disaster," www.guardian.co.uk, December 3, 2009.
87   "Bhopal: The Victims are Still Being Born," www.independent.co.uk, November 29, 2009.
88   Nityanand Jayaraman, "Bhopal: Generations of Poison," www.corpwatch.org, December 2, 2009.
89   "Still Angry about Bhopal Gas Tragedy: Lapierre," www.ibnlive.com, December 3, 2009.

worst industrial disaster pledged to carry forward the fight on their own. For instance, Children Against Dow-Carbide, a youth group, was started in 2008 not only to fight for justice for the Bhopal victims, but to continue the fight once this objective was achieved so that no other company would feel that they could do what UCC did and get away with it.[90] Safreen Khan, one of the co-founders, said, "The Bhopal struggle is not 25 years old. With our entry, the struggle has just entered its youthful phase, and we'll keep the fight alive for as long as it takes."[91]

Experts felt that the on-going struggle against Dow and its eventual outcome would not only have implications for the health and well-being of the people of Bhopal but also have lasting implications for the future of globalization and the labor and environmental movements.[92] According to Hennessey, "But who holds multinational corporations accountable when things go wrong—especially over-seas—and how? And what happens when one company buys another, one that is holding significant public liability?"[93]

90 Eurig Scandrett, "The Demand for Corporate Accountability," http://infochangeindia.org, September 2009.
91 Nityanand Jayaraman, "Bhopal: Generations of Poison," www.corpwatch.org, December 2, 2009.
92 "20 Years After Bhopal," http://dow.radicaldesigns.org, December 2004.
93 Tonya Hennessey, "25 Years and Still Fighting for Justice: When Will Dow Chemical Clean Up its Poisonous Legacy in Bhopal," www.corpwatch.org, December 14, 2009.

EXHIBIT 1 Bhopal Gas tragedy: a timeline

Source: Compiled from various sources.

1934	UCIL is formed.
1950s	UCIL expands into Chemicals.
1969	Agri Products Division is launched.
1978	UCIL obtains license to produce MIC in India.
1979	UCIL plant at Bhopal is inaugurated.
May 1980	The Bhopal plant produces its first gallon of MIC.
1981–84	Cut-backs at UCIL. Many technicians and skilled workers were laid-off leading to shortage in people manning the plant and the tanks containing MIC. In 1983, the principal safety systems in the plant were shut down interrupting the refrigeration of the tanks containing sixty tons of MIC. The flame that burned day and night at the top of the flare tower to burn off any toxic gases emitted into the atmosphere in the event of an accident, was also extinguished. Other essential equipment, such as the scrubber cylinder used to decontaminate any gas leaks, was deactivated.
December 3, 1984	MIC gas leaks at the UCIL plant.
December 4, 1984	The disaster is reported to the UCC plant located in Connecticut. Anderson is placed under house arrest. UCC organizes a team of international medical experts in addition to providing equipment and supplies, to work with the local medical community in Bhopal. The technical team at UCC assesses the cause of the gas leakage.
December 14, 1984	Anderson commits himself to action and assures the U.S. Congress that such an incident will not happen again.
February 1985	UCC offers interim relief and establishes the (UCC) Employees' Bhopal Relief Fund. It also sends medical equipment to UCIL.
March 1985	Disaster program is launched by UCC to study the effects of MIC exposure. The GoI enacts the Bhopal Gas Leak Disaster Act. The UCC technical team reports that a large volume of water was introduced into the MIC tank and that it had led to the disaster.
April 1985	UCC offers US$7 million interim relief out of which US$5 million is for the relief for victims. GoI rejects the offer.
June 1985	UCC funds participation of Indian medical experts.
July 1985	Some samples confirm that water triggered the reaction leading to leakage of gas.
January 1986	UCC offers US$10 million to fund a hospital to treat the victims.
March 1986	UCC proposes US$350 million compensation.

continued

May 1986	The Bhopal litigation is transferred to India from the U.S. District Court. An appeal for decision is made by the victims.
January 1987	The U.S. Court of Appeals affirms transfer of the Bhopal litigation to India.
March 1987	The GoI closes the Bhopal Technical and Vocational Center after determining that UCC had funded the project.
August 1987	UCC offers an additional US$4.6 million in humanitarian interim relief
January– December 1988	Throughout the year, litigations take place before the Indian courts regarding compensation for the Bhopal gas victims.
May 1988	An "independent" investigation by Arthur D. Little concludes that sabotage is the reason for gas leakage.
November 1988	The Supreme Court of India asks UCC and the GoI to reach a settlement.
February 1989	UCC makes a final settlement of US$470 million.
May 1989	The Supreme Court of India explains the underlying principle for the settlement and concludes that the settlement made by UCC is higher than those usually payable under Indian law.
December 1989	The Supreme Court of India authorizes the GoI to act on behalf of the victims.
January– December 1990	Proceedings by the Supreme Court of India to overturn the settlement agreement.
November 1990	The MP state government prepares a list of victims to be compensated and submits it to the Supreme Court of India.
December 1990	The Supreme Court of India concludes review of petitions that sought to overturn the settlement made by UCC.
October 1991	The Supreme Court of India instructs the GoI to purchase medical insurance covering 100,000 people. It cancels UCC's immunity from further prosecution.
April 1992	UCC announces that it will sell its 50.9 percent stake in UCIL.
October 1993	The U.S. Supreme Court denies hearing appeal made by lower courts saying that the Bhopal victims cannot sue for damages in U.S. courts.
April 1994	The Supreme Court of India permits UCC to sell its UCIL stake so that the assets can be used to build the hospital at Bhopal.
November 1994	UCC sells its stake to McLeod Russell (India) Ltd.
December 1994	UCC offers US$20 million to a charitable trust for setting up of the hospital at Bhopal.

October 1995	Hospital charitable trust begins construction.
1999	The charitable has US$100 million funds.
2001	The hospital is open to the public.
February 2001	UCC merges with Dow.
July 2004	The Supreme Court of India orders release of remaining funds to victims.
April 2005	The Supreme Court of India extends the deadline for release of settlement funds to victims to April 30, 2006.
December 2005	The U.S. Federal Court dismisses two of the three claims made in the Janki Bai Sahu (Sahu) case that sought damages for personal injuries due to exposure to contaminated water.
August 2006	The US Court of Appeals Upholds Dismissal of a case of the Bhopal gas victim.
September 2006	Bhopal Welfare Commission clears UCC of all the compensation claims and petitions.
October 2006	MP state government prepares Drinking Water, Healthcare, Environmental Rehabilitation Plan.
November 2006	US Federal District Court dismisses last claim in the Sahu case.
December 2006	Plaintiffs of the Sahu case appeal to the Second Circuit Court of Appeals.
March 2007	Bhopal gas survivors file a new Class Action Lawsuit Filed in New York Federal Court.
November 2007	Indian government asks Dow to deposit a sum of US$22 million for clean-up of the disaster site.
May 2008	Second Circuit Court of Appeals hears oral arguments in the Sahu appeals case.
November 2008	Second Circuit Court of Appeals remands the Sahu appeals case to the U.S. District Court.
February 2009	U.S. Federal District Court rejects mediation request in Sahu appeals case.
July 2009	Chief Judicial Magistrate of Bhopal court re-issues a warrant for the arrest of Anderson.

EXHIBIT 2 A brief note on the Dow Chemical Company

Founded in 1897 by Herbert Dow, The Dow Chemical Company (Dow) is a Michigan-based chemical manufacturer. It began commercial production of bleach in 1898. The company diversified its line of business in 1935 and ventured into the production of plastics with the launch of Ethocel ethylcellulose resins. Over the years, the company offered agricultural products and other specialized products and services in addition to plastics and chemicals. For the year 2009, it had revenues of US$44.88 billion and profits of US$648 million (Refer to Table A for five-year financial summary of Dow).

TABLE A Dow's financial summary: 2005–2009 (In US$ billion)

Source: http://www.dow.com and http://money.cnn.com.

Particulars	2009	2008	2007	2006	2005
Revenues	44.875	57.514	53.513	49.124	46.307
Profits	0.648	0.579	2.887	3.724	4.515
Assets	65.937	45.474	48.801	45.581	45.934
Stockholder's equity	20.555	13.511	19.389	17.065	15.324

The company ranked 127th in *Fortune Magazine*'s Global 500 rankings in 2009. The company ranked second in the Global 500 rankings for the chemical industry (Refer to Table B for a list of top ten companies in the chemical industry).

TABLE B Top ten companies in the chemical industry: 2009

Source: Adapted from "Global 500," http://money.cnn.com, July 20, 2009.

Rank	Company	Global 500 Rank	2008 Revenues (US$ billion)
1	BASF	59	91.19
2	Dow Chemical	127	57.51
3	LyondellBasell Industries	147	50.99
4	Bayer	154	48.18
5	Sabic	186	40.20
6	DuPont	262	31.83
7	Mitsubishi Chemical Holdings	302	28.95
8	Evonik Industries	383	23.71
9	Akzo Nobel	406	22.56
10	L'Air Liquide	484	19.17

Dow entered India in 1957 through a joint venture with Polychem Limited[94] to form Dow India. Over the years, Dow India offered a strong manufacturing base and presence in the country. By 2009, the company had grown to have 1,100 employees. In India, the company offered products in diverse industries such as pharmaceuticals, paints and coatings, water, automotive, water, agriculture, construction, and alternative energies. In India, the company was also engaged in supporting the community by carrying out sustainable drinking water initiatives, supporting physically challenged people through the Jaipur Foot (low-priced prosthetic) initiative, offering school uniforms to local schools, etc. For the year 2009, the company recorded sales of US$500 million in India (Refer to Figure A for a Dow's sales break-up by geographic area).

Dow, which regularly touted its sustainability initiatives, had faced many protests in the past. It was criticized for manufacturing and distributing highly restricted or banned (in the U.S.) chemicals such as DDT, Agent Orange, Dursban (pesticide), and asbestos.[95] It had also earned notoriety for supplying poisons for the U.S.'s chemical warfare in Vietnam.[96]

FIGURE A: Dow's sales break-up by geographic area

Source: adapted from http://www.dow.com

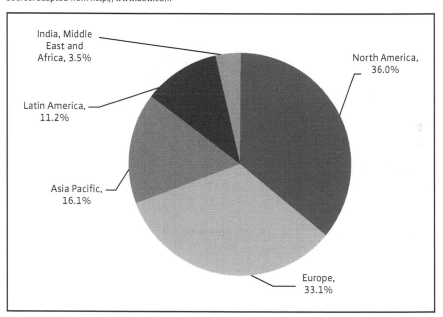

---

94 Established in 1956, Polychem Limited manufactures and sells specialty chemicals.
95 Dow Chemical Company, http://www.greenpeace.org/usa/campaigns/toxics/justice-for-bhopal/dow-chemical-company.
96 "20 Years after Bhopal," http://dow.radicaldesigns.org, December 2004.

About the authors

Debprathim Purkaystha is the Assistant Professor for Marketing and Strategy at IBS Hyderabad, with over 12 years' teaching, research and industry experience. He is the Consulting Editor of *Case Folio,* a refereed journal dedicated to case studies in management. He has written more than 30 case studies focusing on business ethics, corporate sustainability and social entrepreneurship. He has won awards and recognition for case writing from the Association of MBAs (AMBA), ecch, European Foundation for Management Development (EFMD), Emerald, John Molson School of Business, North American Case Research Association (NACRA), oikos International, etc. Many of his cases have been published in global editions of textbooks. He also conducts training and workshops on case writing and case-based learning.

Hadiya Faheem, an MBA graduate from Osmania University, is a former Senior Research Associate at IBS Center for Management Research, IBS Hyderabad, and is currently a freelance case writer. With over seven years' research experience, she has developed several cases on issues related to management. Her research work has also dealt with developing cases on corporate social responsibility and social entrepreneurship. She has won awards and recognition for case writing from the European Foundation for Management Development (EFMD), oikos International, ecch, etc. Her cases have been published in international textbooks and academic journals.

Teaching notes for this case are available from Greenleaf Publishing. These are free of charge and available only to teaching staff. They can be requested by going to:
www.greenleaf-publishing.com/darkside2notes

8

The battle for Middle Earth
New Zealand's bid to save *The Hobbit*[1]

Todd Bridgman
Victoria University of Wellington School of Management, New Zealand

Colm McLaughlin
University College Dublin School of Business

In September 2010 the International Federation of Actors (FIA), which represents performer unions in 100 countries, placed an international boycott on the filming of The Hobbit. The Hobbit films, estimated to cost NZ$670 million, were to be filmed in New Zealand but the FIA, under the advice of an Australian–based actors union, the Media Entertainment and Arts Alliance (MEAA), were unhappy that the production company was refusing to negotiate a collective agreement with local actors. The boycott incensed the film's director Sir Peter Jackson, an icon in New Zealand's flourishing film industry. Jackson was revered for both his creative talents and his success in attracting Hollywood film studios to New Zealand, providing investment, jobs and boosting tourism, which had overtaken agriculture to become the country's biggest export earner. Jackson accused the MEAA of undermining New Zealand's reputation as a desirable location for Hollywood studios, while the MEAA argued that New Zealand actors had struggled for years on non–union contracts. Local film production workers came out in support of Jackson and public opinion was firmly on his side. Pressure on the MEAA increased when Jackson announced that New Line Cinema and Warner Bros executives were coming to New Zealand to make arrangements to move *The Hobbit* offshore. After meeting with Prime Minister John Key, it became clear that the removal of the boycott would not satisfy their concerns. They wanted a change to New Zealand's

---

1 Submission to 'Dark Side X' Case-Writing Competition 2011.

labour laws to prevent any future trouble as well as additional tax breaks and government grants. Following two days of meetings, Prime Minister Key announced a deal had been struck to keep *The Hobbit* in New Zealand. Parliament would be put into urgency the following day to pass a law preventing film production workers from negotiating a collective employment agreement and the government would provide another $NZ33.5 million in financial incentives. The dispute revealed that Jackson's films meant more to New Zealanders then jobs and investment—they had become a symbol of national pride for this small, geographically isolated nation.

October 21, 2010. "Anti-corporate activists sometimes claim that big companies are mightier than governments. This is absurd. Governments can pass laws, raise taxes and declare war. Companies have virtually no powers of coercion" (*The Economist*).[2]

October 26, 2010. Warner Bros executives arrive in Wellington to meet Prime Minister John Key about their concerns with New Zealand's labour laws, which is forcing them to rethink their decision to film *The Hobbit* in New Zealand.

October 27, 2010. Prime Minister John Key stepped to the podium to deliver his much-awaited statement on whether *The Hobbit* would be filmed in New Zealand. He had missed the 6pm news bulletins, but given the intense interest in the outcome, the main television networks had interrupted their normal programmes to carry the press conference live. Earlier in the day Key had assessed the chances of a positive outcome at no better than 50:50. On the line lay not just this NZ$670 million project but potentially the future of New Zealand's big budget film industry.

> I'm pleased to announce an agreement has been reached between the New Zealand Government and Warner Bros that will enable the two Hobbit movies, to be directed by Sir Peter Jackson, to be made in New Zealand ... The Government will introduce legislation tomorrow into Parliament to clarify the distinction between independent contractors and employees as it relates only to the film production industry. It is this clarification that will guarantee that the movies are made in New Zealand.[3]

Parties on all sides of the dispute were relieved the films would stay. The film's director, New Zealander Sir Peter Jackson, thanked the Government for providing reassurance both for local film industry workers and for international film studios. New Zealand Actors Equity (NZAE), the group which had joined an

---

2 *The Economist* (2010) "Companies aren't charities", 21 October.
3 Transcript of press conference, which can be viewed at http://tvnz.co.nz/national-news/film-producer-says-hobbit-deal-terrific-3856571/video.

international boycott of *The Hobbit*, was thankful their action had not led to the film leaving New Zealand. Emotions had run high throughout the dispute and much of the anger was directed at the actors union, with its leaders receiving death threats.[4]

Jackson is an Oscar-award winning director, producer and screenwriter, best known for his *Lord of the Rings* film trilogy, based on the novel by J.R.R. Tolkein, who also wrote *The Hobbit*. Jackson made his name making horror comedy films in New Zealand and produced his first big budget Hollywood film, *The Frighteners* in 1996. Jackson, whose wealth is estimated at $NZ500 million,[5] is revered in New Zealand, especially in his home town of Wellington, colloquially known as "Wellywood". One commentator noted that:

> Instead of running to Hollywood to make movies, he performed some magic of his own and got the money to run to him. He built a Hollywood-style film studio in Wellington, a small windy town on the edge of the world. In rolled the stars, in rolled the millions, in rolled the Oscars. Then the tourists followed. And finally, the Knighthood. If individual resourcefulness and "have-a-go" culture is a religion in New Zealand, then Jackson is something of a god.[6]

His ability to attract Hollywood studios to film in New Zealand saw the industry grow to NZ$2.8 billion in 2009.[7] In addition to providing jobs and investment, Jackson's films had become an important way of promoting New Zealand as a tourism destination, by increasing awareness of the country and showcasing its spectacular scenery. Tourism makes up nearly 10% of New Zealand's GDP and in 2010 it overtook the dairy sector to become New Zealand's top export earner, worth $9.5 billion.[8]

Jackson's big budget films provided more than just an economic boost for New Zealand, becoming an important symbol of national pride for a small, geographically isolated nation. As veteran broadcaster Paul Holmes put it:

> They have more than become our property, as it were. They have become us. We are extremely proud of them. We love what they say about us, not only in terms of the landscape and the gorgeous country that is ours but also in terms of what they say about our creative ability, our creative people and their extraordinary professionalism.[9]

4 Drinnan, J. and Binning, E. (2010). "Death threats fly over Hobbit", *New Zealand Herald*, 29 October.

5 NBR Rich list, 2010.

6 O'Leary, A. (2010) "New Zealand's 'love affair' with The Hobbit", *BBC News*, 25 October.

7 Wither, T. (2010) "Key secures pact for New Zealand filming of 'Hobbit'". *Bloomberg Businessweek*, 27 October.

8 Figures available at http://www.stats.govt.nz/browse_for_stats/industry_sectors/Tourism/TourismSatelliteAccount_MR10.aspx.

9 Holmes, P. (2010) Key's trader skills come to the fore. *New Zealand Herald*, 31 October.

The first most New Zealanders heard of the dispute was on September 26, 2010, when the normally media-shy Jackson launched an attack on Simon Whipp, head of the Media Entertainment and Arts Alliance (MEAA), an Australian union which the NZAE had joined in 2006. MEAA is a member of the International Federation of Actors (FIA), which represents performer unions in 100 countries, including the powerful Screen Actors Guild (SAG) in the United States. On August 17, the FIA sent a letter to 3 Foot 7, Jackson's production company for *The Hobbit*, advising them:

> [t]hat the International Federation of Actors urges each of its affiliates to adopt instructions to their members that no member of any FIA affiliate will agree to act in the theatrical feature film "The Hobbit" until such time as the producer has entered into a collective bargaining agreement with the Media Entertainment & Arts Alliance for production in New Zealand providing for satisfactory terms and conditions for all performers employed on the production.[10]

Jackson was furious that an international boycott had been placed on *The Hobbit* and accused Whipp of taking advantage of New Zealand actors to increase its power and to undermine New Zealand's reputation as a desirable location for Hollywood studios.

> I can't see beyond the ugly spectre of an Australian bully-boy, using what he perceives as his weak Kiwi cousins to gain a foothold in this country's film industry... It feels as if we have a large Aussie cousin kicking sand in our eyes.[11]

The industrial action was another setback for *The Hobbit*, which had been dogged by controversy from the start. In 2005 Jackson announced he was suing New Line Cinema, which owned the rights to *The Hobbit*, for lost revenue associated with the *Lord of the Rings* trilogy. New Line co-chairman Bob Shaye said Jackson would never direct a film for them again, but later backed down and invited Jackson to be executive producer on *The Hobbit*, which would be financed by New Line and Metro-Goldwyn-Mayer (MGM). The movies were scheduled for release in 2011 and 2012 but were delayed by a law-suit from J.R.R Tolkein's estate seeking to block the filming pending a $220 million compensation payment from New Line. That dispute was settled out of court but the film was further delayed by financial troubles at MGM, resulting in director Guillermo del Toro leaving the project, with Jackson taking over as director.[12]

For its part, the MEAA argued that New Zealand actors had struggled for years on non-union contracts, which provided them with inferior working conditions compared with unionised actors in other countries. After Jackson went public,

10   MEAA. (2010*) The Hobbit and Engagement of Performers.*
11   "Peter Jackson's response to union claims", *Dominion Post*, 27 September, 2010.
12   "Hobbit director Del Toro quits", *Dominion Post*, 31 May, 2010.

MEAA responded that all they ever wanted was a meeting with Jackson to discuss working conditions for actors on *The Hobbit*. Jackson was dismissive: "they fail to add that from the outset, they had a gun to our head."[13] He refused to meet with MEAA and held legal advice which stated that to do so would be illegal, since actors on *The Hobbit* would be employed as independent contractors and under New Zealand's labour law, it was illegal to enter a collective agreement with independent contractors. The same conclusion was reached by New Zealand's Crown Law office in advising the Attorney-General, though MEAA received legal advice of its own that showed there were provisions in the act that allowed a collective agreement to be negotiated, with actors classed as independent contractors.

Pressure was mounting on MEAA and NZAE to justify their boycott, but Whipp was now refusing to speak in public. Film workers approached him outside a Wellington restaurant and posted the footage of his refusal on YouTube.[14] The pressure intensified on October 16, when New Line Cinema and Warner Bros confirmed *The Hobbit* would proceed with Jackson as director, but made no mention of where it would be filmed. That day, NZAE and MEAA informed Warner Bros that the boycott would be lifted and the parties set about reaching an agreement on how this would be announced in public.

In the meantime, a protest march was organised by Sir Richard Taylor, the leader of Wellington-based special-effects company Weta, which had already begun pre-production work on *The Hobbit*. Weta was formed by Taylor and Jackson in 1994 and had since acquired international acclaim through its production of the *Lord of the Rings* trilogy and *King Kong*. Taylor had won five Oscars and, like Jackson, had been knighted for his contribution to New Zealand's film industry. Taylor called a meeting of film technicians to discuss the dispute and within hours, 1500 people had gathered at Weta's Wellington studio. The crowd marched to where a meeting was taking place between NZAE and representatives from New Zealand's peak union organization, the Council of Trade Unions.[15] CTU President Helen Kelly, who had now assumed the role of spokesperson for the NZAE, was annoyed Taylor had allowed the protest to go ahead when he knew the boycott had already been lifted. She addressed the crowd but was shouted down when she argued that the union action was a convenient excuse for Warner Bros to reconsider their commitment to film in New Zealand. Since their original decision the NZ dollar had appreciated from 50c to 75c on the $US dollar, making it far more costly. Also at issue, Kelly said, were the financial incentives offered by the New Zealand government to attract overseas films.

Tax breaks for films were abolished in the 1990s, although a deal was done for *Lord of the Rings*, estimated to be worth $200 million in tax breaks.[16] In 2002,

---

13 Peter Jackson—Hobbit media release, *TV3 News*, October 27.
14 Available at http://www.youtube.com/watch?v=7RmzSlCY7_s&feature=related.
15 Cardy, T. (2010) "Jackson hits back", *Dominion Post*, 21 October.
16 "Lord of the tax breaks: A history of capital flight threats", *The Standard*. http://www.thestandard.org.nz.

Taylor warned that New Zealand would lose out on overseas film productions if financial incentives were not reintroduced. The following year, the Large Budget Screen Production Grant Scheme (LBSPGS) was introduced, giving overseas film producers a 12.5% rebate on money spent in New Zealand. In 2009 Treasury, New Zealand's finance ministry, argued the LBSPGS could not be justified on economic grounds, saying grants for *Avatar* and *King Kong* had likely caused a net loss for New Zealand.[17] Jackson, who had been asked to head a ministerial review of the New Zealand Film Commission defended the LBSPGS and recommended that it be kept globally competitive, saying that without it, major overseas projects would not come to New Zealand. "We may think our landscape is unique, but a publicly traded multinational conglomerate won't hesitate to substitute the mountains of Canada, the black forests of Germany or the lush green of Ireland if the numbers point that way."[18]

The day after the Wellington march by film technicians, Jackson announced Warner Bros executives were coming to New Zealand to make arrangements to move *The Hobbit* offshore. Prime Minister Key offered to meet with them in a last-ditch attempt to keep the movies in New Zealand. The executives arrived on October 26 and were transported by limousines to the Prime Minister's official residence for meetings with ministers and officials. A media pack waited outside eager to speak to anyone emerging from the crisis talks. At the day's end, Key predicted the decision could go either way. Warner Bros were now seeking additional financial incentives which New Zealand could not afford to meet. They were not reassured by the NZAE's promise of no further industrial action over *The Hobbit* and wanted a change to New Zealand's labour laws to prevent any future trouble.

At issue was the status of film industry workers under the Employment Relations Act (2000) and the case of James Bryson, who worked for Jackson's production company 3 Foot 6 on special effects for the *Lord of the Rings*.[19] Bryson was eventually made redundant and argued that he was unfairly dismissed. Under the ERA, he could only pursue a personal grievance if he was an employee, rather than an independent contractor. At the Employment Court hearing, the Screen Producers and Directors Association of New Zealand argued that the film industry relied on independent contracts because of the intermittent nature of the work. Giving those workers status as employees would increase their employment rights (through access to such things as personal grievance and redundancy payments) and allow them to collectively bargain as a union. This would seriously affect the viability of film production in New Zealand, which was attractive for overseas film studios because of its non-unionised workforce. The Employment Court found that Bryson's situation was different from standard industry practice. He had not tendered for his position, was in a long-term

17 "Big films cost NZ millions", *New Zealand Herald*, 13 June, 2010.
18 Jackson, P. and Court, D. (2010) *Review of the New Zealand Film Commission*, p.67.
19 3 Foot 6 was the company formed to produce the *Lord of the Rings* trilogy. This is not to be confused with 3 Foot 7, the company formed to produce *The Hobbit* films.

position with 3 Foot 6, had not been working on other projects and had no investment in plant or equipment. Therefore, despite the contract describing him as an independent contractor, the real nature of his employment meant he was an employee and therefore entitled to pursue his personal grievance. The Court of Appeal reversed the Employment Court ruling but Bryson took the case to the Supreme Court and won.

At the end of the second day of negotiations with Warner Bros, Key headed to Parliament to announce that a deal had been struck. The following day the House of Representatives would be put into urgency to pass a law change, meaning it would bypass the usual select committee process. The new law would change the definition of 'employee' under the ERA by excluding film production workers, thereby categorising them as independent contractors and preventing them from negotiating a collective agreement.[20] Opposition Member of Parliament Charles Chauvel said rushing the law through Parliament was unnecessary and likely to result in bad law.[21] John Key acknowledged the circumstances were not ideal, but said the Government had to decide whether or not it wanted the movies kept in New Zealand.

> It's never a perfect process going through urgency, we acknowledge and accept that, even when it's a clarification for law. As a general rule we try and send legislation through a proper process right through to the select committee, just sometimes that's not the case and this is not one of them.[22]

Chauvel accused the Government of sacrificing New Zealand's sovereignty to satisfy a multinational corporation and said Key's claim that the law needed clarification was a sham. Following the Bryson case there had been no other cases concerning whether a worker was an employee or a contractor, which demonstrated the law was settled.[23]

In addition to the law change, Warner Bros' executives were able to negotiate a better financial package for filming in New Zealand. The Government agreed to another NZ$20 million of rebates under the LBSPGS scheme and also offered NZ$13.5 million to assist with marketing the films, bringing the total cost, including the original tax rebate estimates, to nearly NZ$100 million. In return, Jackson would create a promotion for New Zealand as a tourism destination which would be included on DVDs of the movies. It was also agreed that New Zealand would host the world premiere for one of *The Hobbit* movies.

Following Key's announcement, Jackson thanked the government for introducing the new legislation, saying it would "provide much needed stability and reassurance for film workers as well as investors from within New Zealand and

---

20 Roberts, J. (2010) "The Hobbit law—what does it mean for workers?" *New Zealand Herald*, 28 October.

21 "Parliament passes Hobbit labour law change", *Otago Daily Times*, 29 October 2010.

22 Vance, A. (2010) "Hobbit 'better deal than Lord of the Rings'—Key", *The Press*, 29 October.

23 Chauvel's speech to Parliament can be viewed at http://inthehouse.co.nz/node/5924.

overseas".[24] NZAE was pleased the Government had increased the financial incentives to satisfy Warner Bros, but its press release made no mention of the labour law change. The United States' SAG congratulated NZAE for winning "substantial victories" in the dispute, the most important being the first global solidarity campaign among actors.[25] Others, however, concluded it had been a public relations disaster for NZAE and New Zealand's union movement. The boycott had resulted in a law change which weakened workers' rights and allowed a right-wing Prime Minister to emerge as the saviour of New Zealand's film industry.

Glossary

NZAE – New Zealand Actors Equity

MEAA – Media Entertainment and Arts Alliance

FIA – International Federation of Actors

SAG – Screen Actors Guild

MGM – Metro-Goldwyn-Mayer

CTU – Council of Trade Unions

LBSPGS – Large Budget Screen Production Grant Scheme

ERA – Employment Relations Act

About the authors

Todd Bridgman is a Seni or lecturer in the School of Management, Victoria University of Wellington, New Zealand, where he teaches organisational behaviour. He completed his PhD at the University of Cambridge and held research fellowships at Judge Business School and Wolfson College, University of Cambridge. His research interests are located within critical management studies; in 2009 he edited, with Mats Alvesson and Hugh Willmott, *The Oxford Handbook of Critical Management Studies* (Oxford University Press).

24   "Jackson says thanks for Hobbit rescue", *New Zealand Herald*, 28 October.
25   Howard, K. (2010) Letter to New Zealand Actors Equity. Available at https://nzequity .alliance.org.au/images/stories/The%20Hobbit%20Letter%20from%20Ken%20Howard%20 102910.doc.pdf.

Colm McLaughlin is a Senior Lecturer in the School of Business, University College Dublin, Ireland, where he teaches industrial relations, HRM and Business in Society. He is also a Research Associate of the Centre for Business Research at the University of Cambridge. Prior to joining UCD, he was an ESRC research fellow at the University of Cambridge and a lecturer in Management and Employment Relations at the University of Auckland, and has held management positions in local government and the hospitality sector. He graduated from the University of Auckland (BA and MComm) and holds a PhD from the University of Cambridge (Judge Business School). His research interests include comparative industrial relations, labour market protections and gender equality.

Teaching notes for this case are available from Greenleaf Publishing. These are free of charge and available only to teaching staff. They can be requested by going to:
www.greenleaf-publishing.com/darkside2notes

Section C
Ethics and policy

9

Ethical breaches at *News of the World* [1]

Debapratim Purkayastha
IBS Hyderabad

AJ Swapna
IBS Hyderabad

This case study is about the closure of the *News of the World* (NOTW), the 168-year-old national tabloid of the UK, owing to various ethical breaches over the years. James Murdoch, Deputy Chief Operating Officer, Chairman and CEO, News International, announced that the July 2011 edition of the paper would be its last. Many people were arrested, including the former News International CEO Rebekah Brooks and ex-NOTW editor Andy Coulson. News Corp had to withdraw its US$12.5 billion bid for British Sky Broadcasting Group following the public protest and political backlash brought on by the phone hacking scandal.

The case discusses the questionable practices which were common at the tabloid and which eventually led to its fall. The newspaper resorted to hacking phones and bribing police officers in order to publish juicy news. The public backlash over the phone hacking scandal led to a dip in its advertising revenues and ultimately paved the

---

1 This case was a Finalist in the 2012 Dark Side Case Competition organized by CMS Division of Academy of Management. It was written by AJ Swapna, under the direction of Debapratim Purkayastha, IBS Hyderabad. It was compiled from published sources, and is intended to be used as a basis for class discussion rather than to illustrate either effective or ineffective handling of a management situation. @ 2012, IBS Center for Management Research.

ICMR
IBS Center for Management Research
www.icmrindia.org

way for the shutdown of the media giant. News Corp and its senior management came under severe criticism following this scandal. Though News Corp had released a code of ethics in July 2011 and distributed it to all the employees, experts opined that the real challenge before Rupert Murdoch and the senior management was how to enforce this code.

This case study is a critical case study as it deals with the ethically volatile issue of phone hacking. When journalists hack into phones, they violate laws and invade privacy. Following the major public outcry against *News of the World*, several staff members of the tabloid were jailed, the chief executive was arrested, and the tabloid was shut down. Phone hacking by government is useful to fight crime and terrorism, and is permissible within legal limits. Similarly, the media frequently uncovers corruption in public and private sectors and plays a role in keeping everyone honest. Journalists may find information about corruption or that saves lives. Whether it is the media or governments listening into private conversations, both raise ethical concerns. It raises vital questions like: When does hacking violate privacy? Can phone hacking by media ever be justifiable? When is phone surveillance justifiable? Is it ever ethical? Then, the case also includes other questionable practices such as the media group resorting to bribery to gain vital information that could be delivered to its readers as scoops.

> [M]any wonder, amid a parade of arrests and revelation, whether the phone hacking and bribery at NOTW are truly the actions of one News Corp enterprise or an example of the company's overall corporate culture[2] (Patricia Harned, President, Ethics Resource Center[3], in 2011).
> "It is becoming increasingly clear this scandal was not perpetrated by a few rogue reporters, but was systematically orchestrated at the highest levels of News Corp."[4] (Melanie Sloan, Executive Director, CREW[5] in 2011).

"Thank You and Goodbye" read the headlines of Britain's best-selling Sunday tabloid,[6] the *News of the World* (NOTW), as it rolled its last edition off the

---

2 Patricia Harned, "After the Debacle: How News Corp. Can Rebuild Trust," www.business-ethics.com, July 27, 2011.

3 The Ethics Resource Center, a U.S. based non-profit research firm promotes ethical standards and practices for public and private institutions through various programs and publications.

4 "CREW Calls for Congressional Investigation into News Corp.," www.businesswire.com, July 11, 2011.

5 Citizens for Responsibility and Ethics in Washington (CREW), founded in 2003, is a non-profit organization formed with the stated objective of exposing and bringing to light the unethical and corrupt practices followed by various organizations.

6 A tabloid is a newspaper usually in a smaller format and publishes condensed form of news.

presses on July 10, 2011.The tabloid had sold around 4.5 million copies in July 2011, much higher than the average of 2.7 million copies it sold in the preceding weeks[7] (Refer To Exhibit 1 for the first and last edition of the *News of the World*). On July 7, 2011, the parent company of the 168-years-in-print tabloid, News Corporation (News Corp), announced that the NOTW was being permanently closed. The tabloid was forced to shut down after the unethical practices it had been following came to light and kicked off a major controversy in 2011. The tabloid NOTW was entangled in a series of controversies which included hacking the phone lines of celebrities and the royal family, and those of murder and terror victims. It was also accused of paying bribes to police officers for obtaining information and so on. The revelations that the phone of a murdered schoolgirl Milly Dowler[8] had been hacked generated a public outcry. Public enquiry reports later showed that employees of NOTW had also tapped the phones of deceased British soldiers and their families, the victims of the London bombings[9] and their relatives' phone and voice mails. Following the phone hacking controversy, many top senior executives resigned from News Corp and a few, including the former News International CEO Rebekah Brooks (Brooks) and ex-NOTW editor Andy Coulson, were arrested on suspicion of conspiring to intercept communications and unlawfully accessing voicemail messages. News Corp had to withdraw its US$12.5 billion bid for British Sky Broadcasting[10] (BSkyB) Group following a public protest and a political backlash against the phone hacking scandal. Advertisers too began to boycott the tabloid. The loss of revenue eventually led to the tabloid's closure.

The closure of NOTW and the exposure of the scandal brought to the fore the issue of ethical standards at News Corp and the lack of self-regulation. The cut-throat competition in the media industry had paved the way for yellow journalism or 'gotcha journalism'.[11] "Quite simply, we lost our way. Phones were hacked, and for that this newspaper is truly sorry", said a message posted on the tabloid's website. In its last issue, Rupert Murdoch, CEO of the media conglomerate, issued an apology. He acknowledged the fact that NOTW had been involved in phone hacking and had bribed police and investigating officers for information (Refer to Exhibit 2 for the copy of the apology statement issued by Rupert Murdoch). The last edition carried no advertisements and the company decided to donate the sales proceeds to charity. The front page of the last issue had an

---

7 Mark Sweney, "News of the World's Last Edition 'Sells 4.5m Copies," www.guardian.co.uk, July 11, 2011.

8 Thirteen-year-old Milly Dowler was abducted and later murdered. Her murder played a vital role in the NOTW closure.

9 Known as 7/7, the 2005 London bombings were a series of bomb blasts which targeted the general public at the public transport stations.

10 Headquartered in London, British Sky Broadcasting, a satellite broadcasting company, was formed in 1990. As of June 30, 2011, it had 16,500 employees with an operating income of £1,073 million.

11 Gotcha Journalism refers to methods which are used to defame the interviewees by manipulating quotes or opinions.

epitaph, "The world's greatest newspaper 1843–2011", with a strapline: "After 168 years, we finally say a sad but very proud farewell to our 7.5m loyal readers."[12]

In July 2011, News Corp, whose credibility had been questioned following this crisis, released a code of ethics and distributed it to all its employees. The move prompted observers to comment that the next big challenge for News Corp would be the effective implementation of the code. The question before Rupert and James Murdoch and the senior management at News Corp was: Is releasing a code of ethics enough? What else should they do to address this issue?

Background note

American multinational conglomerate, News Corp, was incorporated in 1979 in Australia and was headquartered in New York. Rupert Murdoch was the founder, Chairman, and CEO of the News Group, which was the world's second largest media house in terms of revenue, as of 2011. As of September 30, 2011, the company had total annual revenues of approximately US$34 billion.[13] News Corp had operations in six industry segments: cable network programming; filmed entertainment; television; direct broadcast satellite television; publishing; and others. Apart from these, News Corp had made many acquisitions over the years in the fields of film entertainment, the Internet, magazines, television, and books. One of these was the takeover of the News of the World in 1969 for £34 million[14] (Refer to Exhibit 3 for the list of business units under News Corp).

The first issue of NOTW was rolled out by John Browne Bell on October 1, 1843, in London. By 1939, sales had reached around four million and it had become the world's biggest selling newspaper in 1950.[15] At its peak in 1951, circulation was around 8.4 million issues sold per week.[16] Under Rupert Murdoch, in 1981, *Sunday* Magazine was rolled out along with the NOTW newspaper and in 1984, the newspaper changed its format to a tabloid. In 2007, James Murdoch, son of Rupert Murdoch, became the non-executive chairman and deputy COO of British Sky Broadcasting Group Plc from being the CEO (Refer to Exhibit 4 for the list of senior executives at News Corp). Though the major portion of the news covered in the NOTW was related to scandals, there were occasional stories which were done in public interest.

---

12 Cassandra Vinograd, "News of the World' Bids Farewell to Readers," www.huffingtonpost .com, July 9, 2011.
13 www.newscorp.com.
14 http://news.bbc.co.uk/onthisday/hi/dates/stories/january/2/newsid_2492000/2492157.stm.
15 http://wn.com/News_of_the_World.
16 "News of the World Circulation Data: Who Read it and How Many Bought it?", www .guardian.co.uk, July 8, 2011.

Questionable practices

In its heydays, NOTW took to the path of yellow journalism to increase its circulation and to grow at a faster pace.[17] The editors and the journalists of NOTW used questionable means to obtain information and generated sensational stories to woo the public. Very soon, NOTW became the source of news about scandals and crimes. The cheap price[18] at which it came was also one of the reasons for its success. It was affordable and became popular among middle income grade literates. Some observers believed that the tabloid did not maintain a balance between serious and sleazy news and said that for the NOTW journalists, ethics always took a backseat. The journalists gave ethics the go by when the phones were hacked as they were more interested in obtaining information which their rivals could not get.[19]

While News International was admired for its creativity and energy in surviving in a highly competitive industry, it also attracted criticism as many felt that its employees had adopted Rupert Murdoch's ethos of a "do-whatever-it-takes-to-win attitude".[20] Many considered Rupert Murdoch, who was credited with creating a global media empire from a newspaper in Adelaide, to be one of the most powerful men in the business—brilliant, but with a ruthless streak.[21] His critics often alleged that Murdoch had a reputation for interfering with the editorial decisions to further his own business interests.

On the one hand Britain had the most popular BBC,[22] a very well-respected news organization, and at the same time questions were raised with regard to the unfair means adopted by many journalists across the nation. "It's more important to ask about the culture of journalism in Britain and why it seems to sustain this sort of behavior,"[23] said Stephen Ward (Ward), professor and ethics expert at the University of Wisconsin-Madison Journalism School.

---

17 Yellow journalism refers to those press media techniques where no authentic news is collected and the newspaper depends largely on the use of eye-catching headlines to sell its editions.

18 The NOTW was priced at three pence during its inception in 1843.

19 Geoffrey Robertson QC, "The Paper that Died of Shame," www.thedailybeast.com, July 7, 2011.

20 Robert Marquand, "Rupert Murdoch: His empire Under Attack, A Media Potentate Stumbles," www.csmonitor.com, July 15, 2011.

21 Ian Verrender, "Murdoch's Ruthless Streak May Prove to Be His Own Undoing," www.smh.com.au, July 9, 2011.

22 With around 23,000 employess, British Broadcasting Corporation (BBC) is the largest broadcaster in the world and is headquartered in London.

23 Tony Rogers, "Would a U.S. Newspaper Ever Do What a British Tabloid Did?," http://journalism.about.com/od/trends/a/Would-A-U-S-Newspaper-Ever-Do-What-A-British-Tabloid-Did.htm.

The scandal

The *Guardian*[24] had reported in July 2011 that NOTW had hacked the phones and voicemails of Milly Dowler, relatives of deceased British soldiers, and relatives of the victims of the London bombings.[25] The disclosures, which were reported first in the *Guardian*, generated a huge public outcry and proved to be a turning point for the NOTW. Earlier in January 2007, police investigations had revealed that NOTW had made it a routine practice to hack cell phones. Though it had had to pay huge sums of money as defamation charges, it still did not stop these questionable practices. For instance, the newspaper had paid defamation charges to many people who had been victims of its hackings and scandals. In 2008, Max Mosley a former president of the Fédération Internationale de l'Automobile, won damages against NOTW for false assertions of a Nazi-themed orgy and the paper was found to have breached Mosley's privacy by reporting on his unconventional sexual activities.[26] In 2005, English footballer, David Beckham and his wife, Victoria, filed libel charges against the NOTW for publishing articles that they were on the verge of a split.[27] Also in 2006, the tabloid had to pay Wayne Rooney, another English footballer, damages for publishing false articles about his marital life. Critics opined that NOTW had used the label of "Free Press"[28] to ignore the business ethics which journalists ought to follow.[29]

A former correspondent of NOTW's sister concern, the *Sun*, Bill Coles, had predicted that the tabloid would fall if it continued to use the illegal methods to gain information. The tabloid had a presence in three continents and at all the locations it had lowered journalism standards and ethics frequently, according to critics. It was alleged that Rupert Murdoch often used his lobbying powers and got the rules diluted and that his tabloid often used unorthodox methods[30] to obtain information.[31] According to Ward, "Gotcha journalism is all about intent. If you're going into the interview only to catch someone saying

24 A British national Daily English newspaper, the *Guardian* was founded in 1821 and is head-quartered in London. It works as a part of Guardian Media Group and played a key role in exposing the depth of the News of the World phone hacking scandal.
25 Andrew Sparrow and David Batty, "News of the World Phone Hacking," www.guardian.co.uk, July 6, 2011.
26 Leigh Holmwood and Caitlin Fitzsimmons, "Max Mosley Wins £60,000 in Privacy Case," www.guardian.co.uk, July 24, 2008.
27 Edgar Forbes, "Legal Review of the Year," www.guardian.co.uk, December 28, 2005.
28 Free Press refers to freedom of the press which is not restricted by any Government.
29 Gregory Katz, "Phone Hacking Scandal: Britain's Media Likely to Face New Rules," www.huffingtonpost.com, July 9, 2011.
30 NOTW reporters often used unorthodox methods such as dressing as a housekeeper to steal information ahead of its rival newspapers, paying a bribe to former lovers of Princess Diana to reveal information about her private life, and many such things.
31 Joe Nocera, "The Tables are Turned on Murdoch," www.nytimes.com, July 18, 2011.

something stupid then that's gotcha journalism. The question is, do you have a good justification for what you're reporting?"[32]

Phone hacking

After *The Guardian* report in July 2011, there was a general perception that practices such as phone hacking were widespread in NOTW even before the hacking scandal came to the forefront. According to the report, in 2002, the tabloid hacked the mobile phone of Milly Dowler. The girl, who had gone missing, was found murdered six months later. The reporters of NOTW not only hacked the phone of the girl but also kept deleting old messages from her phone in order to receive new messages. By doing that they confused the investigating police officials and family members, leading them to hope that Milly was still alive (Refer to Exhibit 5 for a Timeline of the phone hacking scandal).

In 2006, former British Prime Minister Gordon Brown (Brown) had accused the journalists of NOTW for hacking bank, legal and medical records of his family. The tabloid had allegedly obtained medical records of Brown's son which indicated that the child had cystic fibrosis.[33] This had upset the couple who wanted to keep the whole affair private. Brown had also claimed that NOTW had targeted his bank and legal files along with his medical files. Sensitive information about his daughter, Jennifer, was also published a week before she died of a brain hemorrhage in 2002. The *Guardian* reported: "The sheer scale of the data assault on Brown is unusual, with evidence of "attempts" to obtain his legal, financial, tax, medical, and police records as well as to listen to his voicemail."[34]

When an initial investigation into phone hacking was called in 2006, the reporters also hacked the phone messages of five senior police officials of Scotland Yard who were investigating the case. This also raised many questions about the quality of the investigation with charges being made that they had been compromised.

The reporters of NOTW used private investigators from 2006 and gained illegal access to the voicemails of hundred of mobile phones. Later in 2007, its correspondent Clive Goodman was jailed on charges of illegally intercepting personal

---

32 Tony Rogers, "Rolling Stone Article on McChrystal Raises Ethics Questions for Journalists," http://journalism.about.com/od/ethicsprofessionalism/a/mcchrystal.htm.

33 A life-threatening disorder, cystic fibrosis, is a disease passed down through families that causes thick, sticky mucus to build up in the lungs, digestive tract, and other areas of the body. It is one of the most common chronic lung diseases in children and young adults. Brown's son Fraser was diagnosed with cystic fibrosis when he was four months old in November 2006.

34 Nick Davies and David Leigh, "News International Papers Targeted Gordon Brown," *The Guardian*, July 11, 2011.

communication. Its editor Andy Coulson resigned in 2007.[35] However, the editor of NOTW, Rebekah Brooks (Brooks), initially denied all the phone hacking allegations. By the end of 2010, investigations proved that the NOTW reporters had been well aware of hacking techniques and that it was a common practice at NOTW. Suspicion arose as to whether Brooks had known about these unethical practices and had allowed them despite knowing that they were against media ethics.

Bribery

The NOTW reporters paid bribes to police officers to learn and use the technology which police used exclusively for investigating cases related to hacking of cell phones of terror activists and for high profile investigations. 'Pinging', a technique used by the police, traced the location of a cell phone user depending on the signal strength.[36] A former reporter of NOTW, Sean Hoare, said that they used the Pinging technique in NOTW and paid the police officials US$500 per trace.[37] By January 2011, the Metropolitan Police had gathered details of the payments made by NOTW, during the period when Andy Coulson was the paper's editor, to the senior police officers who were investigating the phone hacking case between 2003 and 2007.[38] On July 7, 2011, the *Guardian* reported that investigators inside Scotland Yard were trying to identify up to five officers who had been paid a total of at least £100,000 in cash by NOTW in return for evidence or information.[39]

In July 2011, the British police had also informed Prince Charles and his wife at Buckingham Palace that they might be targeted by NOTW.[40] BBC had revealed mails which showed that the reporters had bribed the palace security guards to obtain the phone numbers of members of the royal household in order to hack their phone calls and messages.[41]

Following the public outcry against NOTW in 2011, many news agencies pulled out their advertisements from the tabloid. Several blogs requested advertisers to boycott not only NOTW but also all the other media ventures owned

---

35 On July 8, 2011, Andy Coulson was arrested in connection with the phone hacking scandal.
36 James Robinson and Charles Arthur, "News of the World Accused of Paying Police to Track Stars' Phones," *The Guardian*, July 12, 2011.
37 "James Murdoch Contradicted by his Ex-Legal Manager,"www.updatednews.ca, July 22, 2011.
38 "Cameron's Parliamentary Statement on Hacking," www.economist.com, July 20, 2011.
39 Sandra Laville and Vikram Dodd, "News of the World Paid Bribes Worth £100,000 to Up to Five Met Officers," www.guardian.co.uk, July 7, 2011.
40 Nick Davies, "Prince Charles and Camilla Warned Over Phone Hacking," www.guardian .co.uk, July 11, 2011.
41 "Brown Says Son's Medical Files Hacked," www.thedailybeast.com, July 11, 2011.

by News Corp. Social Networking sites like Twitter[42] kickstarted campaigns[43] which resulted in a dip in the tabloid's advertising revenue, its prime source of revenue.

Government scrutiny

In 1998, phone hacking was made illegal and lack of self regulation in law and journalism ethics was regarded as a serious offence in the UK. Further, the Department of Justice had also opened an investigation into the company affairs. The UK Regulation of investigatory Powers Act 2000 prohibited phone hacking and any form of communication interception. The UK Inquiries Act 2005 was passed to address any scandal without delay and also studied measures to prevent repetition of such scandals. A parliamentary committee of the UK also had investigated the phone tapping. The Federal Bureau of Investigation of the US also conducted investigations to find out whether the phones of the September 11[44] victims had been hacked.[45] In the US, Foreign Corrupt Practices Act (FCPA) set up a public enquiry against News Corp for breach of the Act and stated that if the investigations proved that the company had paid bribes to the police, it would lead to a shutdown of the tabloid.[46]

In July 2011, following the scandal, the British Prime Minister David Cameron (Cameron), declared a public inquiry and investigation into the scandal and also wanted a study on the culture and ethics of the British media. He called for two investigations with regard to this scandal. The first was to re-examine the police investigations and find discrepancies in them, if any. The second investigation was to study the standards of the media industry and to set appropriate protocols wherever necessary. These investigations led to many high profile resignations in the NOTW office and a few other journalists, senior editors, former journalists and former senior executives were arrested by police for hacking. However, experts opined that a newspaper could get away with

---

42 Twitter is a micro blogging and a social networking site owned by Twitter Inc.
43 Melissa Harrison and others developed an online tool which allowed users to generate a pre-prepared tweet: "Dear @TheCooperative, will you be reconsidering your advertising spend with #notw given that we now know they hacked Milly Dowler's phone?". This started off the idea of a mass boycott on Monday, July 4.
44 The September 11, 2001, attacks were a combination of four attacks which were coordinated suicide attacks by the Al-Qaeda on the United States.
45 Dominic Rushe and Jill Treanor, "James Murdoch Could Face Criminal Charges on Both Sides of the Atlantic," www.guardian.co.uk, July 8, 2011.
46 David Folkenflik, "News Corp.'s U.K. Actions Under Scrutiny in U.S.," www.npr.org, September 27, 2011.

anything because the Press Complaints Commission (PCC)[47] was itself owned and managed by the newspapers. The media fraternity along with the general public all over the world was shocked on knowing the truth about the scandal and described the paper's actions as inhumane and heinous.

British Sky Broadcasting takeover deal falls through

Amidst this brouhaha, News Corp's British Sky Broadcasting (BSkyB) takeover bid of June 2010 was called off in July 2011. BSkyB, headquartered in London, was formed in 1990 as a satellite broadcasting and telephony services company with its operations in the UK and Ireland. It was formed by an equal merger of Sky Television and British Satellite Broadcasting and by 2010 it had almost 10 million subscribers.[48] News Corp, which already had a 39.4% stake in BSkyB began its £7.4 billion bid for a complete takeover of the broadcaster in June 2010.[49] Approvals from the European Commission were obtained in November 2010. Top industry players and media groups, however, feared that the largest UK paper and the largest broadcaster would together pose a threat to competition in the business and raised issues of "media plurality"[50,51]. These allegations triggered an eight-month inquiry by the Government and post inquiry, the takeover deal was heaved up to £9.4 billion.[52] The deal was viewed as the biggest deal ever in News Corp's history. The phone hacking scandal of News Corp came to light just two weeks before the proposed deal and the government declared that the bid would be put on hold due to the crisis and regulatory hurdles.

The takeover was an essential part of News Corp's business strategy to have a pan-European presence in television. For BSkyB, it was important because the customers would be offered bundled services at no extra cost. However, the attempts to defuse the scandal failed. Later in July 2011, Rupert Murdoch announced that the takeover proposal had been withdrawn due to the ongoing phone hacking allegations. Experts opined that this deal would have earned News Corp US$8.9 billion every year, which was almost nine times

---

47 The Press Complaints Commission, started in 1991, is an independent body which implements a system of self-regulation for the press.

48 www.corporate.sky.com.

49 Dan Sabbagh, James Robinson and Mark Sweney, "Rupert Murdoch Finally Gets Green Light for Bskyb Takeover—But at a Price," www.guardian.co.uk, June 30, 2011.

50 Media Plurality includes diversity of media ownership and contains diversity in content so that a wide range of views are brought out.

51 Amanda Andrews, "Q&A: News Corp bid for BSkyB," www.telegraph.co.uk, November 4, 2010.

52 Amanda Andrews, "News Corp Takeover of BSkyB a 'Chilling Prospect', Peers Argue in House of Lords," www.telegraph.co.uk, November 4, 2010.

more than the tabloid's profits.[53] According to some analysts, this was a major setback for the corporation. "It is unlikely that approval could be granted until the criminal investigation into phone hacking and subsequent related public enquiries have been completed, which could take years,"[54] opined an analyst.

The judgement day

The investigators pooled evidence against NOTW to claim that the newspaper had deleted all its previous mail conversations from its mail archives to interrupt further investigations by Scotland Yard.[55] NOTW was charged with being non-cooperative with the investigating officers. The archive mails from 2005 could not be retrieved. According to the investigators, a senior executive had deleted emails twice, including once in January 2011, as Scotland Yard was starting its investigation.[56] After initially denying it, the newspaper later accepted that it had resorted to phone hacking and apologized for its unethical practices.

The tabloid was shut down after it lost the support of its advertisers who wanted to distance themselves from it and after police investigations had revealed the cozy relationship between British police and NOTW and between politicians and the powerful Murdoch Empire. The results of a survey conducted by YouGov,[57] showed that almost 86% of the public wanted a public enquiry into the scandal.[58] Media experts and analysts unanimously opined that the media ought to have a set of standards and regulations which had to be complied with. During the investigation, police identified around 4000 names of potential victims of phone hacking over the years.

The closure of the newspaper resulted in 200 journalists being left jobless. Many staff members of News Corp, who had not been aware that the NOTW would be shut down, received the news with utter shock, resentment, and anger. They were allowed to apply for other jobs in the company's sister concerns but were given no guarantee of employment. The impact on the shareholders was significant as well. The corporation lost almost US$5 billion in the share market since

---

53 "Lessons to Learn from Britain's Tabloid Saga," www.expressbuzz.com, July 8, 2011.
54 "Phone Hacking Scandal: Analysts Question BSkyB Bid," www.telegraph.co.uk, July 11, 2011.
55 Scotland Yard refers to the Metropolitan Police Service of London, UK.
56 Nick Davies and Amelia Hill, "Phone Hacking: Police Probe Suspected Deletion of Emails by NI Executive," www.guardian.co.uk, July 8, 2011.
57 Formerly known as PollingPoint, YouGov was launched in the UK in 2000 is an Internet based market research firm.
58 "YouGov on the Phone Hacking Scandal," http://ukpollingreport.co.uk, July 10, 2011.

the phone hacking controversy came to light in July 2011.[59] (Refer to Exhibit 6 for the three-year stock chart of News Corp on the NASDAQ stock exchange)

Many staff of the corporation wore t-shirts with the slogans: "Goodbye, cruel News of the World, I'm leaving you today".[60] The decision to shut down the tabloid was stated to be a collective decision. The corporation also ran advertisements across all national newspapers in Britain to, "apologize to the nation for what has happened". "We will follow this up in the future with communications about the actions we have taken to address the wrongdoing that occurred,"[61] said James Murdoch.

Some analysts were hopeful that the scandal would lead to more government scrutiny and that self-regulations systems would be put in place. Since World War II Britain had been trying to come up with a set of standards for the press and the media.[62] Experts pointed out that Britain had been relying on the PCC 'Editors code of practice' which had a broad set of standards like concealed cameras and recorders being prohibited. However, it also allowed for exceptions if done in the public interest at large.[63] The concept of public interest was often misinterpreted by the media for vested interests. There was a very thin line of demarcation which stood as a barrier.[64] The Press Complaints Commission had suggested having a statutory "press ombudspersons" to address public complaints and redress reforms, which could be used to monitor ethical standards.[65] The newspapers would have to adhere to a set of rules and codes and would be penalized if they violated these rules. Many saw this closure not as an end to yellow journalism but an effective beginning to ethical tabloid journalism.

What happens next?

The NOTW announced that all the sale proceeds from its last issue would be donated to charity. The corporation expressed optimism and said: "Yet when

59 Paul M. Barrett and Felix Gillette, "Murdoch's Mess," www.businessweek.com, July 14, 2011.

60 Cassandra Vinograd, "Final Edition of Britain's News of the World Printed," www.news.com.au, July 10, 2011. Gregory Katz, "Phone Hacking Scandal: Britain's Media Likely to Face New Rules," www.huffingtonpost.com, July 9, 2011.

61 Hasan Suroor, "News International CEO Rebekah Brooks Resigns," www.thehindu.com, July 15, 2011.

62 Gregory Katz, "Phone Hacking Scandal: Britain's Media Likely to Face New Rules," www.huffingtonpost.com, July 9, 2011.

63 Ibid.

64 Roy Greenslade, "News of the World Story Will Go On," www.thehindu.com, July 11, 2011.

65 Geoffrey Robertson QC, "The Paper that Died of Shame," www.thedailybeast.com, July 7, 2011.

this outrage has been atoned, we hope history will eventually judge us on all our years."[66] The closure of the tabloid was followed by the arrest of key executives at News Corp such as Brooks on charges of corruption and bribing the police, and also led to huge criticism of the management at News Corp. According to Richard Greenfield, a media industry analyst with BTIG,[67] a New York-based trading firm, "The newspaper business was such a small pimple for them. Now it's become a hot potato."[68] Many wondered how much the management had known about the questionable practices being adopted at NOTW and how far the rot had set in in the News Corp chain of command. Some even wondered whether it was a reflection of the company's overall culture.

The challenge for the senior management of News Corp was not only how to face this crisis situation and answer the investigators, regulatory authorities, and the general public, but also to take measures to build a new corporate conscience by revisiting and reasserting its corporate values.[69] Following the scandal, in July 2011, News Corp released a code of ethics and distributed it to all the employees. According to an expert, "It will be interesting to see what kind of enforcement measures Murdoch and his staff are talking about, and how exactly they intend to put them into action."[70]

66 Ujala Sehgal, "No Sympathy for News of the World's Proud Final Issue," www.theatlantic wire.com, July 10, 2011.

67 Formed in 2005, BTIG specializes in equity trading and fund services across four countries.

68 Paul M. Barrett and Felix Gillette, "Murdoch's Mess," www.businessweek.com, July 14, 2011.

69 Patricia Harned, "After the Debacle: How News Corp. Can Rebuild Trust," www.business-ethics.com, July 27, 2011.

70 Gloria Goodale, "News Corp. Announces New Code of Ethics. Will it Make a Difference?" www.csmonitor.com, July 20, 2011.

EXHIBIT 1 A collage of the first edition and the last edition of the *News of the World*

Source: www.thehiberniatimes.com

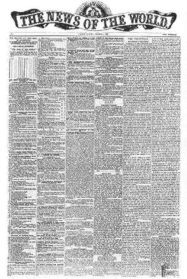

EXHIBIT 2 The apology statement issued by Rupert Murdoch, which appeared in all leading national newspapers

Source: www.forbes.com

We are sorry

The News of the World was in the business of holding others to account. It failed when it came to itself.

We are sorry for the serious wrongdoing that occured.

We are deeply sorry for the hurt suffered by the individuals affected.

We regret not acting faster to sort things out.

I realise that simply apologising is not enough.

Our business was founded on the idea that a free and open press should be a positive force in society. We need to live up to this.

In the coming days, as we take further concrete steps to resolve these issues and make amends for the damage they have caused, you will hear more from us.

Sincerely,

Rupert Murdoch

Rupert Murdoch

EXHIBIT 3 Business units owned by News Corp

Source: www.newscorp.com

Cable Network Programming	Filmed Entertainment
FOX Business Network	Fox Studios Australia
FOX News Channel	Fox Television Studios
Fox Networks	Twentieth Century Fox Film
Fox International Channels	Twentieth Century Fox Home Entertainment
FSN	Twentieth Century Fox Consumer Products
FX Networks	Twentieth Century Fox Television
National Geographic Channel	Shine Group
STAR	
National Geographic Channel Asia	
Television	**Direct Broadcast Satellite TV**
FOX Broadcasting Company	SKY Italia
FOX Sports	BSkyB (equity affiliate)
FOXSports.com on MSN	FOXTEL (equity affiliate)
Fox Television Stations	
MyNetworkTV	
Twentieth Television	
Publishing	**Equity Interests**
News America Marketing	Hulu
New York Post	NDS Group
News International	Education Division
News Limited	Wireless Generation
The Wall Street Journal	
Dow Jones	
HarperCollins	
Other	
Digital Media Group	

EXHIBIT 4 List of News Corporation's senior executives

Source: Compiled from various sources.

Rupert Murdoch—Chairman and Chief Executive Officer
Chase Carey—Deputy Chairman, President and Chief Operating Officer
James Murdoch—Deputy Chief Operating Officer, Chairman and CEO, International
David DeVoe—Senior Executive Vice President, Chief Financial Officer
Roger Ailes—Chairman and Chief Executive Officer, FOX News Channel, FOX Business
Network, Chairman, Fox Television Stations, Twentieth Television
Janet Nova—Interim Group General Counsel
John Nallen—Executive Vice President, Deputy Chief Financial Officer
Beryl Cook—Executive Vice President, Chief Human Resources Officer
Michael Regan—Executive Vice President, Government Affairs
Genie Gavenchak—Senior Vice President, Deputy General Counsel, Chief Compliance
and Ethics Officer
Teri Everett—Senior Vice President, Corporate Affairs & Communications
Reed Nolte—Senior Vice President, Investor Relations

*Data as on August 10, 2011
Source: www.newscorp.com

EXHIBIT 5 Timeline of the phone hacking scandal

Date / Year	Description
2000	Brooks is appointed editor of NOTW. At 32, she is the youngest national newspaper editor in the country. She begins a campaign to name and shame alleged pedophiles, and also campaigns for public access to the Sex Offenders Register, which eventually comes out as "Sarah's Law".
2002	A schoolgirl named Milly Dowler, aged 13, goes missing from London in March. Her body remains are found in September.
2003	Brooks appoints Andy Coulson as her deputy editor. A parliamentary committee was informed that her paper bribed the police for information.
2005	A police inquiry is called for in November by the Royal family after Prince William suffers a knee injury and the NOTW hacks his voice mail messages and publishes a story on it.
2006	Clive Goodman, former reporter and editor of News Corp, and private investigator Glenn Mulcaire were arrested over allegations that NOTW had hacked the mobile phones of members of the royal family.
January 2007	Goodman and Mulcaire are jailed for four and six months respectively. They admit to charges of intercepting communications. Following the arrest, NOTW editor Coulson resigns.
May 2007	Coulson becomes the Conservative Party's Director of Communications under the leadership of David Cameron.
December 2007	James Murdoch is appointed as CEO of European and Asian News Corp's offices.
2008	Gordon Taylor, chairman of Professional Footballers' Association (PFA) is paid £700,000 in April to settle a phone hacking claim.
June 2009	Brooks announced to become the CEO of News International.
July 2009	News Corp Group of newspapers pays more than £1 million to settle cases that threaten to reveal evidence of its journalists' alleged involvement in phone hacking.
September 2009	Brooks bids farewell to *The Sun* and becomes the chief executive of News International.
November 2009	The Press Complaints Commission (PCC) says that the paper's executives did not know what the Goodman–Mulcaire pair was doing.
March 2010	Publicist Max Clifford is paid £1 million to drop any legal action which could have revealed more instances of phone hacking by News of the World reporters.
May 2010	Coulson becomes head of media operation for David Cameron, who forms the new Government after being sworn in as the British Prime Minister.

continued

September 2010	Former NOTW reporters like Sean Hoare and Paul McMullan claim that phone hacking was encouraged at the tabloid and other illegal reporting techniques were also commonly practiced.
November 2010	Metropolitan Police detectives interview Coulson on the phone tapping allegations.
January 2011	A new investigation called 'Operation Weeting' is opened by the British police after actress Sienna Miller, MP George Galloway, and RMT union leader Bob Crow claim that their phones were hacked. Andy Coulson resigns as Cameron's communications chief.
March 2011	BBC reveals that a former NOTW senior executive editor Alex Marunchak had hacked e-mails belonging to an ex-British Army intelligence officer in 2006.
April 2011	Many journalists are arrested on suspicion of conspiring to intercept communications and unlawfully accessing voicemail messages. Claimants such as actress Sienna Miller and football player Andy Gray, receive damage awards. The NOTW publishes apologies on its website and newspaper.
June 7, 2011	News Group formally apologizes to Sienna Miller for hacking into several of her mobile phones, and pays her a settlement of £100,000 for damages and legal costs.
June 20, 2011	As many as 300 emails retrieved from Harbottle & Lewis are handed over to Scotland Yard. They show that Coulson had authorized payments to police officers.
June 22, 2011	Andy Gray is paid £20,000 in compensation for voicemail interceptions.
June 23, 2011	Police arrest Terenia Taras, former partner of Greg Miskiw, who worked in senior roles for the *News of the World* until 2005. Levi Bellfield is found guilty of murdering Milly Dowler in 2002.
July 4, 2011	The *Guardian* reports that the voicemails of Milly Dowler, relatives of British soldiers killed in action, and that of the victims and relatives of the 7/7 attack victims were hacked by NOTW. The victims' lawyer, claim that the NOTW reporters had deleted Milly's voice mails to make room for newer ones, which had misled police and her family into thinking she was still alive.
July 6, 2011	Prime Minister David Cameron announces a government inquiry into the scandal. Joel Klein is appointed as News Corp executive to oversee investigations.
July 7, 2011	News International announces the closure of NOTW.
July 8, 2011	Coulson and Clive Goodman are arrested on the phone hacking charges and for making illegal payments to police.
July 10, 2011	NOTW publishes its last edition.
July 11, 2011	The *Guardian* reports that NOTW reporters had illegally accessed records of former Prime Minister Gordon Brown.

July 13, 2011	News Corp announces withdrawal of its bid for BSkyB.
July 15, 2011	Both Brooks, the chief executive of News International, and Les Hinton, chief executive of Dow Jones & Company, resign.
July 16, 2011	Rupert Murdoch advertises in all national newspapers apologizing for the News of the World's "serious wrongdoing".
July 17, 2011	Brooks is arrested on charges of corruption and phone hacking.
July 18, 2011	David Cameron postpones his parliamentary recess by one day. John Yates resigns as assistant commissioner of the Metropolitan Police. Former NOTW reporter who first made the allegations about phone hacking, Sean Hoare, is found dead in his house.
July 21, 2011	Brooks, Rupert Murdoch, and James Murdoch appear before the London parliamentary media committee for questioning.
July 28, 2011	Fresh allegations emerge stating the NOTW had targeted the mobile phone of Sara Payne, whose eight-year-old daughter Sarah was abducted and murdered in July 2000. Brooks gifted a phone to Sara, which was hacked.
July 29, 2011	PCC chairman resigns over criticism of the PCC's handling of phone hacking investigations.
August 2, 2011	Former NOTW editor Stuart Kuttner is arrested.
August 10, 2011	Former NOTW editor Greg Miskiw is arrested.

Exhibit 6 Three-year stock chart of News Corporation (2009–2011)

Source: www.bigcharts.com

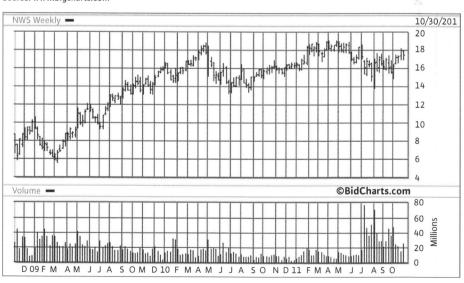

About the authors

AJ Swapna is a Research Associate at the Case Research Center at IBS Hyderabad. She is an M.Com. graduate from Osmania University, Hyderabad, India.

Debprathim Purkaystha is the Assistant Professor for Marketing and Strategy at IBS Hyderabad, with over 12 years' teaching, research and industry experience. He is the Consulting Editor of *Case Folio*, a refereed journal dedicated to case studies in management. He has written more than 30 case studies focusing on business ethics, corporate sustainability and social entrepreneurship. He has won awards and recognition for case writing from the Association of MBAs (AMBA), ecch, European Foundation for Management Development (EFMD), Emerald, John Molson School of Business, North American Case Research Association (NACRA), oikos International, etc. Many of his cases have been published in global editions of textbooks. He also conducts training and workshops on case writing and case-based learning.

Teaching notes for this case are available from Greenleaf Publishing. These are free of charge and available only to teaching staff. They can be requested by going to:
www.greenleaf-publishing.com/darkside2notes

10

Monkey business
The Black Eyed Peas in Halifax[1]

Lawrence T. Corrigan and Jean Helms Mills
Saint Mary's University, Halifax, Canada

In the spring of 2011, it became apparent that the Mayor of Halifax Regional Munici-pality (HRM) and the Chief Administrative Officer conspired to make unapproved and undisclosed payments to a rock concert promoter for an unsuccessful Black Eyed Peas concert held on the Common in Halifax, Canada. This case focuses on the fragility of the democratic process and its potential erosion through seemingly mun-dane, behind-closed-doors, decision-making processes. Of particular interest is the mechanism by which powerful political actors were able to encumber HRM. Funds were transferred outside of the normal municipal financial system and its controls, enabling problematic transactions to go undetected for an extended period of time. Eventually money had to be requisitioned from the HRM payments system and the Chief Financial Officer blew the whistle, informing the Audit Committee and the Halifax Auditor General. Issues around governance and accountability were uncov-ered, along with questionable practices of the management of Trade Centre Limited (a Provincial Crown Corporation which managed some HRM assets). The case follows the action to the point where a formal vote of the Halifax Municipal Council is taken to censure the mayor.

---

1 This case was prepared to provide material for class discussion. The authors do not intend to illustrate either effective or ineffective handling of a managerial situation, or for the case to be used as a source of primary data. The case was written mostly from publically-available sources, although some dramatisation has been included along with the "facts" of the case. Consequently, the interpretation and perspectives presented in this case are not necessarily those of Halifax Regional Municipality or any of its present or past employees.

Introduction: politics and rock concerts

When the Halifax Regional Municipality (HRM) successfully landed major concert deals with recording artist Paul McCartney and later with KISS and the Black Eyed Peas, municipal officials were ecstatic. "Finally, this will make a public statement that Halifax isn't going to let the City of Moncton get all the glory!" said Mayor Peter Kelly.

Kelly worried that Moncton—a small city in a neighbouring province—was winning national attention with its Magnetic Hill concert site. Originally built for Pope John Paul II to hold a papal mass during his tour of Canada, the site was redesigned as a concert venue. The Rolling Stones, whose concert was the largest music event ever held in Atlantic Canada, performed at the Moncton venue in front of 89,000 cheering fans, who spent a lot of money in the local area. This was followed by rockers AC/DC and U2, whose concerts each attracted 75,000 people. The economic importance of these mega-entertainment events was not lost on government officials, including Halifax Mayor Peter Kelly.

Initially, to help Harold MacKay attract big name performers to the Halifax Common site, the Nova Scotia provincial government guaranteed taxpayers' money for a $3.5 million "artist fee." MacKay was the local promoter of Power Promotional Events (PPE), the concert organizer for the 2009 Paul McCartney concert. To sweeten the deal they also provided PPE with a $300,000 repayable loan based on ticket sales. However, with single ticket prices ranging from $114 to $338 for premium seats, sales for The Black Eyed Peas were much slower than anticipated. In the end, sales were not high enough to repay the loan.

Still optimistic, PPE and Harold MacKay promoted the high profile concerts for the 2010 season under the headline "Halifax Rocks." First up would be Kid Rock followed by the Black Eyed Peas. But three weeks prior to the event, the Kid Rock concert was abruptly cancelled, collapsing the two-day event into a single Black Eyed Peas concert held July 24, 2010. When the brilliant stage lights and opening fireworks lit up the crowd, it appeared that the concert was packed with fans. Later it was revealed that security guards at the concert entrance were instructed to let in non-paying spectators to avoid the embarrassment of a very sparse audience.

Slowly, over the next ten months, a much more complicated story began to emerge as it became apparent that Mayor Kelly and Chief Administrative Officer Wayne Anstey may have conspired to make unapproved payments to Harold MacKay. It turned out this was just the tip of the iceberg. At the end of the day, Halifax taxpayers found themselves on the hook for a liability of $400,000. How had this been allowed to happen? Why had nobody said anything? What does this say about the faith we put in our elected officials? It became clear that the business arrangements surrounding the Black Eyed Peas concert had much in common with the name of their hit album – Monkey Business.

'I gotta feeling'

It was a typical foggy March day in Halifax and the weather was doing nothing to help the mood of Cathy O'Toole. Being the chief financial officer for the HRM was a difficult job at the best of times but now it looked like it was about to become more stressful.

Cathy's boss, Wayne Anstey, Chief Administrative Officer (CAO) for HRM and a 32-year veteran with the municipal government, had just hit her with the unexpected news that HRM owed $400,000 to the Halifax Metro Centre. The payment was to cover an authorised cash advance that had been made the previous year to Harold MacKay. Cathy was shocked. She remembered this very issue had been raised following the 2009 concerts when the Legal Department of HRM voiced concerns with Wayne Anstey around insurance issues. At that time, Anstey had made the decision to change future contracts. But, by the time issues for the new contract were sorted out, the 2010 contract for the Black Eyed Peas had already been written by Anstey and signed by Harold MacKay using the old form. Cathy recalled that the Director of Legal Services wasn't too happy at the time. However, the Director had still accepted the CAO's actions due to Anstey's prior lengthy service as City Solicitor.

Cathy remembered the Legal Director's words "If Wayne says it's ok, it must be." And when the Legal Department inquired about the status of the contract negotiations, this assurance was reinforced by a staff person who told them that HRM was "committed to the concerts." On June 25, 2010, Legal Services was contacted by the Mayor's Office to "approve as to form" the two 2010 concert contracts and nobody thought much more about it.

Blowing the whistle

This revelation by Anstey that $400,000 needed to be transferred meant there would be a deficit in the municipal budget and that left Cathy thinking about what she should do. She also wondered if this would ever have come to light if it wasn't for the fact that the bill had come directly to Anstey on Halifax Metro Centre letterhead. Anstey knew that he couldn't make the payment from HRM without involving the Director of Finance and the Halifax Council. Deep down, Cathy knew that she had no choice but to report this to Larry Munroe, the Auditor General for HRM. Although she didn't relish being branded a whistleblower, Cathy knew it was the right thing to do. She also knew, considering the publicity that rock concerts had received the previous year, that the media would relish this story. But what bothered Cathy the most was that Wayne Anstey, the person who had authorised the advance, was her boss. With a bad feeling in her stomach, Cathy called Larry Munroe and asked if she could see him right away.

As an internal auditor, Munroe liked to write things down to get a handle on the situation. So as soon as Cathy O'Toole started to tell her story, Larry started making notes. Once she left, he began to sketch out the details of the timing of tickets sales and advances (see Exhibit 1[2]) and as he did so, he became more uneasy about the overall picture.

Exhibit 1   Black Eyed Peas concert: timing and amount of advances issued and ticket sales

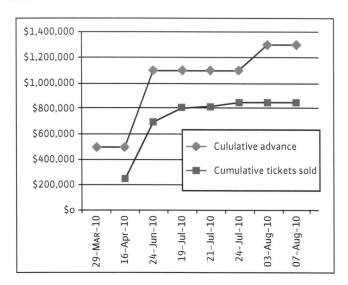

Cathy was right, somebody had not been paying attention and the secret payments to PPE had slipped right past the 23 elected councillors of HRM. At first glance it appeared to Larry that HRM's role had switched from being a venue provider to the riskier position of financial partner. Looking over what he had written, he still couldn't quite believe what he was seeing. From his experience in situations involving misplaced funds, he knew this usually involves a series of well thought out complex events in order to circumvent the control systems. Yet, in this case, it seemed just the opposite had occurred. Clearly no one was actively lying about their conduct and there was no sign that anyone was profiting. But for sure there seemed to be a determined push to finalise the concert deals. Larry Munroe noted that the transactions went undetected for an extended period of time (see Appendix A for a timeline of events).

Larry was puzzled. What had happened to the clear limitations and reporting requirements on concert arrangements that had been discussed in Council meetings? Clearly, the decisions of Council were being ignored. From what Larry could determine, it looked like loans to the concert promoter, Harold MacKay,

2   Excerpt from report of the Auditor General, June 2011.

based on advanced ticket sales, were being approved by Scott Ferguson who was President of the Trade Centre Limited (TCL). TCL is the provincial crown corporation which operates—among other things—Ticket Atlantic and Halifax Metro Centre (the largest sports arena in Halifax) on behalf of HRM. The advances were guaranteed by both Wayne Anstey and Mayor Peter Kelly. Larry intended to find out how this had been allowed to happen. Looking at his notes again, Larry tried to remember the discussions that had taken place after the 2009 concert to see if he could make sense of it.

Like Cathy, Larry remembered that Scott Ferguson had been warned by the auditor at TCL to stop loaning money to promoters from advance ticket sales. These loans often reached a half a million dollars. The auditor was worried that should an event be cancelled, TCL would have to refund the ticket price to people who had bought tickets. In this case TCL had the responsibility to potentially refund all the ticket sales, and if the advanced funds were not returned by the promoter, then the ticket refunds would have to be provided from other sources, i.e. taxpayer pockets. The auditor for TCL knew that it was unlikely that the advanced funds would be returned by the promoter since the money would have been used as a deposit given to the artist. Such deposits are normally not refundable if the promoter cancels the contract.

Reaching for the phone, Larry made a couple of phone calls, and the story started to unfold. It soon became clear to him that both Mayor Peter Kelly and Wayne Anstey had guaranteed the loans that Scott Ferguson had approved from advance ticket sales for the Black Eyed Peas concert. But that was not all. In addition to the event contracts, which included clauses addressing cash advances, Kelly and Anstey on behalf of HRM had also entered into other agreements with the promoter and TCL, using the Halifax Metro Centre bank account. The records in front of him confirmed that Anstey, with the full knowledge of TCL, had entered into numerous agreements between 2008 and 2010 to provide additional cash advances against current and future ticket sales but he had not made Legal Services or Regional Council aware of his actions or the associated financial risk. Worse still, for the Keith Urban concert there were two separate advance payments made to PPE totalling $650,000 which were made without even Mr. Anstey's approval. These were based only on approval by Scott Ferguson.

Larry Munroe was sure of one thing—if TCL not been an active participant in the process of providing cash advances through the Halifax Metro Centre bank account, this mess would never have happened. It was time to talk directly to Anstey, Kelly and Ferguson and get to the bottom of this.

Getting to the truth

Kelly, Anstey and Ferguson sat in front of Larry Munroe trying to explain their actions. When Munroe had first contacted each of them and told them what he had discovered, he had the sense that the three senior officials had become fixated on the competition with the City of Moncton over bringing in big name concerts. That had got in the way of worrying about accountability for their reckless actions in loaning money to concert organizers. In Munroe's reckoning, a "groupthink mentality" seemed to have set-in because none of the many people involved along the way questioned the decisions that had been made. It seemed that all three men were too caught up in putting HRM on the concert map. But Munroe still wanted to find out what had motivated Anstey to start this loan process and how it had gone undetected.

Wayne Anstey knew that the city CAO position is similar to that of corporate CEO, providing professional advice to the board of directors and making major decisions, except that in the public sector the decisions should be in line with the mandate and formal motions of the elected officials. Yet, this is not what happened. Anstey told Munroe that the process of advancing cash to a promoter had begun in 2008, to enable the hosting of major outdoor events in the region and to ensure that the promoter would have the required liquidity of funds to stage the concerts. He admitted that the authorization of the advances exceeded his or any HRM official's authority and that he knew it violated the HRM Charter and put the city at financial risk but he still went ahead.

As they told their story, Anstey and Ferguson confirmed that they felt that as long as each cash advance was able to be supported by ticket sales and the concert was not cancelled, there was little risk of exposing what they had done. This was helped by the fact that the Board of Trade Centre Limited had only one continuous appointment—Mayor Peter Kelly—and three rotating councillor positions. Plus, the financial reporting of the TCL was on a casual basis and at their discretion. So Anstey and others felt that there was little chance that the discrepancy would come to light before the money was re-deposited.

Anstey explained that this worked well for a while, but in the last days leading up to the 2010 concerts, ticket sales were well below the estimated 40,000 people per concert originally proposed. So discussions began in earnest with the Province of Nova Scotia to provide financial support. At this point, Anstey decided to enter into another letter of agreement with PPE. Harold MacKay received another cash advance (through the Halifax Metro Centre) even before receiving word if the Province was prepared to provide financial support. And, unfortunately, financial support was denied by the Province. The concerts appeared in jeopardy of being cancelled at this point in time.

As events unfolded, the sale of tickets was well below the non-repayable threshold and PPE was not required to repay the grant totalling $400,000. TCL later invoiced HRM, on Halifax Metro Centre letterhead, directly addressed to Anstey. It was at this point that Anstey had to go to Cathy O'Toole asking for money to be transferred.

But Larry Munroe was still left with one puzzling question. Why had Legal Services approved the contracts for the Black Eyed Peas and the Country Rocks concerts in 2010? Mayor Kelly filled in the final piece of the puzzle by explaining that there was some confusion about the 2010 concert contracts. He had asked

Legal Services to "approve the contracts as to form." It was his understanding that Legal Services had reviewed and approved the contracts, so that is why he signed them. But, as it turned out, Legal Services thought it was merely approving the intentions of both parties, not taking responsibility for writing the contract. The whole approval process seemed confused. Some people, even the staff, wondered who was really in charge of this big organization. The Chief Administrative Officer? The Mayor? With its complex governance system, by-laws, regulations, a huge $700 million annual budget, Halifax showed all the hall-marks of a formal bureaucracy.

After everyone had left, Larry opened his computer and started to amend his Auditor General's report. Like Cathy, he knew that once his report was released, the press wouldn't leave him alone. His job was going to get busier over the next few months.

Epilogue: The beat goes on

Following the release of the Auditor General's Report, the Black Eyed Peas transactions and the secret payments to PPE received a lot of media attention. It seemed that a new story appeared in the media on a daily basis. In particular, the newspaper headlines in the local paper, the *Halifax Herald*, were numerous and hostile. These stories suggested that the Halifax municipal councillors had been kept in the dark and that the money for the concert had been doled out in a "cavalier manner." All of this unwanted attention was having a big effect on morale at Halifax City Hall. The elected officials were nearly in a state of war. Council meetings were now an endless battle of snide remarks and hurtful accusations. Wayne Anstey was forced to quit in disgrace amidst the controversy. He released a statement saying he felt retirement was the right thing to do. "I would like to first state, that in every instance when I had a choice to make, I truly believed I was making the right choice on behalf of HRM. Of course, if I had to do it over again, I would do things differently."

At least two senior directors had enough of the fighting and decided to retire. Then, unexpectedly, Cathy O'Toole, the CFO who blew the whistle on the whole concert affair, announced that she was leaving to take a job with the Halifax Water Utility. "I'm so happy!" said Cathy when asked about her resignation. "The stuff going on at City Hall wasn't a deciding factor for me but it certainly validated some of the reasons that I'm choosing to go—in terms of the stress and the responsibility. It's going to be good for me and my family."

Perhaps most importantly, HRM Councillor Sue Uteck went on talk-radio to question the lack of democratic process used by the Mayor and other senior officials, saying "23 people got left in the dust, your entire elected regional council, by senior staff that felt there was no need to inform us." It was possible that Sue Uteck was just taking a political shot at Kelly. Uteck was rumoured to be gearing up for a run at the mayor's seat in the next election and she was a consistent complainer of anything that had to do with Peter Kelly. But Councillor Debbie Hum came to a similar conclusion. "No, it doesn't constitute justification," said Hum. "Not if it's contrary to policy that hasn't been complied with in regards to these concerts."

Jumping on the bandwagon, HRM citizens staged a noisy demonstration in a local park and Facebook groups also started popping-up, asking citizens to register their objections by signing on-line petitions. Perhaps the most personal attack against Peter Kelly was a newspaper editorial written by Stephen Kimber on March 21, 2011, entitled "Was our mayor as dumb as he pretends?" It was definitely becoming a losing proposition for Kelly. Kimber proposed two alternative scenarios—either the Mayor was deceitful in failing to admit to his own implication in the concert scandal, or else he actually was disengaged and uncaring in his role as Mayor. Kimber wrote,

> And we must accept that—even after Power Promotions went down the tubes in October—our esteemed mayor didn't say to himself: Perhaps I'd better tell council and taxpayers what we've been doing with their money...And have been doing for years, only this time, uh...we got caught. So I don't want to believe the mayor was as dumb as he claims he was. And I don't.

In a final move towards accountability, the Provincial Auditor General, Jacques Lapointe, who was following events closely, announced that he was going to decide whether or not to initiate an audit of TCL.

In 2008 Peter Kelly was returned by voters, in a landslide vote, as Mayor for a third term. Over the years many people had criticised his leadership style and effectiveness, but, despite his decision making, he still held popular appeal to the general public. Many had felt that the Black Eyed Peas fiasco might be a burden to his re-election because Kelly had not only been the main cheerleader for the concerts on the Common but he had actually taken an active part in the negotiations with PPE and the lobby efforts to (unsuccessfully) get cash contributions from the Provincial government. Ultimately, it was the taxpayers of HRM who were left not only with the concert debt, but with questions surrounding the legitimacy of the decisions made by their elected officials. Where was the accountability? The mayor was not showing any remorse for his actions. Indeed, it appeared that his own interests were superseding the best interests of those who had elected him.

Everything came to a head when Sue Uteck managed to get enough support for a formal motion at the June 21, 2011, HRM Council meeting. Council meetings are usually mundane but this one was a bit of a spectacle. Councillors surprisingly suspended the rules to vote on a motion—that Mayor Kelly should be given a one-week suspension. Later, outside the Council Chamber, Councillor Uteck said that taxpayers deserved to see Kelly held accountable for his role in the concert cash mess. The Mayor refused calls for his resignation, saying "I've got a job to do."

Rising at her place at the Council table, Uteck said "This is the only option available to us and I'm going to take it and see where it goes."

Before Councillor Uteck finally put her motion, the new Chief Administrative Officer, Richard Butts, was asked by a Councillor about whether HRM would try to recoup the unpaid $400,000. The matter had been referred to the HRM legal department and sources said that Harold MacKay had also hired a lawyer. The CAO's reply seemed to sum-up what many were feeling—Butts said "I don't know what the future will hold. I don't know what we're going to do tomorrow."

Mayor Kelly, presiding over a formal motion of the Council for his own suspension, called for the vote.

Appendix A: Halifax concert cash timeline

May 15, 2009—Nova Scotia government guarantees a $3.5-million "artist fee" for a Paul McCartney concert, paid to PPE. Money repaid through ticket sales. Also provides PPE with a repayable loan based on ticket sales—not repaid because not enough tickets were sold.

July 11, 2009—Paul McCartney concert attendance is a disappointment (paid attendance 26,504).

July 18, 2009—KISS concert (paid attendance 21,402).

June 30, 2010—PPE owner Harold MacKay announces the cancellation of the Kid Rock concert scheduled for July 23, the first day of Halifax Rocks. No reason is given.

July 8, 2010—Wayne Anstey becomes acting CAO of Halifax when Dan English retires.

July 21, 2010—Anstey, MacKay and Mayor Kelly meet. Later that day, Anstey authorizes two cheques totalling $400,000 to PPE as a repayable grant if ticket targets are met.

July 24, 2010—The Black Eyed Peas headlines Halifax Rocks, now a one-day event due to cancellation of Kid Rock (paid attendance 8,362).

August 6–7, 2010—Country Rockfest (paid attendance 10,009).

October 2010—PPE goes out of business.

March 3, 2011—Cathie O'Toole, the municipality's CFO, learns from Anstey that HRM owes Halifax Metro Centre $400,000 because the grant to PPE wasn't repaid.

March 10, 2011—The HRM's Audit Committee learns of the cash advances. This information is provided by Cathy O'Toole and Larry Munroe, the municipal Auditor General.

March 17, 2011—Anstey announces his immediate resignation as Chief Administrative Officer, one day after saying he would stay until the end of June.

June 7, 2011—Report by auditor general released. Munroe says Kelly and Anstey risked taxpayers' money and didn't flag concerns.

June 14, 2011—As Facebook groups critical of the cash-for-concerts deal sprout up, Councillor Linda Mosher puts forward a motion requesting a police review. Council votes that down 15–7.

June 16, 2011—MacKay issues a statement saying he did nothing wrong.

June 21, 2011—Halifax Council votes on a motion by Councillor Sue Uteck to censure the mayor. The effect of the motion would be to suspend the Mayor for one week.

About the authors

Larry Corrigan is a PhD Candidate and Assistant Professor at the Sobey School of Business in Halifax, Canada. Larry has extensive experience in the not-for-profit sector. He had previous roles as Vice-President, Finance of Saint Mary's University, President of the Certified General Accountants of Nova Scotia, and was Chief Administrative Officer for the City of Dartmouth. His doctoral research on municipal budget making is inspired by the interpretive tradition of dramaturgy, and will also be informed by actor-network theory and the notion of history.

Jean Helms Mills is a Professor of Management at the Sobey School of Business, Saint Mary's University, Canada, and Professor (part time) at Jyväskylä School of Business and Economics, Jyväskylä University, Finland. In 2009–2010 she was Co-divisional Chair of the Critical Management Studies Division of AoM and served for a number of years on the Administrative Sciences of Canada Executive. Currently, Jean is an Associate Editor of *Gender, Work and Organization* and serves on the editorial boards of a number of other journals. Her books include *Making Sense of Organizational Change* (Routledge, 2003), *Understanding Organizational Change* (Routledge, 2009) and the forthcoming *Routledge Companion to Critical Management Studies*.

Teaching notes for this case are available from Greenleaf Publishing. These are free of charge and available only to teaching staff. They can be requested by going to:
www.greenleaf-publishing.com/darkside2notes

11

Academia accommodating plagiarism? Surely not!

Belinda Luke
Queensland University of Technology Business School

Kate Kearins
Auckland University of Technology

In April 2010, Senior lecturer *A* discovered a new article on strategic entrepreneurship that contained her own words and paragraphs, published under the name of two complete strangers. Over the next eight months, in search of a just outcome, *A* contacted various people and institutions involved: the journal editor and publisher, and more than 20 academics and academic managers at five universities located in four different countries, including vice chancellors, rectors, and university professors. While nobody disputed the plagiarism (which involved at least three documents and more than 50 pages of text, tables, and figures), most were reluctant to act. Disillusioned by institutional responses, *A* had to decide whether to continue pursuing a just outcome at the risk of damaging professional relationships (and her future career), or whether to accept the status quo. She wondered what it would take to change the system to genuinely reject plagiarism.

> Academia is a learning environment, as well as a constant learning process. Sometimes those lessons are really insightful. Other times they are just really sad (*A*,[1] diary note, December 2010).

1 Names have been changed throughout this case study to preserve anonymity. Appendix 1 provides a summary of the main actors involved in the case.

Introduction

There were several unsent drafts in *A*'s e-mail folder. To do nothing about the situation in which she had found herself would be against *A*'s sense of what was just. To press "send" would potentially be career limiting. In early 2010, she had discovered a new article on strategic entrepreneurship, an emerging area of research on which little had been written. *A*'s interest lay in learning about any new developments in this research area, and she printed out the article to read at home. However, her interest in the article dramatically heightened as she began to read her own words and paragraphs, published under the name of two other researchers.

> The whole experience was very surreal (*A,* diary note, April 2010).

Familiar with plagiarism as a concept, and the risk of plagiarism in the classroom, *A* had never really considered the risk of academics taking each other's work and words. One year previously, she had attended an academic conference with a friend, and watched a presentation by a PhD student (now associate professor) whom the friend had informally mentored and supervised. At the end of the presentation, *A*'s friend calmly commented that the PhD student had presented his work as her own.

> It's awful, but I laughed. I laughed at the ludicrousness of the situation, the fact that he (my friend) was so calm, and that she (the PhD student) was so confidently presenting another person's work to a room full of strangers (*A,* diary note, April 2010).

One year later, at the centre of a similar case involving different players, *A* had lost her sense of humour.

> I'm just astounded by the whole issue. It's been such a learning process. I think the real issue now is finding a balance between persevering in the attempt for a just outcome at the risk of becoming an angry or bitter person, or letting the issue go and moving on to preserve my mental and emotional well-being (*A,* diary note, October 2010).

When sorry isn't enough

The paragraphs in the article were immediately familiar, but *A* sent a copy to her former supervisors to check that she wasn't being paranoid. They confirmed *A*'s suspicions, and after tracing the paragraphs to *A*'s individual documents, A then contacted both authors.

> As a researcher of strategic entrepreneurship I was interested to read your recent article. I was, however, surprised to find that this article includes sentences, paragraphs, and figures replicated from my own work, without any referencing. I would appreciate your comments on this issue. I will be contacting the [journal] editor to notify him of this issue. You may wish to do the same (*A*, e-mail correspondence, April 2010).

The editor responded to *A*'s e-mail immediately, noting the issue would be investigated. His e-mail signature included the tag-line "today, not tomorrow—not only words, but real action!" A similar e-mail followed from the journal publisher.

The first author, based in the United Kingdom, also responded immediately, acknowledged the duplication, apologised profusely, and advised that he wrote the back-end of the paper, where there was no such duplication. The front-end had been written by his co-author based in Greece.

> I am absolutely horrified to learn of this information. I am truly, truly stunned. I truly regret being ignorant of the [plagiarised] material and I am dreadfully sorry that this situation has occurred. I have now severed all ties with my co-author (*UK co-author*, e-mail correspondence, April 2010).

The *UK co-author* advised that he would be contacting his Head of Department, as well as the journal editor, advising them of the plagiarism identified and requesting a retraction of the article.

One day passed without a response from '*K*', the co-author based in Greece, and so a follow-up e-mail was sent.

> Dear *K*, I have now heard from your co-author and the journal editor. I am awaiting your response. As mentioned previously, I would appreciate you reviewing your other publications and awards[2] carefully to check there is no further replication of my work. I will be doing a similar review and taking this matter further (*A*, e-mail correspondence, April 2010).

K responded with words similar to her co-author's British English, noting she was *dreadfully sorry* and suggested it may have been a referencing issue.

> I would like to let you know that I am very very sorry for all this situation. By no means do I have the intention to duplicate your work without referencing you and this was done unintentionally. You have

---

2 A review of *K*'s profile on her university website revealed a number of papers on strategy and entrepreneurship, and an academic award for one paper in particular.

> my word on this. One reason for which this might have happened is
> that I... got really confused as to the sources and the exact referenc-
> ing. I will do whatever I have to in order to make up for this situation
> (*K*, e-mail correspondence, April 2010).

A then requested copies of *K*'s related publications, thesis and award doc-
umentation and was advised these would be sent later that day. Three days
passed without any documents being sent; only a message from *K* stating she
was "so sorry for all this trouble" and wanted to contact *A* by phone.

> I understand that this matter is not resolved just by stating how sorry
> I am. I feel so depressed and I ask for your sincere apology (sic) (*K*,
> e-mail correspondence, April 2010).

K's mood had lowered, as had the quality of her written English. *A* responded
that there was no need to speak at this stage and reiterated her request for all relevant documents, noting that these documents would also be requested through
other channels. In particular, *A* was interested to see *K*'s PhD, as the *UK co-author*'s
understanding was that *K*'s PhD was the source material for the journal article.

Documents were not sent by *K*, and *A* then proceeded to contact the university in Athens where *K* had graduated, outlining details and attaching evidence
of the plagiarism. A response promptly followed from *K*'s former supervisor,
Associate Professor S, at the Athens-based university.

> Thanks for your message, which unfortunately raises a very critical
> issue that also has taken me by total surprise. I see with stupefaction
> that in *K*'s thesis there are some additional parts that are copy paste
> (*Associate Professor S*, e-mail correspondence, April 2010).

A copy of *K*'s thesis (in English) was provided by *Associate Professor S*, with
further plagiarised sections highlighted. A paper presented at the Academy of
Management Meetings was also provided, where *Associate Professor S* again
highlighted plagiarised sections.

> I feel also cheated to some extent as a supervisor, although I also have
> part of the responsibility in the sense that this duplication and omis-
> sion of referring you escaped my attention. Just for your info and not
> as an excuse, my field of research expertise is not entrepreneurship
> and I have neither before nor after supervised any similar work. I
> supervised the particular thesis due to internal university procedures
> that unfortunately now I see the negative effects of (*Associate Professor
> S*, e-mail correspondence, April 2010).

Associate Professor S undertook to continue a comparison of the two theses,
and present information to the University President for possible further disciplinary action.

I can only at the moment apologize of (sic) the behalf of our university and ensure you that we will pursue our own investigation and reinforce our procedures of duplication identification (*Associate Professor S*, e-mail correspondence, April 2010).

A updated her former supervisors (whom she continued to publish with) on the developments.

Thanks for keeping us up to date. It is really important to see *K*'s other papers, because we have to assess what it means for our other papers (will it look like we are plagiarising?) (*A*'s former supervisor, e-mail correspondence, April 2010).

The issue had gone beyond violation of property rights and now jeopardised *A*'s right to publish her own work without appearing dishonest.[3]

One day later, *A* received an update from *Associate Professor S*, advising he had spoken with the Director of Postgraduate Studies, and the corrective actions they required from *K* were as follows:

- She will send a letter to the seven-member committee explaining that her PhD contains material that have (sic) not been elaborated and referenced appropriately

- She will proceed with changes to and deletions of duplicated content, and, of course, additionally reference you properly

- The new version of the thesis will be distributed to the seven committee members, as well as to myself in electronic form. Hence, there will be a replacement of the unpublished PhD thesis after the appropriate corrections.

- We see very seriously on this, and hope that the above actions will contribute to resolving the situation amicably (*Associate Professor S*, e-mail correspondence, April 2010).

As *A* read the response, she thought about the past week which had become a routine of 10 hour days in the office, followed by several hours at home each night reviewing documents and e-mailing various parties in Europe who had been drawn into this issue. The plagiarism in *K*'s PhD thesis extended to more than 50 pages of *A*'s work, including text, tables, and figures which had been directly copied and pasted. Despite *A*'s tiredness, she was very clear this was not

---

3 A publication by Kock (1999) subsequently reviewed by *A* revealed this was a very real issue faced by Kock, himself a victim of plagiarism, when the person who plagiarised threatened to take legal action against Kock as the original author. Under the legal system in the US (where both authors were based), the defence process was going to be both time consuming and costly—up to US$10,000.

a referencing issue, and that the suggested actions were less than appropriate. A matter of plagiarism had now become one of politics.

Institutional responses sought

A continued to request documents from *K,* but received nothing other than e-mails advising that the documents would be sent. *A* was increasingly becoming disillusioned with the academic systems in place. As a senior lecturer at an Australian university working in an academic discipline different to the area in which she published, *A* felt her case was not being taken seriously, and so turned to others for assistance.

The response from staff at *A*'s university was consistent.

> Everyone keeps telling me "you should really do something about this", but nobody has come forward to actually help me. It is an extremely lonely and isolating experience (*A*, diary note, April 2010).

A contacted her Head of Department, inquired about university legal services, and approached the Faculty and University Research Directors, as well as senior library and copyright staff. While they each acknowledged the situation as a clear case of plagiarism, no-one seemed willing to get actively involved. It was repeatedly suggested that this was an issue for the overseas university which *A* had graduated from, rather than the Australian university where *A* currently worked.

> The only time assistance was offered was if I was a student who had been accused of plagiarism. In that case, legal representation and counselling was on hand. When I advised that I was a staff member whose work had been plagiarised rather than a student who had plagiarised, the response was "we don't have services for that" (*A*, diary note, April 2010).

The New Zealand university which *A* had graduated from was supportive but cautious. *A*'s former supervisor, *Professor C* (now Associate Dean Research), requested copies of the documents, and a review by the postgraduate and research librarian confirmed the extent of the plagiarism. *A* communicated her feelings at this point.

> I am a bit disappointed with the [e-mail sent by *Associate Professor S* yesterday], as this is not a referencing issue. It is a very clear case of plagiarism, involving repeated acts of dishonesty and misrepresentation (*A*, e-mail correspondence, April 2010).

A's former supervisor, *Professor C*, agreed with *A*'s assessment.

> This matter is shameful for the person concerned and something that affects her institution as well... you are correct, I believe, in stating it is not a referencing issue or one that can necessarily be so readily "patched up"—and the question of whether the PhD should be revoked is a very real one in my view. Since you are in contact, perhaps you should tell the supervisor that. But first what was the legal advice from [your university]? (*Professor C*, e-mail correspondence, April 2010).

Correspondence once again showed support for *A*'s concerns, but emphasised the reality that legal issues (which everyone seemed eager to avoid) took precedent over moral ones. Empathy was evident, but the issue was consistently conveyed as someone else's problem. *A*'s own institution suggested it was a matter for the overseas university where she had graduated. The overseas university considered it was a matter for the institution where *A* now worked and published.

An e-mail to this effect was sent by *A* to her former supervisor. The response:

> Let's see if [this university] is any better in helping you (*Professor C*, e-mail correspondence, April 2010).

Attempts by *Professor C* to bring in the New Zealand university's legal counsel were unsuccessful, although there was interest from the postgraduate director who had been copied in on the e-mails on the basis that the university might have some interest in protecting its students' intellectual property. That interest took the form of encouraging the supervisor to inform the university research committee of a rather alarming occurrence, but no action on the part of the university itself.

A responded to the university in Athens highlighting the case as one of extensive and repeated plagiarism rather than a referencing issue, and requested more appropriate action be taken.

> If we judge that actions beyond our first suggested are not enough, we will activate our internal disciplinary procedure (*Associate Professor S*, e-mail correspondence, April 2010).

Knocking on new doors

Dissatisfied with the lack of progress being made, *A* turned to the regional university in Greece where *K* now worked. Whilst being a relatively young university financed jointly by the European Union and the Greek State, its website referred to its "internationally renowned executive education and business courses".

Other promotional material noted it was "committed to priorities of academic excellence, meeting the needs of society". Yet contact information on the university website was scarce, with many of the academics being visiting faculty, so *A* identified a professor in the relevant department and contacted him.

> Dear Professor, the reason I am writing is to inform you of a series of reviews being undertaken in relation to *K*'s research. I believe this affects your institution, as *K* is representing both herself and [your institution] (*A*, e-mail correspondence, April 2010).

The response was prompt and seemingly positive.

> Thank you for bringing this to my attention. This is clearly a very serious matter that definitely requires further investigation. I will be awaiting the results of the investigations from [the Athens-based university] as the PhD awarding institution, the publishers of the paper, and *K*'s comments on this matter. I would be grateful if you could keep me informed on future developments (*Professor*, regional Greek university, e-mail correspondence, April 2010).

Such correspondence had perhaps prompted *K* to act, and one day later *K* e-mailed two abstracts relating to her papers from the Academy of Management meetings.

> Please try to understand the situation I find myself in since the last week has been like living in hell for me, so this does not aid me to act quickly. There are many issues now I have to handle and this is the reason for delaying to send you anything. But you already have almost everything there, so I will send you the rest of the material. As I mentioned in my first email, I intend to take all corrective actions to repair this damage (*K*, e-mail correspondence, April 2010).

K had somehow become the victim of a situation created from her own dishonesty. Despite repeated requests, *K* had provided nothing other than two abstracts. Yet the abstracts provided little if no opportunity to check for plagiarism, and *K*'s former supervisor, *Associate Professor S* had already identified plagiarism in one of the Academy of Management meetings papers. Further, it seemed the "issues" *K* was handling involved hiring a lawyer to argue against any wrong-doing, as indicated by the *Publisher* in a subsequent e-mail.

Editorial licence

Approximately two weeks had passed since initial contact with the journal, when the *Publisher* contacted *A* with a proposed course of action.

I have now had a chance to look through the [journal] materials, and it is evident (and agreed by all sides) that there is a lack of attribution to your work in the first half of the paper. It's clear that *K* has used your material [in her PhD] also (*Publisher*, e-mail correspondence, April 2010).

The *Publisher* advised that he could update the journal article as appropriate and publicise any changes.

I believe the action required is to add a detailed corrigendum outlining how the work has failed to reference your own. In drawing this conclusion, I am using the guidelines of the Committee on Publication Ethics, which suggest that because the article also contains original content of merit (primarily the UK author's contribution) it should remain as part of the scholarly literature.

An alternative course of action would be to formally retract the article, but I have a feeling that would be too harsh. We see several of these cases, and they tend to fall into two camps: naivety and deliberate intent to deceive. In my view, having spoken at length with *K*, this is a case of the former. That doesn't excuse it in any way (and I emphasise that), but since *K* has admitted fault and, I understand, apologized to you and [her co-author], a corrigendum seems an appropriate response. It will be published online alongside the article, with a unique DOI reference, and will also appear in the next issue of the journal. Please can you let me know your thoughts? (*Publisher*, e-mail correspondence, April 2010).

A's thoughts were clear. First, this was not a referencing issue, nor an act of naivety. The plagiarism extended to at least three documents, and involved more than 50 pages of cut and paste text, tables, and figures. *K* had shown little remorse, obtaining legal representation to protect her status as a Doctor of Philosophy, researcher, and published author. Second, *A* felt her concerns were not being taken seriously. With a growing awareness that she could not rely on the systems within academia to produce a just outcome, *A* turned to two individuals at her own institution—the current Assistant Dean Research, and the former Assistant Dean Research—requesting help. She had met with both people briefly on previous occasions, and while not knowing them personally, she wondered if they would be able to offer direction and support from a professional perspective.

The current Assistant Dean Research was attentive, but reluctant to act.

The correspondence you have received indicates appropriate investigations have commenced. Essentially, we need to await the outcomes. If necessary our Deputy Vice Chancellor of Research will correspond with his counterparts (Vice-Chancellors or equivalent) at the universities concerned seeking appropriate action or explanation (*Assistant Dean Research*, e-mail correspondence, May 2010).

A felt she had been very clear in her requests.

> [The Assistant Dean Research] asked many times "what do you want me to do?" I very clearly requested she send an e-mail to those people I had been dealing with overseas requesting appropriate action—retraction of the journal article, review of the PhD award by the Athens-based university. Her response was increasingly vague and indecisive, and ultimately she noted that I had already done these things, so there was no point her e-mailing anyone (*A*, diary note, May 2010).

In contrast, the former Assistant Dean Research, *Professor D*, internationally renowned in the field of entrepreneurship, questioned why *A* had contacted him (as he no longer held the Assistant Dean Research role), suggested who she should contact within the university where they worked, and then sent numerous e-mails throughout Europe to colleagues and journal editors he knew both personally and professionally, alerting them to the issue.

Her confidence buoyed, *A* again wrote to the *Publisher*.

> I see this as a blatant and repeated plagiarism issue, rather than a referencing/attribution issue. I would strongly request the article be retracted (*A*, e-mail correspondence, April 2010).

The *Publisher* appeared open to reconsideration.

> Certainly: I am quite prepared to retract the article as requested. My original proposal was certainly not to condone poor practice, but an attempt to retain the valuable aspects of the paper for future research. Having read [the UK co-author's] e-mail to you [supporting retraction], I'm more than happy to agree to a retraction. I am currently out of the office and will lay out the expected course of action as soon as I return on Thursday—earlier if possible. Please let me know if this is acceptable to you (*Publisher*, e-mail correspondence, April 2010).

A read the response with relief, feeling that after much effort, progress was finally being made. Developments were also seemingly underway at the Athens-based university.

> Our President has been informed last Friday (upon his return) and we are in the process of reviewing the issue. I will transmit your input to him and the three member supervising committee that will meet regarding the issue. We have already ordered K and our internal services to withdraw the unpublished PhD thesis from any possible place of storage, electronic or printed (*Associate Professor S*, e-mail correspondence, April 2010).

A lesson in Greek ethics

One of the concerns which was hinted at but not openly discussed, was potential cultural differences on the topic of ethics. *A* had broached this issue in an e-mail to her former supervisor, *Professor C*, and the text was later incorporated in an e-mail sent by the former supervisor to the Athens university.

> There are several institutions which have been drawn into this issue... each of which promotes high academic standards. The promotion of independent thought and protection of intellectual property is a key feature of these standards. I request therefore that you act to remedy the situation including considering the possibility of revising your earlier decision to recommend the PhD degree for *K* who has breached academic standards and whose work as it stands, does not merit this degree (*Professor C*, e-mail correspondence, May 2010).

The e-mail had been copied to various parties involved in the case, one of whom, the postgraduate and research librarian, congratulated *Professor C* on her wording. The response:

> Dare I admit it but 50% or more of my e-mail is plagiarised from various e-mails written by *A* (*Professor C*, e-mail correspondence, May 2010).
>
> I read that e-mail and laughed out loud. My sense of humour had returned (*A*, diary note, May 2010).

A reply from *Professor Y,* the Vice Rector Academic Affairs at the Athens-based university to *Professor C* followed.

> I can assure you that we will look into the matter with all the seriousness it deserves on my return next week. I would also like to certify that our University shares very high academic standards and fully supports the protection of intellectual property rights (*Professor Y*, e-mail correspondence, May 2010).

Professor C forwarded the e-mail to *A*.

> ...it would now seem *K* is set to suffer serious consequences of her actions. There are a bundle of lessons here—and one is that I should not have taken the initial advice that I did take and not weigh in sooner. Part of that was being busy and seeing an easy way out of a tricky situation which I suspect is also what some others here were doing when they passed the ball back to me. On the other hand, people like [the postgraduate and research librarian] here, do seem to genuinely care about the issue of plagiarism and authors' rights. Equally for you, *Professor D*'s action was to the point and secured a response.

> For all the work (for you) and upset this caused, I guess we both have more ideas about how to handle it. I am sure it would make a very readable piece if you ever wanted to write it up! (*Professor C*, e-mail correspondence, May 2010).
>
> We all saw a case study coming out of this (*A*, diary note, May 2010).

Two weeks later, *Professor C* received an updated response from the Vice Rector Academic Affairs at the Athens-based university.

> I have met today the three-member committee of *K*'s PhD thesis, *Professors P* and *L* and *Associate Professor S*. We have discussed in detail the case. There was unanimous agreement that there has been a very serious misconduct involving plagiarism. The committee also unanimously agreed to refer the case to the Board of the relevant University Department which awarded the PhD to *K*, with the recommendation that the PhD thesis award is retracted subject to what the University Legal Counsel will advise in relation to the practical steps of implementing this recommendation (*Professor Y*, e-mail correspondence, May 2010).

The response was promising. However action continued to be governed by legal issues. *Professor C* responded, thanking the Athens-based university management for their reply.

> We are grateful that the matter has been taken seriously and that a recommendation has been made for retraction of the PhD thesis award. In order to ensure closure on this matter, we request you to send myself and the author of the original thesis (now Dr) *A* a copy of the official letter retracting the award in due course as evidence that such has actually occurred (*Professor C*, e-mail correspondence, May 2010).

Sense and sensibility

An update from the *Publisher* to *A* revealed *K* had indeed hired a lawyer, but also highlighted the complexity of communication throughout this ordeal.

> You may know *K* engaged a lawyer to represent her. Have you heard from this lawyer? I was given the impression she was going to speak with you regarding the [journal] article, in an attempt to mitigate the situation. If you haven't, that's fine, but I'm just trying to work out who has said what to whom! (*Publisher*, e-mail correspondence, May 2010).

A had not heard from *K*'s lawyer, but certainly acknowledged the challenge of having open and transparent communication. E-mail correspondence over the past two months had involved a number of people and groups, but it was often difficult to share views openly at times, without occasionally feeling that perhaps too much liberty had been taken when forwarding e-mails. Nothing had been expressly stated as "confidential", but sharing of e-mails had also not been expressly authorised—particularly with regard to some of the more candid views expressed. *A* reflected wryly on the situation.

> I have tried to be transparent but also respectful of people's privacy throughout this process, which at times has been a difficult balancing act. I was not trying to make friends or enemies along the way; simply wanting to reach a just outcome, which I initially thought would be through institutional channels. If people knew plagiarism was even remotely acceptable in practice, why wouldn't they risk borrowing a few PhD chapters from a stranger occasionally, instead of slaving away by themselves for three plus years? (*A*, diary note, June 2010).

A's views were a mix of pragmatic rule following as well as a naive trust in the institutions of academia. Given that, institutionally, plagiarism in academia was promoted as unacceptable, it seemed somewhat confusing that such acts were effectively being accommodated rather than readily admonished in practice.

Greek wheels turn slowly

Over a month had passed since the Athens-based university's last correspondence, so *Professor C* requested an update.

> While we are pleased your university saw fit to make the recommendation for the retraction of the PhD thesis award, I am wondering whether you may now be in a position to attend to the requests below to ensure closure on this matter (*Professor C*, e-mail correspondence, June 2010).

The response from *Professor Y* seemed promising, with a final note that *Professor P*, the university Rector, would provide updated information in due course.

> According to Greek Law PhD theses are assessed by a 7-member academic committee following a recommendation by the student's 3-member supervisory committee. The same 7-member committee has to look at issues related to plagiarism.
> I understand that the 7-member committee has convened and a hearing of *K* took place where they explained to her exactly the situation. Following this, a few days ago *K* sent to the committee in writing her views and responses. So this process has been finalized. The 7-member committee has now to convene again and make a recommendation to the Board of the Academic Department that will then take the final decision concerning the retraction of the thesis. (As I have mentioned before the

3-member supervisory committee in its first meeting that I also attended recommended that the thesis is retracted. However this recommendation has to reach the Board of the Department by the 7-member committee and the Board takes the final decision) (*Professor Y*, Athens-based university, e-mail correspondence, June 2010).

Two months passed, and *Professor C* again asked for an update. The response was that the university was closed until the end of the month, with all functions resuming in September. *Professor P* advised that he would be in contact by the end of September.

More cautious action from the publisher

In September the *Publisher* e-mailed *A* with an unexpected update.

I am writing to update you about the *K* paper published earlier this year. As you recall, my intention was to retract the paper, since there were clear problems with the originality of the material. I held off doing this, however, because I was waiting for *K*'s university to make a decision about her PhD status, and it seemed appropriate to let those events take their course. This is a note to let you know:

1) that I am still waiting to hear from the university

2) that in the meantime I will be placing an 'Expression of concern' on the online version of the paper to flag that all is not well

3) that a retraction will follow as soon as things are clearer at *K*'s end

Please let me know if you have any questions (*Publisher*, e-mail correspondence, September 2010).

A had many questions. Once again, she had become disillusioned at the position taken by those in the role of institutional "leaders", as hopes of any substantive progress faded. Once again, *A* turned to the former Associate Dean Research, *Professor D*, at her own institution for guidance.

Sorry to raise this issue with you again, but it seems that while there is an acceptance that *K* has clearly plagiarised my work (both in the [journal] article and her PhD thesis), there is a reluctance to take any decisive action to date.

I am obviously disappointed, and more than a little disillusioned by academic institutions which seem to be acknowledging but also accommodating this act of dishonesty (*A*, e-mail correspondence, September 2010).

Professor D offered a considered response.

> Thanks for your update. Unfortunately, people and institutions often choose to act cowardly because they are less uncomfortable with that than with having to stand up for justice in what threatens to be a legal process ...
>
> I think you and *K*'s co-author should again, jointly, demand that the journal article be retracted. Since the co-author has determined that it is clearly a case of plagiarism (with which he does not want to be associated), the journal should be able to make an independent decision and not hide behind the eventual outcome of a possible lengthy process in an individual country which may not fully share the views on plagiarism that should govern the journal in question (what if the degree were earned in Somalia?).
>
> *K*'s chances for an international or internationally active (publication-wise) career is probably effectively barred already—(as I recall it I alerted some journal editors and she also withdrew a submission from AoM—the Program Chair also knows about her case). Withdrawal of the article is much more important, and that should be achievable (*Professor D*, e-mail correspondence, September 2010).

Concerns raised by *A* with the *Publisher* were responded to. In particular, the *Publisher* made reference to the Committee on Publication Ethics (COPE), to which his organisation was a signatory.

> I appreciate your concern about the timeframe here.
>
> [Under COPE] guidelines when dealing with manuscript disputes, if an allegation of misconduct related to a potential retraction results in a disciplinary hearing or institutional investigation, it is normally appropriate to wait for the outcome of this before issuing a retraction (but an expression of concern may be published to alert readers in the interim).
>
> This is why we've not yet been able to close things off. If there's a delay regarding the thesis retraction because *K* wants to defend herself, then it's appropriate that we wait also. It's not a question of failing to make an independent decision, but because [our] relationship with COPE brings additional credibility to the decisions we make, we are also committed to follow their procedures (*Publisher*, e-mail correspondence, September 2010).

Comedy or tragedy?

Another month passed. Another follow up e-mail was sent by *Professor C* to the Athens-based university requesting confirmation of closure. *Professor Y* responded that he had no idea (seemingly no longer interested or affected by the matter), and advised her to contact *Professor P*, the Rector at the Athens-based university.

Professor C did so and received the following response.

> I would appreciate it if you stopped bombarding us with your e-mails about this issue, and wait for my updating you on progress, when I have some news to report to you (*Professor P,* e-mail correspondence, September 2010).

A timeframe of almost six months to resolve the issue by management at Greece's "leading economics and business higher education institution" was apparently not long enough. The Athens-based university claimed on its website to have a "high sense of responsibility—educating tomorrow's leaders". Yet, monthly e-mail requests had become *bombardment*. It also seemed to A that for the University Rector, who referred to goals of openness and excellence on the university website, the best form of defence was attack.

In an e-mail exchange between A and *Professor C*, A noted:

> It's interesting in an earlier e-mail that [the Athens-based university] alluded to wanting to adhere to international standards, but I would hope that most western universities would address issues such as this one more efficiently and perhaps professionally (A, e-mail correspondence, September 2010).

Professor C, feeling chastised after the accusation of bombardment, duly acknowledged her former student's turn of phrase.

> Great reply. I will file and perhaps we can use some of this in the next e-mail if we have to send one (*Professor C*, e-mail correspondence, September 2010).

A further two months passed without a response from the Athens-based university. *Professor C* sent another follow up e-mail to the Rector.

> I have waited a further two months but have heard nothing from you. I wonder if at last there is some news or you could indicate a date when the matter is due to be finally resolved (*Professor C*, e-mail correspondence, November 2010).

Several weeks passed, without response.

Exhausting final options

In November 2010, the Faculty of Business where *A* worked was in the process of re-applying for several international accreditations. As part of this process, *A* had been asked to participate in two panel discussions, each involving 15–20 staff. In preparation for the panel discussions, staff were reminded of various programmes, resources, and initiatives in the Faculty which made it a great place to work and study.

> While we were being prompted to say positive things, which we did believe anyway, there was certainly no shortage of suggestions for improvement either (*A*, diary note, November 2010).

The first panel discussion was less structured, and dominated by academic staff in the public relations school, doing what they do best. The second panel discussion involved each staff being asked to identify one good thing and one thing in need of improvement within the institution. One of the first suggestions from an economics colleague was that parking (a scarce commodity in a city campus) needed to be improved. Brief light-hearted discussion followed, with the panel concluding that if supply was limited, the price obviously needed to increase.

A put forward a suggestion regarding better mentoring, but left the room wondering if she had violated her own morals, and wasted her last opportunity of attempting to be heard.

> When my turn came, I had longed to say "better support for protection of intellectual property, given that my work has been extensively plagiarized and the university has done nothing". But the comment would have been career limiting, leaving the room stunned, and the Dean with a cardiac arrest once the details were relayed to him. While I have always had a reasonably clear sense of what is "just", I had never been a controversial or "problem" employee, and didn't intend to start being one now (*A*, diary note, November 2010).

In a last attempt, *A* e-mailed details of the situation to her own University *Research Director* (who was away when she first contacted his office). At that time, the Assistant Research Director noted that *A* had taken appropriate action and should wait for a response from the Greek universities. That department would be able to assist if the response from the Greek universities was not satisfactory.

A, feeling she had reached the point herself of having too many unsatisfactory responses, contacted her University *Research Director* and again requested assistance. More than two weeks passed before *A* received a response.

> I apologise for the delay in responding to your email. I have reviewed the various e-mails you have provided and concur with the previous

advice provided by [the Assistant Research Director]. As the matter relates to your PhD thesis and not to work undertaken as part of your employment at [this university] it would not be appropriate for [this university] to enter into this matter (*Research Director*, e-mail correspondence, November 2010).

A wondered how much time the *Research Director* had spent on this issue. The position outlined was inconsistent with previous advice from the Assistant Research Director, and the matter related to plagiarism of *A*'s Master's thesis, not PhD. Moreover, it directly impacted on *A*'s rights and ability to continue to publish her own work—something by which *A*'s performance was judged. The institution's aim was to "provide an outstanding learning environment", and "sustain excellence and impact in serving communities nationally and internationally". Its actions seemed somewhat different. Another door closed.

As the year came to an end, *A* reflected on the matter as an insightful but disappointing learning process.

> If this ever happened to one of my students, I am very clear that I would do everything possible to pursue a just outcome. If I was ever to be in a senior management position, I would also expect my colleagues to support this course of action (*A*, diary note, December 2010).

Checking her inbox, *A* saw a reminder e-mail from her own university's Vice Chancellor, requesting suggestions from staff on how to make the university a better place to work. *A* considered and drafted another potentially career limiting e-mail detailing the overwhelming lack of support she had received from various areas of the university throughout the past eight months. She then saved it to the draft folder with a number of other potentially career limiting drafts. It was still not clear to her whether she should press "send" and pursue the fight for a course of action personally viewed as just, try to change seemingly flawed institutional systems, or leave the issue behind at the risk of becoming a bitter or at least bitterly disappointed person.

Appendix 1: Main actors involved in the case

Actor	Description
A	Academic whose thesis had been plagiarised, subsequently working at an Australian University.
K	Academic who graduated from the Athens-based university and then worked at a Greek regional university, responsible for plagiarism in a published article, PhD thesis (containing more than 50 pages of *A's* Master's thesis), and Academy of Management Meeting submission.
UK co-author	Co-author of the plagiarised journal article, who requested that the article be retracted once he was aware of the plagiarism.
Publisher	European-based publisher of a B ranked journal (under Australia's journal ranking system), who felt the case needed to be considered by the Athens-based university before acting in relation to the plagiarised journal article.
Associate Professor S	*K's* former PhD supervisor at the Athens-based university, who was not an expert in the research area of *K's* thesis, and was unaware that the thesis and Academy of Management Meeting paper contained plagiarised material, but was co-operative in providing documents to *A*.
Professor Y	Vice Rector Academic affairs at the Athens-based university where *A* graduated from.
Professor P	Academic Rector of the Athens-based university where *A* graduated from, who felt "bombarded" by monthly e-mails requesting updates. After eight months, the issue remained unresolved.
Professor C	*A's* former supervisor, Associate Dean Research at the New Zealand university which *A* graduated from.
Professor D	Internationally renowned researcher in the field of entrepreneurship and former Assistant Dean Research at the university where *A* worked, who considered the plagiarised article should be retracted immediately, and alerted other colleagues and journal editors about the issue.
Assistant Dean Research	Current Assistant Dean Research at the university where *A* worked, who was reluctant to act.
University Research Director	Research Director at the university where A worked, who felt (in contrast to the advice previously provided by the Acting Research Director) that it was not appropriate for the university where *A* worked to become involved in the matter.

About the authors

Belinda Luke is a senior lecturer in the School of Accountancy at Queensland University of Technology, Australia. Her research interests include accountability, the public sector, and the third sector. Belinda's research has a strong case study based focus, and she has been awarded finalist in two Academy of Management Dark Side Case study competitions.

Kate Kearins is Professor of Management and Deputy Dean in the Faculty of Business and Law at Auckland University of Technology, New Zealand. She has an eclectic research base around organisational power and politics. A major focus of her work in recent years has been on business and sustainability, moving from a critical focus to one that explores potentialities in new forms of organising. One of Kate's favourite research activities is case-writing, and she has won numerous awards for co-authored cases. Her interest in publication ethics derives from both unfortunate experiences like the one profiled in the case in this volume and her work on the Academy of Management Board of Governors where she takes an ethics focus.

Teaching notes for this case are available from Greenleaf Publishing. These are free of charge and available only to teaching staff. They can be requested by going to:
www.greenleaf-publishing.com/darkside2notes

12

Milk or wine come rain or shine

Culture and politics in a Dutch–Belgian banking group after an international takeover[1]

Alexandra Bristow

Surrey Business School, University of Surrey

This case explores some of the consequences of the seemingly unstoppable drive for internationalisation for the workforce of a European banking group. Set in 2004, it tells the story of Roger, a student at a UK university, who joins a small unit in the banking group—the Dutch merchant bank Seers—on an internship designed to investigate the socio-cultural implications of the group's latest international acquisition. On the commencement of his internship, Roger immediately gets sucked into the tug of war between the Dutch and the Belgian parts of the group's merchant banking. As Roger's interview count grows, he develops an affinity for the Dutch side of the battle, which his Amsterdam colleagues see as a fight for economic rationality set against Belgian politicking. But when Roger is sent on a reconnaissance mission to Brussels, the Belgians have a different story to tell, which leads to the Group Headquarters back in the Netherlands. After a trip to the very top of the organisation and having been shown 'the big picture' by a Group CEO, how will Roger position his report at the end of the internship?

Roger, a business student at a UK university, was delighted to learn that he had been successful in obtaining an internship with the Dutch merchant bank Seers. He had heard of Seers as a small but highly prestigious investment house, famous for building long-term relationships with very rich clients, including members of

---

1 This case study is based, with very slight alterations, on a real-life story. All names of people and organisations have been changed to protect research participants.

the Dutch Royal family, and typically offering high returns on substantial deposits. He also knew that the bank was part of Ridder—a large Dutch banking group that a few years back had been involved in a reverse takeover with a formerly state-owned Belgian bank called Savant. After speaking to Gerda—a Dutch head of department at Seers who was going to be his immediate superior during the internship—Roger was hoping to use his time in Amsterdam to carry out research into the socio-cultural consequences of the international acquisition on Seers. The report that he would deliver to the bank at the end of his internship would then also form the basis of his degree project at university.

When Roger arrived in Amsterdam to start his placement, he was surprised to discover that Gerda had in the meantime left the company. Frank, her replacement, explained to Roger that Gerda had been 'forced out by the Belgians', because she had openly disagreed with the changes being pushed through from Brussels. 'They've put me in charge,' Frank told Roger, 'because I'm a Belgian, but I've actually lived in the Netherlands for over 20 years. I think they are hoping that I can keep the peace for a while, but my loyalty is with the Dutch.' Frank seemed very interested in Roger's proposed research topic and spent a while explaining that there were major cultural and political issues between the Dutch and the Belgian parts of the banking group. 'The reason for these issues is rooted in the histories of the Dutch and Belgian nations', he said to Roger: 'whereas the Dutch have built their empire through open fighting and have always directly resisted their enemies, the Belgians survived through surrender, diplomacy and back-stage politics. These different histories are still reflected in the different ways in which the Dutch and the Belgians do business.'

Frank then handed Roger a magazine. 'This is Seers' company newsletter—this particular edition came out shortly after the reverse takeover had taken place', he said. 'The picture—and the story—on the front page will tell you quite a lot about what's been going on here.' Roger looked at the newsletter. The cover had a large image of a knight triumphing over an evil-looking wizard. The knight seemed victorious, but the wizard was clearly only pretending to be defeated. In fact, on closer inspection the knight turned out to be a marionette doll, and it was the wizard who held the strings. The article next to this image was written in the form of a fairy tale and ran along similar lines. It related the story of an evil magician, who envied a neighbour's kingdom but could not defeat him in open battle. Eventually, the story went, the wizard had a cunning and devious plan and... surrendered. He then proceeded to poison his neighbour's mind with a secret potion so that he could gain control and slowly destroy the knight's kingdom. 'You see, Roger,' commented Frank,

> Savant had tried to take over Ridder a few times, but it hadn't worked. So they changed their plans and let themselves be taken over instead, but on such terms that it had effectively meant that the Belgians are now in charge. They are in charge of a lot of companies that had belonged to Ridder, including Seers. And they are destroying Seers because we are in competition to their own bit of merchant banking.

> They don't care that Seers is a lot more successful and profitable than Savant merchant banking, or that we've got an extremely loyal and extensive customer base and a highly distinct and reputable brand. They're only interested in politics and preserving their own bit of the company rather than rational economic thought. The latter comes much more naturally to the Dutch than the Belgians, I'm afraid.

Roger had not been expecting to come across such strength of feeling against Savant, but as he proceeded with interviews, informal conversations and observation, he realised that Frank's position was widely shared across Seers. Roger also could not help to begin to feel more personally involved with Seers' situation as he learnt more about the merchant bank. In many ways, it seemed to have a perfect organisational culture. Everybody was friendly, and there was a lot of good-natured humour and laughter in offices and corridors. People seemed to genuinely enjoy coming in to work. Colleagues went out into town to have lunch together and socialised after work as well. The hierarchy was quite flat and also informal—everyone from the trading floor to the CEO of Seers had the open-door policy (which was actually actively used) and had the power to circulate all-staff emails or call a meeting (which was occasionally used). Internal Seers meetings were sites of lively debate, with subordinates openly raising objections and superiors accepting criticisms. Personally, Roger felt that he was made very welcome from his very first day, being invited along to business meetings, training events and lunches. He was also surprised at how willing people were to take part in his research and how open they were in the interviews and conversations. Nobody turned down his request for interviews or refused to answer a question—if anything, Roger felt overwhelmed by information, and people kept turning up at his desk to say that they had heard about his study and wanted to take part in it.

He soon began to get an impression as to why there was so much interest in his research at Seers. It appeared that members of staff in Amsterdam were struggling to get their opinions heard and understood by their new Belgian 'masters'. After trying all kinds of channels of communication they were exasperated at being ignored and saw Roger's study as yet another option to try. Sometimes Roger even thought that he was actually running some sort of therapy sessions for the particularly disaffected. As his interviews and conversations progressed, he began to see the depth of unhappiness within Seers that was lurking just beneath the veneer of cheerfulness. Roger realised that his Amsterdam colleagues believed themselves to be not only in immediate danger of losing their jobs, but also persistently unfairly treated by management in Brussels.

Roger began to piece together parts of the Dutch side of the story. It was clear that colleagues in Savant were seen as quite different, and were neither liked nor trusted (yet this dislike and mistrust did not seem to apply to Frank or to a couple of other Belgians working in Amsterdam, who were treated as honorary Dutch). As Frank first pointed out, Savant Belgians were seen as secretive, backstage politicians, who carefully observed formal hierarchies and were largely driven by considerations of power and status, playing their cards close to their chests, spinning their own networks and excluding any outsiders (the Dutch in particular) from any relevant decision-making. Because of their own secret power games, they were apparently unwilling to engage in rational economic planning, feasibility studies or performance evaluation, could not bear to take open criticism in meetings, avoided putting decisions down in writing, often changed their minds on important subject matters, were ambiguous and unpredictable, instigated changes that lacked clear goals and directions and that were not properly prepared, set intentionally unrealistic targets and expectations to undermine Seers, and, perhaps most seriously, routinely and often grossly manipulated information—including key financial figures—to serve their own political ends. Alongside the above crimes, even the gastronomic behaviour in Savant was held up to scrutiny and often presented as the epitome of the importance of politics in daily business lives in Brussels. In particular, Savant Belgians were said to attribute tremendous importance to lunches, which often lasted as long as three hours and tended to incorporate large quantities of wine.

After a while, Roger started to wonder whether the Belgians would now be seen in a more friendly light by the Dutch if the whole process of change following the reverse takeover had been managed differently. As he watched and listened, Roger was getting convinced that the amount of Merlot consumed by the average Belgian between the hours of 12 and 15 on a working day would be less of an issue if it were not for the past few years of company history. In particular, it seemed strange to him that, even though the takeover itself had taken place 4 years before his internship, some very basic attempts at integration were only taking place now. 'They tried to instil fear in us by making us wait and guess,' one of Roger's interviewees said: 'suddenly, two years after the takeover, they announced that they were creating new international business lines, so we would have one Dutch–Belgian Merchant Banking, and they created a new CEO in Brussels to be in charge of that. Except that, you know,' the interviewee laughed,

> they did that without taking away the old structure, and they haven't specified the relationship between the old and the new structures. So there's now the CEO of Seers here in Amsterdam, and the CEO of Savant Commercial Banking in Brussels, and the new CEO of Merchant Banking, also in Brussels, and they're all fighting over who is in charge. Now it seems that the Brussels CEOs have won.

That victory, it appeared to Roger, took just under two more years, during which no further attempts at integration had been made. Then, just a few months before Roger's arrival, an event took place that colleagues at Seers referred to as 'the February presentation' (in the sort of way that people talked about 'Bloody Sunday', Roger thought).

One morning in February an urgent all-staff meeting was called at Seers. The CEO of Merchant Banking had arrived from Brussels—apparently unannounced—to deliver a presentation on 'The Future of Merchant Banking at

Ridder: the Road to Internationalisation'. Colleagues at Seers were surprised at this unexpected visit and somewhat unsettled, as it coincided with the absence of several senior Seers managers, including Gerda and the CEO of Seers, who had apparently been called to an important training event running simultaneously in Brussels. Nevertheless, the meeting room was full when the February presentation was delivered. In just half an hour, the Belgian CEO announced the imminent creation of a Single Legal and Booking Entity (SLBE), a single dealing room and the centralisation of mid- and back-office operations in Brussels. Effectively, this spelt the end of Seers. 'When he finished speaking, all hell broke loose,' said Janke, one of Roger's office mates at Seers,

> after a moment's silence, because everyone was so shocked, people got off their seats and were all talking and screaming and waving hands. They wanted to know what would happen to their jobs and what would happen to the company's clients and brand. They wanted to know why they had no notice of this happening and why no consultation or feasibility study had taken place. But the Belgian guy avoided giving us any direct answers. In fact, he told us that he was running late for another meeting and was gone inside five minutes. I'm surprised he managed to get out with his suit still intact!

The next day, when the missing senior managers came back to Seers, they went straight back to Brussels on hearing what had happened. They returned the following day bearing no good news—it seemed they were now powerless to stop the demise of Seers from happening. Later on that day came a phone call from Savant Information Systems Services in Brussels, requesting the Seers electronic risk management system to be shut down immediately in order to make way for the transfer of risk management functions to its Belgian counterpart. Gerda, Head of Risk Management at Seers, refused on the basis that it was impossible to stop the system without interrupting reporting to the Central Bank of the Netherlands, which remained a legal requirement for as long as Seers existed. 'They knew they were asking the impossible,' Frank told Roger: 'so everybody at Seers rightly interpreted the request as a power move by Brussels.'

Roger had been at Seers for about two weeks when he went to interview Hans, the Dutch CEO of the company. Like everybody else at Seers, Hans was very keen to get his views heard by Roger. 'It's not even the fact that they are shutting us down that has upset people so much,' he said.

> Here at Seers, we prefer the direct and open approach and we understand the economics of running a business. So we understand that sometimes in business you need to make harsh decisions, and we're ok with that. But it's the politicking, the back-stabbing, and the fact that they are destroying a thriving, very profitable business with an established, highly respected brand for purely political ends, and it doesn't make sense economically. And they are doing so in such secretive,

> devious ways that we can't stop them because we're not used to that sort of a game.

Hans paused and added:

> you know, after the February presentation it turned out that they hadn't even carried out an economic study of the proposed changes. They just hadn't evaluated them at all. After we insisted on having one done (we had to involve the Group Board to get our way on this), they did one, and it was full of basic mistakes and obvious bias. Even so, they were only able to show a total benefit of a maximum of 2 million Euros. This is nothing in terms of the profit we bring in each year.

Then Hans sighed.

> The worst thing is that they won't tell us exactly what is going to happen to people's jobs and when. From time to time they will call certain people over to Brussels and try to persuade them to move across, but it all seems a bit random and unstructured. People are living and working with this uncertainty, and, given that many of them are in charge of millions of Euros each day, this is not a good situation. If we didn't have such a strong company loyalty at Seers, I would be even more worried. But now all of us are job-hunting.

Hans paused again. 'This is why, Roger,' he said finally

> we need you to go to Brussels and bring us back some information. You are more likely to be seen as a neutral party, neither Dutch nor Belgian, carrying out research for a university degree. Anything you can find out would help us. Can you do that? You need to interview them anyway, don't you?

As Roger walked back to his office, he pondered how strange it was that he, a humble student intern, became a spy in this international job massacre. Partially, he was flattered, but he was also very worried. Could he carry it off and help Seers in any way? And should he even try—was he not meant to remain neutral as part of his study? However, he could not help sympathising with the Dutch. From everything he had learnt so far, his colleagues at Seers had been horribly treated. He knew that there was probably a Savant part of the story as well that could also make sense, but the Belgians now had to convince him. He walked to his computer and decided it was time to get in touch with Brussels.

Just then he noticed that he had a new email waiting for him. As he opened and read it, he could not believe his eyes—it was from Jean, Head of Risk Management at Savant, telling him that he had heard of Roger's research and was offering him an interview in a few days' time. 'Have they read my mind??!' Roger exclaimed out loud. 'I wouldn't put it past them,' said Janke at the next desk: 'I certainly wouldn't put it past them to have read your emails. They monitor everything around here.' Roger looked worried. 'He probably wants to talk to you because he wants to know what you've found out here in Amsterdam. Be careful what you say when you go to Brussels, Roger,' Janke added. Still somewhat bewildered, Roger wandered across to Frank's office. 'Ah', said Frank when he heard the news: 'I'm afraid it might have been my fault. When I was last in Brussels I might have mentioned your study and the fact that your final report would be going to the Group Executive Board.' 'It will?!' asked Roger: 'Why did you tell them that?' Frank smiled: 'To prepare the way,' and he winked at Roger.

The next few days were a whirlwind of phone conversations as Roger tried to set up more interviews for his visit to Brussels. He decided he would stay overnight and do two full days of interviewing before returning to Amsterdam. His schedule was filling up quickly—he soon learnt that the way to get interview requests accepted by Belgians was to mention other important Belgians he was already interviewing, as well as key Seers players that he had already interviewed in Amsterdam. Janke listened with a smile as Roger told the PA of the reluctant CEO of Commercial Banking that he had already interviewed the CEO of Seers and had a meeting set up with the CEO of Merchant Banking in Brussels at 3 pm on a Wednesday. 'My final report will be going to the Group Executive Board,' he added. 'One moment please,' said the PA. Then she returned: 'Mr Tournet will see you at 4 pm on Wednesday.' 'If you're not careful, Roger,' said Janke as Roger triumphantly put down the phone, 'you will turn into a Belgian yourself.'

A few days later, it was at last time to travel to Belgium. As he sat in the train, Roger felt nervous but determined. Unlike his colleagues at Seers, he did not have a job to lose—so what could the Belgians do to him? Yet he also decided that he would keep an open mind as much as possible. After all, he had only heard one part of the story so far.

Savant did not disappoint Roger's expectations of cultural differences. He noticed that everybody was a bit less smartly dressed than in Amsterdam, and, as he arrived at the headquarters at nine o'clock, he was nearly trampled in the stampede of the employees trying to get into the building. At the end of the working day, at five o'clock on the dot, a similar stampede joined in the exodus from work. This was very different from Seers, where there was an accepted flexibility in working hours and where people quite often stayed late at work to finish off various tasks of the day. Roger also noticed more ingrained hierarchy and power distance at Savant—superiors seemed to be treated much more formally and a strict meeting-by-appointment system was in operation. Roger also noticed that there appeared to be fewer female managers in Brussels, and, by contrast, mostly female PAs. At lunchtime, Roger was impressed by the quality of food in the company canteen, and yes, there were glasses of wine on every table around him. None of Roger's interviewees offered to accompany him to lunch however—he was clearly an outsider. He ate alone until he saw a couple of Seers managers, also on a visit from Amsterdam. They joined Roger with the typically Dutch trays of filled baguettes and glasses of milk, which markedly stood out against the Belgian tables laden with three-course meals and wine. 'You know, they call the Dutch 'babies' because we drink milk with lunch,' said one of the managers. 'Better a baby than a drunk,' responded the other: 'I don't know how they manage to do business during the rest of the day after all *that*.' Despite his feelings of loyalty towards Seers, Roger felt embarrassed by these remarks. He was worried that Belgian colleagues might have overheard the last comment and he thought that a bit more tact and flexibility would have been more helpful.

This made Roger think back to the interviews he had carried out that morning. Those interviews had turned out to be more work than he had expected, and certainly much more work than the interviews in Amsterdam. The problem was that the Belgians were reluctant to talk. Janke had been right—they were much more interested in listening. In fact, a lot of the time Roger had felt that he was the one being interviewed. The Belgians wanted to know as much as possible about Seers—dates, numbers, names, as well as opinions and rumours. They were prepared to trade some information but not to give it freely. The Dutch were right—the colleagues in Brussels seemed a lot more adept at politics.

To get any information out of the Belgian interviewees, Roger had to give something back. He tried to make guesses in reporting what he thought was already known or was the least damaging and personal. He made sure he maintained everybody's anonymity. He got some information back, but somehow he could not escape the feeling that he might have betrayed something or someone of Seers, and that there might be repercussions for Amsterdam. Despite the difficulties in gaining information, during his stay in Brussels he did begin to get the idea of the Belgian part of the story, although he was aware that it was a lot more limited than his view of the Dutch side. He began to see, for example, how differently the Dutch actions and behaviour were interpreted in Brussels and what detrimental effects this had on the communication and relationship between the two parts of the company. He realised, for example, that what the Dutch saw as direct, open and honest, the Belgians mostly interpreted as aggressive, rude and tactless; that they valued politeness, diplomacy and personal humility; that they believed in respect for authority and thought Dutch confrontational behaviour in meetings unacceptable. When Roger interviewed the CEO of Merchant Banking and asked him why colleagues at Seers were not given answers to their questions following the February presentation, the Belgian replied that he was so affronted by the personal attacks following his speech that he had to leave. 'Instead of discussing the actual event, they were extremely rude to me personally,' he said.

> They implied that I personally engineered this situation after months of planning because of some sort of covert jealousy of Seers. They did not want to know that the decision to centralise in Brussels had been made by the Executive Board at the Group level, and that I came to tell them about it as soon as I knew. If you want to verify that this was the case, you should speak to Gerard Van Doorn. He is the Group CEO for Strategy and he was responsible for the decision. He is Dutch and is based at the Group headquarters in Rotterdam.

Upon his return to Amsterdam, Roger decided to follow the above advice. He got in touch with Gerard's PA and was amazed to be given an appointment the very next day. First thing the following morning, he arrived at the tall, futuristic ivory-and-glass building that was the Group's headquarters. As he stepped inside the huge glass atrium, the outside town noise magically died away, and all around him was peace and beauty. He waited in the comfortable armchair at the reception, observing smartly-dressed people arriving for work and glass elevators moving quietly and swiftly between the building's many floors. Finally, he was asked to go up. 'He is on the 37th floor – it's the very last one,' the receptionist said helpfully. Slightly surprised that he was not going to be accompanied, Roger took one of the glass elevators to the top of the building. As he exited it, he was faced with a wide corridor laid with a thick, soft carpet; framed by white walls covered in abstract paintings and punctuated by broad, hardwood doors. Everything looked very expensive, but the corridor was completely silent. Roger noticed that most of the offices seemed empty. 'Nicolaas Zeeman, Group CFO', 'Matthijs Ronderdam, Group CEO Marketing', 'Renee Minous, Group CEO Operations', 'Vincent Wevers, President', Roger read the labels by the doors. If this is where the Group power resided, then where were most of its agents?

Finally, he came to a door that was open. A tall, grey-haired man rose from behind his desk to shake Roger's hand. 'You must be Roger. It's a pleasure to meet you. I'd heard of your study and was delighted that you wanted to come and talk to me.' Roger was pleased by the friendliness and flattered to have become so well-known. Yet he was determined not to become so easily seduced by the attention from the powerful. He was here to ask some difficult questions after all. So he told Gerard that he believed that Seers staff had been badly treated and asked for the rationale behind the decisions that had been made over the last few years. In response, Gerard motioned to Roger to come over to the window that faced inside the atrium from his office. Far below, Roger could see the tiny figures of company employees criss-crossing the reception area, little more than ants. 'You see, Roger,' Gerard said,

> we're right at the top here, and some people say we are so far removed that we don't care. This is not true. These people that you see far below, I know each one of them by name. But what we do get up here at the top is the big picture, which these people at the bottom don't get. We have the big picture and we have to make the decisions that we think are best for the whole of the Group in the long run. And, for banking right now, this means international growth—mostly through mergers and acquisitions—and internationalisation. It has been like that for quite a few years. So Seers and Savant might be deeply involved in their cultural Dutch–Belgian battles, but what they don't see is that we are involved in much bigger wars at the global level—with the British, and the Americans, and the Asian, and everybody else. I know that the Dutch in Seers complain about having to move to Brussels if they want to stay with the company. But we're not asking them to do anything

that we are not having to do ourselves. Did you notice that most of the offices in this corridor were empty? This is because members of the Executive Board are always abroad, fighting global battles for their employees. You were lucky to get an appointment with me so quickly, because today is my one-day-break from a month of non-stop travelling. Last night I came back from the States and tomorrow I'm off to Hong Kong, looking at the next possible merger. I hardly get to see my family once in a few weeks nowadays. So yes, personal sacrifices for the sake of the company are necessary and the Dutch at Seers have to accept that. International growth is essential if we are to survive as a Group and there are very likely to be further international acquisitions. So my advice to Seers would be 'accept that change is necessary, move with the times and make the most of the emerging opportunities'.

'It was nice meeting you, Roger', Gerard added when the interview was over, 'and I look forward to receiving your report.'

Back at Seers, Roger sat at his computer and pondered. He had accumulated a lot of information from over 50 in-depth interviews, and it was now time to start writing that report that was going to be read at all levels in Amsterdam, in Brussels and even at the Group headquarters. When he had just started his internship, Roger could not anticipate such exposure. Now he realised that what he said in the report was likely to affect the people he knew at Seers. Or would it? Had not the senior management already made up their minds? Whatever the case, he knew that people were waiting to hear what he had to say. He sighed and started to type.

About the author

 **Alexandra Bristow** is a Lecturer in Organisational Behaviour at the University of Surrey, UK, and is passionate about encouraging students to question and critique organisational realities. Alex's research is located within the field of critical management studies and currently focuses on the changing nature of academic work, identity and knowledge within the increasingly managerialist and neoliberalist global Higher Education context. Prior to taking up her position at Surrey, Alex was a PhD researcher at the Lancaster University Management School, UK. Her doctoral thesis, which investigated the work of academic journal editors, is a co-winner of the Academy of Management Best Dissertation Award (2011), in the Critical Management Studies Division.

Teaching notes for this case are available from Greenleaf Publishing. These are free of charge and available only to teaching staff. They can be requested by going to:
www.greenleaf-publishing.com/darkside2notes

13

'Alisha in Obesity-land'
Is food marketing the Mad Hatter?[1]

Sonya A. Grier
Kogod School of Business at American University, Washington, D.C., USA

Guillaume D. Johnson
Université Paris–Dauphine, France

The case explores the aggregate influence of corporate marketing practices on public health. It examines the topical issue of the role of targeted marketing strategies by the food and beverage industries in the obesity epidemic. Specifically, it engages a discussion about a significant yet overlooked dimension—that of targeted marketing to ethnic minority children. Although U.S. government reports readily cite the disproportionate rates of obesity among ethnic minority youth, limited attention is paid to understanding whether the factors that contribute to obesity among children in general may have an excessive impact on ethnic minority youth. However, research suggests that individual characteristics of minority youth (e.g., high media use, consumer

---

1 A first version of this case study was the winner of the 2010 Dark Side Case Writing Competition organized by the Critical Management Studies Division of the Academy of Management (AOM).

© HEC Montréal 2011. Reproduced with the permission of the HEC Montréal Case Centre. All rights reserved for all countries. Any translation or alteration in any form whatsoever is prohibited.

The *International Journal of Case Studies in Management* is published on-line (www.hec. ca/revuedecas/en), ISSN 1911-2599.

This case is intended to be used as the framework for an educational discussion and does not imply any judgement on the administrative situation presented. Deposited under number 9 10 2011 002 with the HEC Montréal Case Centre, 3000, chemin de la Côte-Sainte-Catherine, Montréal (Québec) Canada H3T 2A7.

orientation) and contextual characteristics (i.e., the amount and nature of the targeted food and beverage marketing) may contribute to disproportionate health outcomes. This case explores these issues and challenges the reader to specifically consider the potential effects of ethnically targeted food and beverage marketing to minority youth from an aggregate perspective, along with any responsibility of the food and beverage industry. At the same time, the case allows students to narrow their focus from the aggregate view to also consider the influence that the strategies of a particular company may have on the behaviours of specific target segments.

The case provides background on issues relevant to the obesity epidemic and targeted food marketing from the perspectives of both the general children's market and the ethnic minority child sub-segment. Specific corporate strategies and tactics are detailed. The case then describes individual and contextual considerations that may contribute to the excessive impact of target marketing on ethnic minority children. Corporate responses to the obesity epidemic in the form of corporate social responsibility (CSR) programs are summarized and broad mentions of policy attempts are made. The case ends with a summary of the central issue: In the debate over necessary interventions specifically related to food marketing, limited attention has been focused on children who are in groups at the highest risk for obesity. If, as Alisha's typical day suggests (in the introduction to the case), ethnic minority youth are exposed to more food marketing than other children, is there a need for targeted interventions related to food marketing in order to halt the obesity epidemic among ethnic minority children like Alisha?

Introduction

Imagine for a moment that you are a 12-year old African-American girl living in the inner-city of a major U.S. metropolis; your name is Alisha. Every day when you wake up, your mother has already left for work. You quickly brush your teeth, take a shower, get dressed and then pour yourself a bowl of Reese's Puffs cereal, humming the catchy rap from their website. You eat the cereal as you watch a new episode of your favourite morning TV program. The 30-minute show, sponsored by a candy brand, features the life of a young Black girl struggling with her adolescence. The program is interrupted four times for advertising purposes. Eighteen commercials are broadcast, more than half of them promoting food-related products such as soft drinks (e.g., 7UP, Sprite, Dr Pepper) or fast food (e.g., Domino's Pizza, Dunkin' Donuts, Wendy's).[2]

2　All examples are drawn from research and trade press articles describing actual marketing tactics used by specific companies and brands, including the following: http://www.reeses puffs.com/; Gabriel Packard, *U.S.: Unhealthy Food, Figures Feature in TV for Blacks – Study*, Inter Press Service, August 13, 2003, McDonald's Corporation, *What is McDonald's 365 Black?*, Kate MacArthur and Hillary Chura, "Urban Warfare: Hip-Hop and Street Savvy Are

At the end of the show, you rush to the corner of your street to catch the bus to school. After showing the driver your report card featuring the logo of the pizza store located opposite the school, you find a seat in the back. You are thinking of the conversation you and your mother had with the doctor during your check-up yesterday, and trying to understand what he said about you being "pre-diabetic" and needing to lose weight. Despite all your resolutions, your health is not getting better. Your weight is 135 lbs for 4 feet 7 inches and your Body Mass Index (BMI) of 31.4 indicates that you are obese. So are many of your classmates, friends and family members.

As you stare out the window, lost in thought, you notice billboard after billboard promoting alcoholic beverages, tobacco products, soft drinks and various fast-food items. You also see the shops shifting from fast-food outlets to liquor stores to fast-food outlets. On the 10 blocks that separate your house from the school, the bus passes about 10 food-related billboards (e.g., Coca-Cola, Burger King), eight fast-food outlets (e.g., Pizza Hut, Subway, Crown Fried Chicken) and one small corner store. Once at school, you give away the banana and drink the juice drink that your mother packed in your bag, and spend your pocket money earned from babysitting on chips and cookies from the school vending machines. At lunch you sometimes eat some of the food in the free school lunch, but more frequently buy a slice of pizza, a taco or a burger from the Taco-Bell outlet at the school canteen. You sit on the sidelines during the 30 minutes of afternoon gym class, as each movement of your body requires extra effort and you easily feel out of breath.

After school, you usually go to the library. Recently there was a photo-exhibition in honour of Black History Month that you thought was very cool. You noticed that the entire exhibition was funded by McDonald's. Walking to the bus stop from the library, you see a crowd of your friends gathered around a van, embellished with the Pepsi brand logo. You join in as the popular local DJs ask the youth to sing and rap for various Pepsi-labelled promotional items, and workers distribute free bottles of soda. After this, you take the bus home. You go inside, as your mother does not like you hanging outside when she is not home. As you wait for your mother, you either watch TV, play video games or surf on the Web.

Your favourite video game is Afro Samurai, an animated game mixing hip-hop and Japanese themes. You won this game as well as the gaming console at Church's Chicken, a fast-food outlet down the street. On the Internet, you and your mother recently joined a digital community, called "We Inspire," run by PepsiCo, where you share personal and inspirational thoughts. However, you can only access this website with your mother, and so more often you use your mobile via "Be Heard," a program supported by Coca-Cola and Church's Chicken, which lets you interact with your friends via inexpensive text messages. You are

Soda Marketers' Weapons in the Battle for Minority Kids," *Advertising Age,* 2000; Eric Bush, *Church's Chicken Teams w/Surge to Promote Afro Samurai,* 2009; Kenneth Hein, *Pepsi Program Targets African-American Moms*, 2009 [cited 2010 March 8th]; Mickey Alam Khan, *Coca-Cola Debuts Ambitious Mobile Push for Sprite*, May 18, 2009.

also a member of the recently launched Sprite mobile network and have encouraged more of your friends to join.

Your mother arrives home around 8:00 pm. Because of the lack of supermarkets in the neighbourhood as well as the absence of a car or reliable transportation to go to the closest one several miles away, she brings home a bucket of chicken from the Kentucky Fried Chicken (KFC) located one block away. She has bought a new flavour that you requested after seeing it advertised on TV and several neighbourhood billboards and bus shelters. After dinner, you go to your bedroom to watch your favourite evening TV show "Victoria Justice" while surfing on the Web and flipping through your mom's *Essence Magazine*. At 11:03 pm, you fall asleep and you miss your mother who comes in 30 minutes later to turn your TV and computer off.

Alisha is one of many overweight children around the world. Societies globally are debating what steps are necessary to halt the rates of childhood obesity that have been characterized as an "epidemic" and to decrease the related health, economic and social costs. Although lack of physical activity, parental feeding practices, the composition of school lunches and many other factors are recognized as important contributors to the epidemic, food marketing targeted to children has captured significant societal attention. Numerous policies and programs have been proposed and enacted by advocates, government agencies and food marketers. However, in the debate over necessary interventions specifically related to food marketing, limited attention has been focused on children like Alisha, who are in groups at the highest risk for obesity. If, as her typical day suggests, she is exposed to more food marketing than other children, is there a need for targeted interventions related to food marketing in order to halt the epidemic among ethnic minority children like Alisha?

The obesity epidemic

Background

Obesity[3] among children and adolescents[4] has become a major societal concern in developed as well as developing countries, including places where

---

3 The definition of obesity in children is having a body mass index or BMI level (which is calculated by dividing weight in kilograms by the square of height, in metres) that is at or above an age- and sex-specific cutoff point (the 95th percentile) on standard curves published by the Centers for Disease Control and Prevention (CDC). Overweight is defined as a BMI at or above the 85th percentile and lower than the 95th percentile (Flegal *et al.*, 2010).

4 The term "children" generally refers to ages 6 to 11, whereas "adolescents" and "teens" refer to youth 12 to 19 years old. Nevertheless, the present case study uses the terms "children" and "youth" to refer to both the child and adolescent categories, although we recognize they are not identical.

undernutrition and underweight have historically been issues. More than 100 million children worldwide are overweight (World Health Organization, 2009) and obesity has been characterized as an "epidemic" given that it is now a characteristic of populations, not only of individuals (World Health Organization, 2003). In the U.S., the prevalence of obesity has steadily increased over the past 30 years, creating a major public health challenge, as shown in Box 1.

Box 1 Obesity epidemic in the U.S.

- Overweight and obesity have increased among all age groups, tripling among children and adolescents since 1980 (Ogden *et al.*, 2006; Wang and Beydoun, 2007).
- In 2007–2008, nearly one-third of children and adolescents were overweight or obese (Flegal *et al.*, 2010; Ogden *et al.*, 2010).
- More than 60% of adults are overweight or obese, with one-third of adults being classified in the obese range.
- If the trends continue, in only 20 years it is expected that these rates of overweight and obesity will double among children and rates will reach almost 90% among American adults (Wang *et al.*, 2008).

Overweight and obesity are of societal concern given their association with serious chronic conditions and an increased risk of asthma, diabetes, cardiovascular disease (e.g., hypertension), sleep apnea and orthopedic complications (Caprio *et al.*, 2008). Many overweight and obese children are developing formerly "adult" diseases, including Type 2 diabetes and hypertension, and are at increased risk for heart disease, stroke, and some types of cancer. Excessive weight has many social, psychological, and economic consequences for both the affected individuals and for societies. The economic impact is especially salient in health-care costs. It is projected that medical expenditures attributed to overweight and obesity will increase from accounting for 9.1% of total U.S. medical expenditures (US$78.5 billion) in 1998 to accounting for one in every six dollars spent on health care by 2030, with costs ranging from US$860.7 to 956.9 billion (Wang *et al.*, 2008). Moreover, the current U.S. generation of children may have a shorter life expectancy than their parents if the obesity epidemic cannot be controlled.

Ethnic disparities in the obesity epidemic

Alisha is even more likely to be overweight than children in general, as obesity rates differ significantly by gender and ethnicity. Rates are generally higher for girls than boys, and for African-American and Hispanic children than white children (see Appendix 1). The statistics are most alarming for young African-American girls like Alisha. In 2007–2008, 46.3% of African-American girls between the ages of 12 and 19 were overweight or obese—the highest prevalence of any age group by gender or ethnicity (see Appendix 1). By comparison, 29.9% of

White adolescent girls were overweight or obese. It is projected that if current trends continue, the largest increases in overweight and obesity prevalence will be among Hispanic-American adolescents (a two-fold increase) and African-American teens (a 1.8-fold increase) (Wang *et al.*, 2008).

Despite the common assumption that ethnic disparities in obesity result from income differences, there is also variation in the association between socioeconomic status (SES) and obesity by ethnicity. Although obesity declines with parental SES among White children, the rates may increase with income or not reflect any consistent pattern among Black and Hispanic children (Ogden *et al.*, 2008). For example, among girls aged 10–17 years old, like Alisha, obesity rates were highest among African-American girls at the highest socioeconomic status level (Wang and Beydoun, 2007). Nonetheless, given the large numbers of Blacks and Hispanics that are of lower income, there may be stronger effects among lower income ethnic minority youth. These "obesity disparities" also exist among adults, as ethnic minority adults, especially women, also have higher rates of overweight and obesity than White adults (see Appendix 2). The epidemic is not new for ethnic minority populations, as high levels of obesity were documented in a 1985 government report on minority health, whereas the current obesity epidemic in the U.S. population was not recognized until the early nineties (Kumanyika, 2002). Some researchers argue that a lack of effective action has allowed the problem to balloon.

Obesity is just the beginning of health troubles for children like Alisha. She has almost a one-in-two chance of developing diabetes during her lifetime (Narayan *et al.*, 2003) and her life expectancy is already shorter than that of her mother (Olshanksy *et al.*, 2005). Alisha might well die before her 40s from a cardiovascular disease, as the occurrence of cardiovascular disease also reflects the ethnic disparities in obesity. Further, Box 2 shows how ethnic minority youths are more likely to develop diabetes than other children.

Box 2 Consequences of ethnic disparities in childhood obesity

- White boys born in 2000 have a 26.7% risk of being diagnosed with diabetes during their lifetime, while Hispanic and Black boys have a 45.4% and a 40.2% lifetime risk, respectively.
- White girls born in 2000 have a 31.2% risk of being diagnosed with diabetes during their lifetime, while Hispanic and Black girls have a 52.5% and a 49% lifetime risk, respectively.

As society searches for causes in order to stall the rise in obesity among children, many factors have been implicated and responsibility has been attributed to a variety of stakeholders. The basic cause of obesity is an imbalance between the amount of energy taken in through eating and drinking and the amount of energy expended through metabolism and physical activity. General cultural trends such as sedentary lifestyles, unhealthy dietary patterns, the prominence in the American diet of fast and convenience foods that are often of higher caloric and lower nutritional value, and related agricultural policies, are seen as important. Of the many presumed causes of the obesity epidemic, marketing by the food and beverage industry is among the most heavily criticized and debated. Researchers, advocates and government officials attribute the obesity epidemic to marketing factors such as the expanded availability of junk and fast food, increased portion sizes, relative food prices and, most often, food advertising. Issues of individual responsibility and the food industry's right to free speech as supported by the First Amendment often dampen serious consideration of intervention in marketing efforts directed to adults. However, society's concern for children has cast a harsh spotlight on food marketing targeted to children and adolescents.

Targeted food and drink marketing

Targeted marketing involves strategically talking to specific consumer groups—i.e., "target markets"—in a way that prompts them to think, feel and act in line with marketing objectives—usually product consumption. The strategies may influence awareness of specific products, stimulate the creation of meanings about those products, affect brand attitudes, provoke trial and contribute to food-related knowledge, beliefs and norms (Grier, 2009). Targeted marketing strategies are based on consumer research which explores the beliefs, attitudes and behaviours of target segments, how they respond to specific marketing tactics and how, when and where to best reach them with marketing efforts. Given that the industry is self-regulated, marketers themselves develop, transmit and enforce their own codes of practice regarding these activities.[5] The general youth market (comprised of both children and adolescents) and the ethnic minority youth markets reflect two overlapping target segments of importance to the food and drink industry.

Targeted marketing to children

Children and adolescents are attractive target markets for businesses. They have considerable and growing buying power, they influence parental purchases and they offer the opportunity to develop lifelong relationships and brand loyalty. Children and adolescents are also increasingly easy to reach and target given their heavy use of media and rapid adoption of new media technologies, such as the Internet and cell phones (Calvert, 2008; Larson and Story, 2008; McGinnis *et al.*, 2006). The children's market in the U.S. alone is now estimated at US$165 billion for purchases made with children's own money and US$200 billion when

5 See http://www.caru.org for additional information.

child-influenced purchases are included (Story and French, 2004). The food and beverage industry is arguably one of the sectors that has most benefited from this buying power. For example, cereal companies, historical targeters of children, spend more than US$156 million per year marketing to children (Harris *et al.*, 2009). A 2008 analysis of 44 food and drink companies by the U.S. Federal Trade Commission (FTC) found that marketers spent approximately US$1.6 billion to promote food and beverages to children aged 2-17 (FTC, 2008). The US$1.6 billion represented 17% of the spending on these specific products, yet may also underestimate spending. Additional expenditures through unmeasured media exposure targeted to youth such as in-school and event marketing, sampling and package design may further increase this amount. Marketing may be targeted to children as young as two years old, as strategies attempt to get children to ask their parents to buy advertised foods and beverages for them (Larson and Story, 2008; McGinnis *et al.*, 2006). Box 3 highlights the evolution of targeted marketing to children.

Box 3 From the Mickey Mouse Club to the school

Marketing to children has come a long way since the 1950s when marketers began to embed promotional messages in child-oriented TV shows such as *The Mickey Mouse Club*. Today, marketers use a multitude of creative and diverse strategies to target children and adolescents. In addition to traditional TV advertising, marketers make frequent use of digital marketing, licensed characters, outdoor advertising on billboards or transit, customized packaging, product placement in entertainment, youth-oriented sales promotions and loyalty programs (Hastings *et al.*, 2003). Stealth marketing techniques, such as strategically provoking word-of-mouth among peers, are also increasingly used in lieu of more traditional, visible approaches. Marketers may also infiltrate social networks or create their own, or place promotional messages in music and video games. Some argue that these newer techniques may be especially influential since they may not be recognized as advertising (Grier and Kumanyika, 2010).

School marketing has become its own industry, with companies providing needed financial support and other resources to cash-strapped schools in exchange for exposure to the captive audience of students. School marketing involves a variety of strategies and tactics including:

• Marketing research; e.g., surveys and tracking student Internet usage;
• Indirect promotions; e.g., corporate sponsorship of curricula or report cards and corporate-sponsored contests such as free pizza for reading a certain number of books;
• Direct promotions; e.g., advertising on book covers, in-school posters or sampling;
• Product sales; e.g., pouring contracts with soft drinks or contracts allowing fast-food franchises to sell food in school cafeterias (U.S. General Accounting Office, 2000);
• Channel One, an in-school TV channel with a 10-minute news program and two minutes of ads, is in 80% of all classrooms (U.S. General Accounting Office, 2000).

Targeted marketing to ethnic minority children

Marketers reach African-American and Hispanic children like Alisha with their general youth targeting efforts, but also design strategies specifically to reach these groups. Although children and adolescents in the U.S. tend to live more ethnically integrated lives than their parents and grandparents did, there are characteristics that make them identifiable and especially attractive targets within the general youth category. In the U.S., ethnic minorities such as African-Americans and Hispanics are crucial to the viability of food and beverage marketers, as they comprise the fastest-growing segments of the youth population (Frey, 2003; Humphreys, 2006; Zhou, 1997). Ethnic minorities are predicted to comprise almost half of all American youth by 2050 (U.S. Census, 2008). Ethnic minority families are also growing at a faster rate than the total population and are expected to comprise more than half of families with children by 2025 (Nielsen Company, 2009). A 2004 study showed that most spending on ethnic target marketing is geared toward Hispanics and African-Americans (totals of US$3.9 billion and US$1.7 billion respectively) (Huang, 2006). In 2008, the buying power of Hispanics was US$951 billion and US$913.1 billion for African-Americans, amounts that have steadily increased (Humphries, 2008). A study of kids aged 6–14 found that the yearly "income" (comprised of lunch money, allowance, gifts, earned income and other money) for African-Americans was US$1,549 and US$1,192 for Hispanics (vs. US$1,644 for all children and US$1,811 for White children) (Nickolodeon and Group, 2006). As a Nielsen vice-president noted, "While some companies have multicultural marketing initiatives in place today, by 2020, multi-cultural marketing will be a necessity—rather than an option—for doing business. This shift will impact product selections, product flavours, and the methods marketers use to reach their new target audiences" (Nielsen Company, 2009).

Marketers are aware that ethnic minority youth are heavy consumers of soda, fast food, candy and snack products. Food and beverage advertising expenditures represent a significant proportion of overall ethnically targeted marketing. For example, Coca-Cola re-established a dedicated African-American marketing group in 2006, that includes five people who also work on programs targeting Hispanic Americans and is making efforts to better connect with "key consumers, including teens, moms and multicultural consumers" (Zmuda, 2009a; Zmuda, 2009b). In 2009, ad spending on Spanish-language and African-American media fared better than the overall ad market, with quick-service restaurants as the top-spending category for both. These "fast-food" restaurants increased ad spending by 13.9% in Spanish-language media and 19.2% in African-American media (Bachman, 2010).

The strategies marketers use to target ethnic minority youth include those used to reach youth in general, as well as appeals related to some aspect of ethnic identity, beliefs or behaviours. Marketers use popular ethnic celebrities, music, ethnic symbols and cues and cultural values, beliefs and norms to promote the consumption of specific food products. Indeed, research shows that Black and Hispanic consumers are more likely to pay more attention to and identify with and trust spokespersons of similar ethnicity, and to have more positive attitudes and purchase intentions towards a brand when it features ethnic cues (Appiah, 2001). Box 4 presents examples of food marketing targeted towards minority youth.

Box 4 Examples of food and beverage marketing targeted to minority youth

'Sprite Yard'

In 2007, Coca-Cola's Sprite unveiled the "Sprite Yard" program for mobile handsets, to interact with its "mostly African American youth target audience." This program supports interacting with others via texting, allows picture sharing and downloading, and sends users company information (Khan, 2007). Sprite is one of the youngest brands in Coca-Cola's portfolio, with about 54% of consumers under age 24 and a consumer base that is about 30% African American and 15% Hispanic (MacArthur and Neff, 2004).

'365 Black'

This McDonald's campaign promotes a 365-days-a-year celebration of African-American culture through ads that feature African-American celebrities such as Venus Williams, sponsorship of music festivals and posters in its fast-food outlets. The program also distributes Black history booklets in schools in collaboration with Coca-Cola and supports community events including an academic achievement program for Black middle-school students and a Black college tour (McDonalds Corporation).

Pepsi

Pepsi used hip-hop celebrity Busta Rhymes to increase relevance and awareness of Mountain Dew and Code Red to urban consumers, because, as Charlee Taylor-Hines, director of urban and ethnic marketing for Pepsi, noted, "Among African-American and Latino youth, celebrity power is very compelling." Furthermore, this ad campaign was broadcast on radio, as ethnic minority youth spend more time with radio than the rest of the population. Pepsi reported that the results of their campaign led to "all-time highs in awareness and conversion of the two brands among African Americans and Latinos" (Radio Advertising Bureau, 2010).

'Fast-food marketing'

A 2011 study of fast-food marketing to youth concluded that in addition to targeting children and youth in general, fast-food marketing specifically targets Hispanic and African-American children and teens with TV advertising, targeted websites and banner ads. The study noted that African-American children and teens see at least 50% more fast-food ads than other children and teens (Harris et al., 2010).

Despite the recognition in major governmental reports that ethnic minority youth are at a higher risk for obesity, targeted marketing efforts toward this audience are rarely discussed at the same level of detail or focus as efforts targeted toward children in general.[6] One reason may be a lack of detailed information.

---

6   The term "ethnic minority youth" is used here to refer to the focal groups of interest, Black and Hispanic youth. Nonetheless, it is acknowledged that, in general use, this term may also refer to other groups (e.g., Asian Americans and Native Americans).

The amounts spent to target ethnic minority children specifically are not publicly available and individual companies do not generally report their ethnically targeted expenditures. The aforementioned analysis of food marketing expenditures aimed at children by the FTC did not report the data at this level of detail. A 2006 joint Health and Human Services and FTC workshop on *Marketing, Self-Regulation, and Childhood Obesity* brought together representatives from food and beverage companies, medical and nutrition experts, consumer groups and advertising specialists for an open discussion on industry self-regulation concerning the marketing of food and beverages to children. Although the disproportionate rates of obesity and the potential for different exposure to marketing efforts relative to White children was noted, discussion of ethnic group-specific challenges was absent when the discussion turned to industry self-regulatory solutions. In response to a question regarding how ethnic differences might affect self-regulatory options, the three panellists who responded each described a lack of ethnic group-specific knowledge or tradition of focus (Lascoutx, 2005; Miller, 2005; Montgomery, 2005).

There is also limited academic research on marketing strategies targeted to ethnic minority youth. For example, a systematic review on the effects of food promotion to children (Hastings *et al.*, 2003) examined over 100 articles, but fewer than five of the reviewed articles examined effects among ethnic minority children, and most of this research was more than 10 to 15 years old. Despite the limited academic research, there is a large commercial industry that conducts market research on ethnic minority youth to support the development of targeted marketing strategies.

As the details of Alisha's day suggest, ethnic minority youth may be likely to be exposed to more food and beverage advertising. Children like Alisha see and respond not only to marketing targeted specifically to ethnic minority children and to children in general, but also to marketing based on ethnic appeals aimed at adults and marketing targeted to the general population. Consider the Pepsi program targeting African-American mothers through a digital community that Alisha participates in with her mom. The effort serves as the cornerstone of Pepsi's African-American marketing outreach for 2010 utilizing Facebook and print ads in Black magazines (e.g., *Essence* magazine), featuring popular Black actresses (e.g., Queen Latifah, Taraji P. Henson and Raven Simone) reflecting on their love for their mothers (Hein, 2009).

Some researchers, advocates and public health proponents argue that interventions related to food marketing targeted to youth must explicitly consider ethnic minority youth who are most affected by the obesity epidemic. Some note the different cultural contexts such as the "normative" presence of obesity in the community and related acceptance of larger body sizes among ethnic minorities (Colabianchi *et al.*, 2006; Kumanyika and Grier, 2006). Other researchers note that certain individual and contextual characteristics of ethnic minority youth, including access to healthy foods, language ability, marketplace experience and marketplace segregation, may interact with marketing strategies and make their impact on minority youth even stronger than on children in general (Grier and Kumanyika, 2008; Penaloza, 1994). Three such factors are: (1) levels of media usage; (2) content of targeted marketing; and (3) receptiveness to targeted marketing (Grier and Kumanyika, 2008).

The Kaiser Family Foundation conducts a nationwide periodic study of media use among American youth ages 8 to18. The studies examine children's media use across various media, including TV, computers, video games, music, print, cell phones and movies. Results of the 2009 study showed that Black and Hispanic youth average about 13 hours of media exposure daily, compared to about 8.5 hours among White youth (Rideout *et al.*, 2010) (see Appendix 3 for specific differences in media use by ethnic groups). Although Black and Hispanic youth also spent more time with media than White youth in the 2004 study, these recent figures reflect significant growth in ethnic-related differences in media use over the past five years (see Appendix 4). The study also found that fewer Black and Hispanic youth report having rules about the content of the media they use than White children. Interestingly, the ethnic differences in media use hold up even after controlling for other demographic factors such as age, parent education or whether the child is from a single- or two-parent family. This heavy media usage also extends to certain digital media. For example, 2.5 million Hispanic teens aged 12–17 have a mobile phone and their usage is expected to grow at a rate of two to three times that of the overall U.S. teen market over the next five years (Grier, 2009). Further, ethnic minority youths' use of specific mobile tools such as text messaging has been described as "the core of successful mobile marketing" due to higher rates of usage than the general population (Briabe Media, 2007).

Levels of media exposure are of interest because repeated exposure can increase awareness of specific products, attach meanings to those products, affect brand attitudes, shape food-related norms and contribute to people's receptivity to marketing efforts (Hornik, 2002). Research on the relationship between media usage and obesity shows that increased media usage, especially TV, is associated with viewers eating and weighing more. This relationship is driven, at least in part, by increased consumption of frequently advertised high-calorie foods (Escobar-Chaves and Anderson, 2008; Wiecha *et al.*, 2006). For example, a study found that the odds of being overweight were almost five times greater for youth aged 10 to 15 who viewed five hours of TV per day vs. those who viewed two or less hours. Further, given their high levels of media consumption, ethnic minority youth consumers are an easily accessible target, a point that marketers understand and utilize in their strategies.

The content of targeted marketing

African-American and Hispanic youth likely encounter more food marketing that promotes less healthful foods and is less likely to support positive nutrition. A review of the marketing strategies over a 14-year period (1992–2006) to which African Americans were exposed as compared to White Americans identified 20 academic articles that consistently demonstrated that the most frequently promoted and most accessible products were high-calorie and low-nutrition foods and beverages (Grier and Kumanyika, 2008). For example, the TV shows most watched by African Americans have more food commercials that promote candy, soda and snacks than general prime-time shows (Henderson and Kelly, 2005; Triodkar and Jain, 2003). One study found that African Americans aged 12–17 view 14% more food product advertisements than their White peers—a difference that may have been even larger if the greater amount of time African-American adolescents spend watching television were considered (Powell *et al.*, 2007b). Ads with Black characters are also more likely to promote convenience and fast foods and less likely to include overweight characters or foods consistent with dietary recommendations (Harrison, 2006). Analyses of in-store and outdoor advertising have also found significantly greater promotion of less-healthful foods in African-American and Hispanic communities relative to White communities (Hillier *et al.*, 2009; Lewis *et al.*, 2005; Yancey *et al.*, 2009).

Minority youth are also exposed to similarly unhealthy strategies near and within their schools. Youth with more fast-food restaurants around their schools or with fewer supermarkets in their neighbourhoods are more likely to over-consume unhealthy food and to be overweight or obese (Davis and Carpenter, 2009; Powell *et al.*, 2007a) and both situations are more common for Black and Hispanic youth. Commercialism in schools may also have a significant negative impact on ethnic minorities. Although limited research focuses specifically on ethnic minority youth, the research that does exist characterizes the "obesegenicity" of the marketing environment in which minority youth live, learn and play as unlikely to support healthy eating. Researchers argue that without environmental changes, such as in corporate marketing practices, the effectiveness of solutions targeting individual change (e.g., dietary habits) will be limited or nonexistent (Grier and Kumanyika, 2008; Hillier *et al.*, 2009; Kumanyika and Grier, 2006; Larson *et al.*, 2009; Yancey *et al.*, 2009).

Targeted marketing receptiveness

Black and Hispanic youth are viewed by marketers as heavily consumer oriented and trendsetters. As the Coca-Cola assistant VP of African-American marketing noted in an interview in *Ad Age,* "teens really are the future of America, and African-American teens, in particular, have proven to be trendsetters in the U.S. Their ability to shape culture is really critical." Surveys have found that minority youth are more interested in, positive towards and influenced by media and marketing than White youth (Korzenny *et al.*, 2006). Furthermore, they are viewed as willing to try new products and receptive to companies that do good for their communities, which suggests that the numerous corporate sponsorships and support of ethnic minority cultural institutions may be quite effective (Korzenny *et al.*, 2006). Research also suggests that ethnic minority youth may be more positive towards marketing targeted to them on the basis of their ethnicity than majority youth (Appiah, 2001).

Targeted food and beverage marketing and corporate social responsibility

The targeted marketing strategies and tactics of the food and beverage industry directed towards children have been criticized by diverse organizations worldwide, including government agencies, NGOs, medical associations, scholars, ethicists and parents' councils. While some argue for government oversight and intervention, others say increased parental responsibility or increased media literacy is key to helping children navigate food marketing and hinder any negative effects. Various members of Congress have issued statements reflecting their concern (Harkin, 2007; Markey, 2007). The FTC, the Federal Communications Commission (FCC) and other government agencies have conducted hearings, issued reports on the topic and convened an inter-governmental Task Force on Media and Childhood Obesity (FTC, 2008; Holt, 2007). In 2004, the Institute of Medicine (IOM), in response to a Congressional directive, conducted a review of the role of food marketing as a contributing factor to childhood obesity (McGinnis et al., 2006). Box 5 presents a summary of the results of this report.[7] The IOM noted the disproportionate rates of obesity among ethnic minority groups and cited a need for additional empirical evidence to support concerns that food marketers disproportionately target these groups.

Box 5 IOM Report

The IOM Report, released in 2006, determined that food and drink advertising targeted at children influences their product preferences, requests and what they eat. The report also concluded that "food and beverage marketing practices geared to children and youth are out of balance with healthful diets, and contribute to an environment that puts their health at risk," and that "food and beverage companies, restaurants, and marketers have underutilized potential to devote creativity and resources to develop and promote food, beverages and meals that support healthful diets for children and youth" (McGinnis et al., 2006).

Since the industry is self-regulated, marketers themselves enforce their own codes of practice regarding their activities. In response to being put in the "hot seat" by the IOM report, food and beverage companies developed guidelines

---

7 See http://www.nap.edu/openbook.php?record_id=11514 to review the full report.

individually and in concert with each other. A major response was the launch of the Children's Food and Beverage Advertising Initiative (CFBAI) by the council of Better Business Bureaus (BBB) in November 2006 as a "transparent and accountable advertising self-regulation mechanism" (Council of Better Business Bureaus, 2004). The CFBAI lists membership from many of the nation's largest food and beverage companies. The initiative "is designed to shift the mix of advertising messaging to children to encourage healthier dietary choices and healthy lifestyles" (Council of Better Business Bureaus, 2004). Some company actions suggest that they have integrated societal concerns about obesity into their corporate social responsibility (CSR) programs to drive long-term corporate growth (Herrick, 2009). For example, both Kraft Foods and Pepsi created their own umbrella branding for healthier products (Sensible Solution and Smart Spot respectively) in order to cultivate consumer trust and brand value through appeals to choice, provision of information and adherence to government dietary guidelines (Herrick, 2009).

Some observers applaud the actions taken by corporations in response to the obesity epidemic. For example, at a 2005 summit on "Health, Nutrition and Obesity," then-governor of California Arnold Schwarzenegger awarded the distinction of "Honor Roll" to Kraft Foods Inc. This distinction was the result of Kraft's commitment to modifying its marketing strategies towards children (e.g., eliminating in-school advertising of junk food, not advertising to children under age six and advertising to children under age 12 only products that meet specific nutrition criteria) (Kraft Foods Inc., 2010). Similarly, the agreement signed by the Alliance for a Healthier Generation with the major companies of the beverage industry such as Coca-Cola, PepsiCo and Dr Pepper Snapple Group (formerly Cadbury Schweppes) has created an 88% reduction in beverage calories shipped to U.S. schools since 2004 (Alliance for a Healthier Generation, 2010). This reduction is seen as making schools, where children drink and eat almost half of their daily calories, healthier environments (Lavizzo-Mourey, 2010).

Other observers have criticized these CSR initiatives for focusing the debate on "good" versus "bad" individual lifestyles, which frames obesity as based on rational consumer choices between the vast varieties of products available in the marketplace (Herrick, 2009; Hornik, 2002). From this perspective, CSR actions imply that youth and other individuals such as parents and teachers are primarily to blame for unhealthy lifestyles (Ajuha, 2005). These critics consider that CSR programs, by favouring an individualized explanation of health status, overlook the social determinants of poor health and hold the potential to undermine wider agendas to address environmental and structural contributors to the obesity epidemic (Herrick, 2009).

In 2009, Children Now, an advocacy organization, commissioned an independent evaluation of the CFBAI and its impact on children's television food marketing environment (Kunkel *et al.*, 2009). The study concluded: "The Children's Food and Beverage Advertising Initiative has not improved the overall nutritional quality of ads targeting children. Moreover, the food and beverage industry has failed to meet the Institute of Medicine's principal recommendation to voluntarily shift the balance of children's food marketing away from low-nutrient, high-density foods to advertising strategies that promote healthier foods, beverages, and meal options." Similarly, a recent study of the amount and nutritional content of cereal advertising to children on television found that the breakfast cereals that most frequently and aggressively target children are those that are least healthy, despite being noted as "better-for-you" choices according to the CFBAI (Harris *et al.*, 2009). The one ethnically targeted cereal that was identified (based on the marketing tactics), Reese's Puffs, received the worst nutritional rating of all the cereals.

In March 2010, the Center for Science in the Public Interest released a report card that rates food, restaurant and entertainment companies' policies on food marketing targeting children (Wootan, 2010). Amongst the 128 companies evaluated, three-quarters obtained an "F" for having a weak marketing policy or none at all. Some advocates argue that since not all food and beverage marketers are involved in the initiative, the program may not have the necessary population impact. The authors conclude that "without more significant progress in the next two years, the country will need to rely on government regulation, rather than self-regulation, as the means to address food marketing to children" (Wootan, 2010). An April 2011 study commissioned to examine the five-year progress of private- and public-sector stakeholders in meeting the IOM report recommendations found that none of the key stakeholder groups had made extensive progress. The study noted that while some progress had been made by food and beverage companies and schools, limited progress was made by restaurants, trade industry associations, media and entertainment companies and government (Kraak *et al.*, 2011).

Some food and beverage companies have implemented CSR campaigns directed at minorities, often aimed at influencing individual behaviour. For example, Coca-Cola's *Vida Activa* initiative provides dedicated health advice to the Latino community (Herrick, 2009). Similarly, Kraft and the National Latino Children's Institute have developed *Salsa, Sabor y Salud*. This wellness program aims to bring a healthy lifestyle to Latino families with children of 12 and younger by creating awareness about healthier food choices and promoting physical activities (National Latino Children's Institute, 2004). In 2007, *Salsa, Sabor y Salud* received the American Dietetic Association/American Dietetic Association Foundation Presidents' Circle Award for Best Nutrition Education (National Latino Children's Institute, 2004). Food and beverage companies also support significant African-American-oriented community organizations and policy-oriented agencies such as the Congressional Black Caucus Foundation (CBCF), as presented in Box 6. However, within the societal focus on food marketing to children, interventions focused on the potential for excess or differential effects of ethnically targeted food marketing on obesity among ethnic minority youth have been absent.

Box 6 The CBCF and the food industry

The CBCF is a non-profit organization linked to the Congressional Black Caucus (CBC), which is comprised of the majority of Black members of the United States Congress. The CBCF aims to "help disadvantaged African-Americans by providing scholarships and internships to students, researching policy and holding seminars on topics like healthy living" (Lipton and Lichtblau, 2010). The food and beverage industry is the fourth largest donor of this organization (up to US$3.7 million), behind the makers of drugs and medical devices (up to US$7.8 million), the alcohol and tobacco industry (up to US$3.9 million) and the finance and lending industry (up to US$3.7 million) (Lipton and Lichtblau, 2010).

Some observers have argued that these donations are made in order to influence the votes of CBC members on related issues. For instance, the caucus split over the possible ban of menthol cigarettes (bought by 75% of Black smokers) that might play a role in the disproportionate share of smoking-related cancer among African Americans, but whose producers are some of the historical donors (Saul, 2008). However, others emphasize that economic realities drive the need for corporate support. As the chief executive of the foundation, Elsie L. Scott, acknowledged: "Black people gamble. Black people smoke. Black people drink. And so if these companies want to take some of the money they've earned off of our people and give it to us to support good causes, then we take it" (Lipton and Lichtblau, 2010).

Societal recognition of the role that the "obesogenic" environment may play in perpetuating the childhood obesity epidemic (Wang *et al.*, 2008) increases the call for solutions that address environmental factors in addition to individual behaviour. Stakeholders emphasize the need for strong collaboration among the public and private sectors in order to develop creative solutions having the power to effect large-scale change. Consistent with this view, the U.S. president, Barack Obama, announced on February 9, 2010, the creation of a childhood obesity task force (Eggerton, 2010). This task force, which includes the heads of the Departments of Interior, Agriculture, Health and Human Services, and Education, and the Office of Management and Budget, will develop a plan to overcome childhood obesity through coordinated federal responses. This task force comes in addition to First Lady Michelle Obama's national initiative "Let's Move," launched in January 2010. This program encourages the involvement of actors from every sector (i.e., the public, non-profit and private sectors, as well as parents and youth). The four pillars of the campaign are: empowering parents and caregivers; providing healthy food in schools; improving access to healthy and affordable foods; and increasing physical activity.[8]

While launching her project, Mrs. Obama acknowledged the ethnic disparities within childhood obesity, mentioned the problem of "food deserts" (i.e., neighbourhoods that lack a full-service grocery store) and toured the Fresh Grocer supermarket in North Philadelphia (Let's Move, 2010). This US$15 million store

---

8 See http://www.letsmove.gov/ to read more about the campaign.

opened in December 2009 in a predominantly Black neighbourhood that had been without a grocery store for more than a decade. It led to the creation of 270 jobs and has a 96% minority workforce (Let's Move, 2010). However, there was no broader mention of ethnically targeted marketing strategies, a point noted by observers (Nestle, 2010).

In addition to action at the federal level, states and local communities can also become involved in obesity prevention efforts that seek to influence food marketing strategies to children. Many states have consumer protection laws and state attorneys general can use this authority to address marketing practices that involve health (NPLAN, 2010). Thus, specific marketing-related policy tools are also being explored to address obesity at not only the federal, but also state and local levels. Menu labelling bills, taxes on sodas and fast-food moratoriums such as that seen in Los Angeles are but a few of the approaches designed to address the issue (Chaufan *et al.*, 2009; Powell and Chaloupka, 2009; Severson, 2008; Simon *et al.*, 2008; Sturm and Cohen, 2009). Still, it is unclear how policy solutions will affect ethnic minorities, as most research has not examined the effects of such interventions on minority youth.

Conclusion

As American society continues to debate the role of food marketing to children and appropriate interventions, it is unclear what effects developed programs and policies will have on children like Alisha who are the hardest hit by the obesity epidemic and who represent a growing proportion of the U.S. population. The absence of a focus on ethnically targeted food marketing, in particular, seems to fit with Alice in Wonderland's response to the Mad Hatter's offer of tea: "I've had nothing yet, so I can't take more." However, those who argue for this focus seem to echo the Mad Hatter's response: "You mean you can't take less; it's very easy to take more than nothing." As the fates of children like Alisha hang in the balance, the question remains: Is "nothing" or "more" the appropriate response for food marketers with regard to focused attention towards halting the epidemic among ethnic minority children?

Appendix 1: Prevalence of obesity and overweight among U.S. children by age, ethnicity and gender 2007–2008[9]

	Gender	Age	White American	African American	Hispanic American
Prevalence of obesity (BMI > 95th percentile of the CDC growth charts)	Boys	2 to 5	6.6	11.1	17.8
		6 to 11	20.5	17.7	28.3
		12 to 19	16.7	19.8	25.5
	Girls	2 to 5	12.0	11.7	10.4
		6 to 11	17.4	21.2	21.9
		12 to 19	14.5	29.2	17.5
Prevalence of overweight (BMI > 85th percentile of the CDC growth charts)	Boys	2 to 5	15.6	28.1	30.7
		6 to 11	34.6	36.4	43.7
		12 to 19	32.6	33.0	42.7
	Girls	2 to 5	19.5	23.9	24.3
		6 to 11	34.3	38.9	41.5
		12 to 19	29.9	46.3	39.7

Appendix 2: Prevalence of among U.S. adults (aged 20 years or older) by ethnicity and gender 1999–2008[10]

	Gender	White American	African American	Hispanic American
Prevalence of obesity (BMI > 30)	Men	31.9	37.3	34.3
	Women	33.0	49.6	43.0
Prevalence of overweight (BMI > 25)	Men	72.6	68.5	79.3
	Women	61.2	78.2	76.1

9   Appendix 1 is adapted from the results of Ogden *et al.* (2010).
10   Appendix 2 is adapted from Flegal *et al.* (2010).

Appendix 3: Total media exposure among U.S. youth (8–18) by ethnicity 2009[11]

	Media	White American	African American	Hispanic American
	TV content	3:36	5:54	5:21
	Music/Audio	1:56	3:00	3:06
In a typical day, average amount of time youth (8–18) spent with:	Computer	1:17	1:24	1:49
	Video games	:56	1:25	1:35
	Print	:39	:33	:34
	Movies	:13	:43	:33
Total Media Exposure		8:36	12:59	13:00

Appendix 4: Media exposure over time among U.S. youth (8–18) by ethnicity and platform[12]

Media	White American			African American			Hispanic American		
	change	2009	2004	change	2009	2004	change	2009	2004
Computer	+:15	1:17	1:02	+:32	1:24	:52	+:55	1:49	:54
Music/Audio	+:15	1:56	1:41	+1:17	3:00	1:43	+1:27	3:08	1:41
Video games (total)	+:10	:56	:46	+:21	1:25	1:04	+:42	1:35	:53
Console video games	+:02	:32	:30	−:08	:32	:40	+:11	:45	:34
Handheld video games	+:09	:24	:15	+:29	:53	:24	+:30	:50	:20
TV content (total)	+:06	3:36	3:30	+:49	5:54	5:05	+1:13	5:21	4:08
Live TV	−:31	2:14	2:45	−:42	3:23	4:05	−:15	3:08	3:23
Videos/DVDs	−:07	:27	:34	+:01	:35	:34	+:08	:36	:28
Pre-recorded TV	−:02	:09	:11	−:12	:14	:26	−:10	:07	:17

11 Appendix 3 is adapted from Rideout *et al.* (2010).
12 Appendix 4 is adapted from Rideout *et al.* (2010).

	White American			African American			Hispanic American		
Media	change	2009	2004	change	2009	2004	change	2009	2004
On Demand		:11	–		:21	–		:11	–
TV on other platforms		:35	–		1:21	–		1:18	–
Print	–:03	:39	:42	–:05	:33	:38	–:13	:34	:47
Movies	–:04	:13	:17	–:05	:43	:48	+:04	:33	:29
Total Media Exposure	+:38	8:36	7:58	+2:49	12:59	10:10	+4:08	13:00	8:52

Bibliography

Ajuha, Anjana (2005). "Obesity: Don't Swallow Everything You're Told," *Times Online* [online], [March 8th, 2010]. http://www.timesonline.co.uk/tol/life_and_style/article532129.ece.

Alliance for a Healthier Generation (2010). "Beverage Industry Delivers on Commitment to Remove Regular Soft Drinks in Schools, Driving 88% Decline in Calories," [online], [March 10, 2010]. http://www.healthiergeneration.org/media.aspx?id=4399.

Appiah, Osei (2001). "Ethnic Identification on Adolescents' Evaluations of Advertisements," *Journal of Advertising Research,* Vol. 41, No. 5, p. 7-22.

Bachman, Katy (2010). "Multicultural Ad Spend Fared Better in '09," *Mediaweek* [online]. http://www.mediaweek.com/mw/content_display/news/media-agencies-research/e3i888c20 be761d1d659a7ad31dc4dc5c0c.

Briabe Media (2007). "Briabe Media Offers Multicultural Mobile Marketing Assessments for Brands Seeking to Better Connect with Hispanic and African American Customers," [online], [May 15, 2009]. http://www.prwebdirect.com/releases/2007/2/prweb507171.htm.

Calvert, Sandra L. (2008). "Children as Consumers: Advertising and Marketing," *Future of Children,* Vol. 18, No. 1, p. 205-234.

Caprio, Sonia, Stephen R. Daniels, Adam Drewnowski, Francine R. Kaufman, Lawrence A. Palinkas, Arlan L. Rosenbloom and Jeffrey B. Schwimmer (2008). "Influence of Race, Ethnicity, and Culture on Childhood Obesity: Implications for Prevention and Treatment," *Diabetes Care,* Vol. 31, No. 11, p. 2211-2221.

Chaufan, Claudia, Gee Hee Hong and Patrick Fox (2009). "Taxing 'Sin Foods': Obesity Prevention and Public Health Policy," *The New England Journal of Medicine,* Vol. 361, No. 24.

Colabianchi, Natalie, Carolyn E. Ievers-Landis and Elaine A. Borawski (2006). "Weight Preoccupation as a Function of Observed Physical Attractiveness: Ethnic Differences among Normal-Weight Adolescent Females," *Journal of Pediatric Psychology,* Vol. 31, No. 8, p. 803-812.

Council of Better Business Bureaus (2004). "Children's Food and Beverage Advertising Initiative," [online], [March 8th]. http://www.bbb.org/us/childrens-food-beverage-initiative/.

Davis, Brennan and Christopher Carpenter (2009). "Proximity of Fast-Food Restaurants to Schools and Adolescent Obesity," *American Journal of Public Health,* Vol. 99, No. 3, p. 505-510.

Eggerton, John (2010). "Obama Announces Creation of Childhood Obesity Task Force," *Multichannel News* [online], [March 8th]. http://www.multichannel.com/article/448417-Obama_Announces_Creation_Of_Childhood_Obesity_Task_Force.php.

Escobar-Chaves, Soledad Liliana and Craig A. ANDERSON (2008). "Media and Risky Behaviors," *The Future of Children,* Vol. 18, No. 1, p. 147-180.

Flegal, Katherine M., Margaret D. Carroll, Cynthia L. Ogden and Lester R. Curtin (2010). "Prevalence and Trends in Obesity among US Adults, 1999-2008," *Journal Of The American Medical Association,* Vol. 303, No. 3, p. 235-241.

Frey, William H. (2003). "Married with Children," *American Demographics,* Vol. 25, No. 2, p. 17-19.

FTC (2008). Marketing Food to Children and Adolescents. A Review of Industry Expenditures, Activities, and Self-Regulation.

Grier, Sonya A. (2009). "African American & Hispanic Youth Vulnerability to Target Marketing: Implications for Understanding the Effects of Digital Marketing," *Second NPLAN/BMSG Meeting on Digital Media and Marketing Effects of Digital Marketing.* Berkeley, CA, NPLAN Marketing to Children Learning Community.

Grier, Sonya A. and Shiriki K. Kumanyika (2008). "The Context for Choice: Health Implications of Targeted Food and Beverage Marketing to African Americans," *American Journal of Public Health,* Vol. 98, No. 9, p. 1616-1629.

Grier, Sonya A. and Shiriki K. Kumanyika (2010). "Targeted Marketing and Public Health," *Annual Review of Public Health,* Vol. 31, April, p. 11.1-11.21.

Harkin, Tom (2007). "Preventing Childhood Obesity: The Power of Policy and Political Will," *American Journal of Preventive Medicine,* Vol. 33, No. 4, Supplement 1, p. S165-S166.

Harris, Jennifer L., Marlene B. Schwartz and Kelly D. Brownell (2009). Cereal F.A.C.T.S.: Nutrition and Marketing Ratings of Children's Cereals. Rudd Center for Food Policy & Obesity.

Harris, J Jennifer L., Marlene B. Schwartz and Kelly D. Brownell (2010). Fast Food F.A.C.T.S.: Evaluating Fast Food Nutrition and Marketing to Youth. Rudd Center for Food Policy & Obesity.

Harrison, Kristen (2006). "Fast and Sweet: Nutritional Attributes of Television Food Advertisements with and without Black Characters," *Howard Journal of Communications,* Vol. 17, No. 4, p. 16.

Hastings, Gerard, Martine Stead, Laura McDermott, Alasdair Forsyth, Anne Marie Mackintosh and Mike Rayner (2003). Review of Research on the Effects of Food Promotion to Children. *Report to the Food Standards Agency,* Glasgow, UK, Center for Social Marketing, University of Strathclyde.

Hein, Kenneth (2009). "Pepsi Program Targets African-American Moms," *Brandweek* [online], [March 8th]. http://www.brandweek.com/bw/content_display/news-and-features/direct/e3i0d52172227325f2841b53acba5ad865b.

Henderson, Vani R. and Bridget Kelly (2005). "Food Advertising in the Age of Obesity. Content Analysis of Food Advertising on General Market and African American Television," *Journal of Nutrition Education and Behavior,* Vol. 37, p. 191-196.

Herrick, Clare (2009). "Shifting Blame/Selling Health: Corporate Social Responsibility in the Age of Obesity," *Sociology of Health and Illness,* Vol. 31, No. 1, p. 51-65.

Hillier, Amy, Brian L. Cole, Tony E. Smith, Antronette K. Yancey, Jerome D. Williams, Sonya A. Grier and William J. McCarthy (2009). "Clustering of Unhealthy Outdoor Advertisements around Child-Serving Institutions: A Comparison of Three Cities," *Health Place,* Vol. 15, No. 4, p. 935-945.

Holt, Debra, Pauline M. Ippolito, Debra M. Desrochers and Christopher R. Kelley (2007). Children's Exposure to TV Advertising in 1977 and 2004: Information for the Obesity Debate. Washington, DC, Bureau of Economics Staff Report.

Hornik, Robert C. (2002). "Exposure: Theory and Evidence About All the Ways It Matters," *Social Marketing Quarterly,* Vol. 8, No. 3, p. 31-36.

Huang, Julia (2006). The 'Invisible' Market: Asian Americans Are a Sizable Population with Considerable Spending Power, So Why Aren't More Marketers Speaking Directly to This Audience? *Brandweek.*

Humphreys, Jeffrey M. (2006). *The Multicultural Economy 2006*, Atlanta, The University of Georgia, Selig Center for Economic Growth.

Humphries, Jeffrey M. (2008). *The Multicultural Economy 2008*, Atlanta, The University of Georgia, Selig Center for Economic Growth.

Khan, Mickey Alam (2007). "Coca-Cola Debuts Ambitious Mobile Push for Sprite," *DM News* [online], [May 18, 2009]. http://www.dmnews.com/Coca-Cola-debuts-ambitious-mobile-push-for-Sprite/article/95828/.

Korzenny, Felipe, Betty Ann Korzenny, Holly McGavock and Maria Gracia Inglessis (2006). "The Multicultural Marketing Equation: Media, Attitudes, Brands, and Spending," Center for Hispanic Marketing Communication, Florida State University.

Kraak, Vivica I., Mary Story and Ellen A. Wartella (2011). "Missed Opportunities for Private- and Public-Sector Stakeholders to Achieve the Institute of Medicine Report Recommendations for Food Marketing to American Children and Adolescents, December 1, 2005 – January 31, 2011," *Commissioned paper completed for the Robert Wood Johnson Foundation's Healthy Eating Research National Program Office.*

Kraft Foods Inc. (2010). "Communications: Advertising Responsibly to Children," [online], http://www.kraftfoodscompany.com/Responsibility/healthandwellness/communications.aspx.

Kumanyika, Shiriki (2002). "The Minority Factor in the Obesity Epidemic," *Ethnicity and Disease,* Vol. 12, No. 3, p. 316-319.

Kumanyika, Shiriki and Sonya Grier (2006). "Targeting Interventions for Ethnic Minority and Low-Income Populations," *Future Child,* Vol. 16, No. 1, p. 187-207.

Kunkel, Dale, Christopher McKinley and Paul Wright (2009). *The Impact of Industry Self-Regulation on the Nutritional Quality of Foods Advertised on Television to Children*, Children Now.

Larson, Nicole and Mary Story (2008). "Food and Beverage Marketing to Children and Adolescents. What Changes Are Needed to Promote Healthy Eating Habits?" Robert Wood Johnson Foundation.

Larson, Nicole I., Mary T. Story and Melissa C. Nelson (2009). "Neighborhood Environments: Disparities in Access to Healthy Foods in the U.S.," *American Journal of Preventive Medicine,* Vol. 36, No. 1, p. 74-81.e10.

Lascoutx, Elizabeth L. (2005). "Current Self-Regulatory and Other Standards for Marketing Food to Children Panel," Joint Workshop of the Federal Trade Commission and the Department of Health and Human Services: Perspectives on Marketing, Self-Regulation & Childhood Obesity, (July 14–15), Washington, DC.

Lavizzo-Mourey, Risa (2010). "Robert Wood Johnson Foundation Statement Regarding Evaluation of School Beverage Guidelines," [online], [March 10, 2010]. http://www.rwjf.org/childhoodobesity/product.jsp?id=56748.

Let's Move (2010). "America's Move to Raise a Healthier Generation of Kids," *Let's Move.gov* [online], [March 8th]. http://www.letsmove.gov/.

Lewis, LaVonna Blair, David C. Sloane, Lori Miller Nascimento, Allison L. Diamant, Joyce Jones Guinyard, Antronette K. Yancey and Gwendolyn Flynn (2005). "African Americans' Access to Healthy Food Options in South Los Angeles Restaurants," *American Journal of Public Health,* Vol. 95, No. 4, p. 668-73.

Lipton, Eric and Eric Lichtblau (2010). "In Black Caucus, a Fund-Raising Powerhouse," [online], http://www.nytimes.com/2010/02/14/us/politics/14cbc.html?em=&pagewanted=all.

MacArthur, Kate and Jack Neff (2004). "Sprite Shifts Gears in Quest for Street Cred," *Advertising Age.*

Markey, E. (2007). "Let's Give Parents the Tools to Fight Unhealthy Media Images," [online], [June 22, 2007]. http://markey.house.gov/index.php?option=com_content&task=view&id=2933&Itemid=88.

McDonalds Corporation "What Is McDonald's 365 Black?," [online], [May 29, 2009]. http://www.365black.com/365black/whatis.jsp.

McGinnis, J. Michael, Jennifer Appleton Gootman and Vivica I. Kraak (2006). *Food Marketing to Children and Youth. Threat or Opportunity?* National Academies Press.

Miller, Patti (2005). "Current Self-Regulatory and Other Standards for Marketing Food to Children Panel," Joint Workshop of the Federal Trade Commission and the Department of Health and Human Services: Perspectives on Marketing, Self-Regulation & Childhood Obesity, (July 14–15), Washington, DC.

Montgomery, Kathryn (2005). "Current Self-Regulatory and Other Standards for Marketing Food to Children Panel," Joint Workshop of the Federal Trade Commission and the Department of Health and Human Services: Perspectives on Marketing, Self-Regulation & Childhood Obesity, (July 14-15), Washington, DC.

Narayan, K. M. Venkat, James P. Boyle, Theodore J. Thompson, Stephen W. Sorensen and David F. Williamson (2003). "Lifetime Risk for Diabetes Mellitus in the United States," *Journal of The American Medical Association,* Vol. 290, No. 14, p. 1884-1890.

National Latino Children's Institute (2004). "Salsa, Sabor Y Salud," [online], http://www.nlci.org/salsa/indexSSS.htm.

Nestle, Marion (2010). "What Michelle Obama's Childhood Obesity Campaign Misses: Food Marketing to Kids," *AlterNet.*

Nickolodeon and C.A. Group (2006). "U.S. Multicultural Kids Study 2006," *Advertising Research Council Annual Youth Meeting.*

Nielsen Company (2009). "Nielsen Projects Older, Multi-Cultural, and Low-Income Consumers Driving Consumer Packaged Goods Trends in 2020," *Reuters Business Wire* [online], [May 12].

Nplan (2010). *Consumer Protection: An Overview of State Laws.*

Ogden, Cynthia L., Margaret D. Carroll, Lester R. Curtin, Molly M. Lamb and Katherine M. Flegal (2010). "Prevalence of High Body Mass Index in U.S. Children and Adolescents, 2007–2008," *Journal of the American Medical Association,* Vol. 303, No. 3, p. 242-249.

Ogden, Cynthia L., Margaret D. Carroll, Lester R. Curtin, Margaret A. McDowell, Carolyn J. Tabak, Katherine M. Flegal (2006). "Prevalence of Overweight and Obesity in the United States, 1999–2004," *Journal of the American Medical Association,* Vol. 295, No. 13, p. 1549-55.

Ogden, Cynthia L., Margaret D. Carroll and Katherine M. Flegal (2008). "High Body Mass Index for Age among U.S. Children and Adolescents, 2003–2006," *Journal of the American Medical Association,* Vol. 299, No. 20, p. 2401-2405.

Olshanksy, S. Jay, Douglas J. Passaro, Ronald C. Hershow, Jennifer Layden, Bruce A. Carnes, Jacob Brody, Leonard Hayflick, Robert N. Butler, David B. Allison and David S. Ludwig (2005). "A Potential Decline in Life Expectancy in the United States in the 21st Century," *New England Journal of Medicine,* Vol. 352, p. 1138-1145.

Penaloza, Lisa (1994). "Border Crossings: A Critical Ethnographic Exploration of the Consumer Acculturation of Mexican Immigrants," *Journal of Consumer Research,* Vol. 21, No. 1, p. 32-54.

Powell, Lisa M., M. Christopher Auld, Frank J. Chaloupka, Patrick M. O'Malley and Lloyd D. Johnston (2007a). "Associations between Access to Food Stores and Adolescent Body Mass Index," *American Journal of Preventive Medicine,* Vol. 33, No. 4 (Suppl.), p. 301-307.

Powell, Lisa M. and Frank J. Chaloupka (2009). "Food Prices and Obesity: Evidence and Policy Implications for Taxes and Subsidies," *Milbank Quarterly,* Vol. 87, p. 229-257.

Powell, Lisa M., Glen Szczypka and Frank J. Chaloupka (2007b). "Adolescent Exposure to Food Advertising on Television," *American Journal of Preventive Medicine,* Vol. 33, No. 4 (Suppl.), p. S251-6.

Radio Advertising Bureau (2010). "Pepsi Pumps the Vibe on the Streets," *Radio Advertising Bureau* [online], [March 8th]. http://www.aef.com/pdf/rab_pepsi.pdf.

Rideout, Victoria J., Ulla G. Foehr and Donald F Roberts (2010). *Generation M2: Media in the Lives of 8-18 Year Olds,* Kaiser Family Foundation.

Saul, Stephanie (2008). "Blacks in Congress Split over Menthol Cigarettes," *The New York Times.*

Severson, Kim (2008). "Los Angeles Stages a Fast Food Intervention," *The New York Times* [online], http://www.nytimes.com/2008/08/13/dining/13calo.html?_r=1&pagewanted=all.

Simon, Paul, Christopher J. Jarosz, Tony Kuo and Jonathan E. Fielding (2008). *Menu Labeling as a Potential Strategy for Combating the Obesity Epidemic: A Health Impact Assessment*, Los Angeles, Public Health Division of Chronic Disease and Injury Prevention.

Story, Mary and Simone French (2004). "Food Advertising and Marketing Directed at Children and Adolescents in the U.S.," *International Journal of Behavioral Nutrition and Physical Activity,* Vol. 1, No. 1, p. 3.

Sturm, Roland and Deborah A. Cohen (2009). "Zoning for Health? The Year-Old Ban on New Fast-Food Restaurants in South L.A." *Health Affairs,* Vol. 28, No. 6, p. 1088-1097.

Triodkar, Manasi A. and Anjali Jain (2003). "Food Messages on African American Television Shows," *American Journal of Public Health,* Vol. 93, No. 3, p. 439-41.

U.S. Census (2008). "An Older and More Diverse Nation by Midcentury" [online], [May 12, 2009]. http://www.census.gov/Press-Release/www/releases/archives/population/012496.html.

U.S. General Accounting Office (2000). *Public Education: Commercial Activities in Schools*, IN OFFICE, U.S.G.A. (Ed.). Washington, DC.

Wang, Youfa and May A. Beydoun (2007). "The Obesity Epidemic in the United States—Gender, Age, Socioeconomic, Racial/Ethnic, and Geographic Characteristics: A Systematic Review and Meta-Regression Analysis," *Epidemiological Review*, Vol. 29, p. 6–28.

Wang, Youfa, May A. Beydoun, Lan Liang, Benjamin Caballero and Shiriki K. Kumanyika (2008). "Will All Americans Become Overweight or Obese? Estimating the Progression and Cost of the US Obesity Epidemic," *Obesity,* Vol. 16, No. 10, p. 2323-2330.

Wiecha, Jean L., Karen E. Peterson, David S. Ludwig, Juhee KIM, Arthur SOBOL and Steven L. Gortmaker (2006). "When Children Eat What They Watch: Impact of Television Viewing on Dietary Intake in Youth," *Archives of Pediatrics and Adolescent Medicine,* Vol. 160, p. 436-442.

Wootan, Margo G., Ameena Batada and Ona Balkus (2010). *Report Card on Food-Marketing Policies: An Analysis of Food and Entertainment Company Policies Regarding Food and Beverage Marketing to Children.* Center for Science in the Public Interest.

World Health Organization (2003). *Controlling the Global Obesity Epidemic*, [online], [10/2/06]. http://www.who.int/nutrition/topics/obesity/en/.

World Health Organization (2009). "Childhood Overweight and Obesity," [online], [February 23]. http://www.who.int/dietphysicalactivity/childhood/en/index.html.

Yancey, Antronette K., Brian L. Cole, Rochelle Brown, Jerome D. Williams, Amy Hillier, Randolph S. Kline, Marice Ashe, Sonya A. Grier, Desiree Backman and William J. McCarthy (2009). "A Cross-Sectional Prevalence Study of Ethnically Targeted and General Audience Outdoor Obesity-Related Advertising," *Milbank Quarterly,* Vol. 87, No. 1, p. 155-184.

Zhou, Min (1997). "Growing up American: The Challenge Confronting Immigrant Children and Children of Immigrants," *Annual Review of Sociology,* Vol. 23, p. 63-95.

Zmuda, Natalie (2009a). "Coca-Cola Lays out Its Vision for the Future at 2010 Meeting," *Advertising Age* [online], [March 8th]. http://adage.com/article?article_id=140664.

Zmuda, Natalie (2009b). "How Coke Is Targeting Black Consumers," [online], [March 8th]. http://adage.com/bigtent/post?article_id=137716.

About the authors

Sonya Grier conducts interdisciplinary research on topics related to target marketing, race in the marketplace, the social impact of commercial marketing, and social marketing. Her current research investigates the relationship between marketing activities, and consumer health, with a focus on obesity. She has published her research in leading marketing, psychology and health journals. Professor Grier has policy experience based on two years at the Federal Trade Commission, and also has practical industry experience in Market Research, Brand Management and Marketing consulting. She serves on the Editorial Board for the *Journal of Public Policy and Marketing*, and the Advisory Boards for Transformative Consumer Research and the Villanova Center for Marketing and Public Policy. She also serves as a member of the Board of Scientific Counselors for the Centers for Disease Control and Prevention (CDC) National Center for Health Marketing. She received her Ph.D. in Marketing, with a minor in Social Psychology, from Northwestern University and also has an MBA from Northwestern University, with an emphasis on marketing, non-profit mgmt and international business.

Guillaume D. Johnson is an associate researcher at Dauphine Recherches en Management (DRM), UMR CNRS 7088, Université Paris-Dauphine, Paris, France. Previously he held positions at the University of the Witwatersrand, Johannesburg, South Africa as the Head of the Marketing Division and Senior Lecturer. His research interest focuses primarily on multicultural marketing and the implications of the coexistence of multiple cultures within the marketplace. He has explored these issues in France, South Africa and the United States. His work has been published in the *Journal of Public Policy and Marketing*, the *Journal of Advertising*, the *Journal of Business Research*, and the *International Journal of Advertising*, amongst others.

Teaching notes for this case are available from Greenleaf Publishing. These are free of charge and available only to teaching staff. They can be requested by going to:
www.greenleaf-publishing.com/darkside2notes

14

The Olivieri case

An ethical dilemma of clinical research and corporate sponsorship[1]

Heidi Weigand and Albert J. Mills
Saint Mary's University, Canada

The "Olivieri case" was a high-profile series of ethical disputes concerning multiple institutions and individual researchers involved in the clinical research on a new drug. The drug was developed during the mid-1980s to the mid-1990s to treat an inherited, potentially fatal blood disorder called thalassemia. The initial dispute arose from an attempt to advise patients of potential side effects of a drug referred to clinically as Deferiprone (L1). It was subsequently compounded by oversights, mistakes and misjudgements by individuals, public institutions, a private corporation and inquiry panels. This case focuses on issues of research ethics and academic freedom so important to the public interest that it attracted national and international attention. The primary conflict involves Apotex Inc., a private pharmaceutical manufacturer; the Hospital for Sick Children (HSC) in Toronto, a teaching hospital affiliated with the University

---

1 A first version of this case study was shortlisted in the 2010 Dark Side Case Writing Competition organized by the Critical Management Studies Division of the Academy of Management (AOM).

© HEC Montréal 2011. reproduced with the permission of the HEC Montréal Case Centre.

All rights reserved for all countries. Any translation or alteration in any form whatsoever is prohibited.

The International Journal of Case Studies in Management is published on-line (www.hec.ca/revuedecas/en), ISSN 1911-2599.

This case is intended to be used as the framework for an educational discussion and does not imply any judgement on the administrative situation presented. Deposited under number 9 40 2011 043 with the HEC Montréal Case Centre, 3000, chemin de la Côte-Sainte-Catherine, Montréal (Québec) Canada H3T 2A7.

of Toronto; Dr. Nancy Olivieri, a clinical researcher; and Dr. Gideon Koren, associate director for clinical research at the HSC. Drs. Olivieri and Koren were both associated with the University of Toronto. Additional parties are the Hospital Medical Advisory Committee (MAC), the Canadian Association of University Teachers (CAUT), and, not least, the sick children and their parents who constituted the patient group primarily affected by the drug trials. The case centres on ethical decision making in a context of competing ethical demands and expectations.

"You do not know about Emrich?"

"That she had emigrated to Canada. But she was still working for KVH [the multi-national drug company]."

"You do not know what her position is now—her problem?"

"She quarrelled with Kovacs."

"Kovacs is nothing. Emrich has quarrelled with KVH."

"What on earth about?"

"Dypraxa. She believes she has identified certain very negative side-effects. KVH believes she has not."

"What have they done about it?" asked Justin.

"So far they have only destroyed her reputation and her career."

"That's all."

"That's all."

John le Carré, *The Constant Gardener*, 2001, pp. 361-362

Preface

As she watched *The Constant Gardener*—the movie based on John le Carré's novel of the same title—Nancy Olivieri reflected on her life over the past eight years. She had never met le Carré, but the movie, and especially the book on which it was based, contained "intriguing parallels" to her own case.[2] Like Lara Emrich, one of the book's key characters, Olivieri is a Canadian-based doctor

---

2 Quoted in the *Globe and Mail*, September 3, 2005 (http://meds.queensu.ca/medicine/histm/ oilivieri/globe constant.htm—accessed July 7, 2010).

and researcher whose "troubles begin when she signs a contract with a drug company, forbidding her to publish findings from a clinical trial without the company's consent."[3] Olivieri reflected that years earlier she had "signed a similar research contract, approved by [the Toronto Hospital for Sick Children]. Like me, Lara studied a drug to be prescribed in poorer countries and, when she sought to disclose her subsequent concerns about the drug, was met with vigorous opposition within her hospital."[4] These thoughts brought back "memories of [her] own unhappy experience" at the Sick Children's Hospital and the "years of harassment, false accusations and legal threats" that she faced as the result of her decision to inform patients of the potentially dangerous side-effects of the drug she was administering.[5] As she noted, the book's description of "anonymous hate mail" sent to the heroine, warning her to stop "poisoning decent people's lives" was similar to those that she and her colleagues had received warning them to "stop poisoning the air and fabric" of "decent people" at the Sick Children's Hospital.[6] Vindicated by the Ontario College of Physicians, the Canadian Association of University Teachers (CAUT) and other independent bodies, Olivieri would nonetheless continue to be vilified by some in the medical profession and sections of the media.[7] Applauding *The Constant Gardener's* dramatization of "the exploitation of vulnerable patients in medical research conducted by certain drug companies,"[8] Olivieri could not be blamed for pondering the very difficult and ethically problematic road she had travelled to this point. Nonetheless, as the case will show, there are still debates around her approach to the ethics of the case.[9]

3 Ibid.
4 Ibid.
5 Ibid.
6 Ibid.
7 In 2005, for example, a fairly influential book on the case accused Olivieri of being an "ambitious, vindictive scientist [who] unfairly trashes the reputation of a good drug for a rare disease" (Shuchman, 2005, cited in Brody, 2007, http://brodyhooked.blogspot.com/2007/02/olivieri-case-she-said-they-said.html—accessed July 7, 2010). Brody (2006), who included his own account of the case in his book on ethics and the medical profession later recanted some of his support for Olivieri. He now argues that, based on his reading of the Shuchman (2005) book, he is "pessimistic that we will ever know the truth about this case. The people in a position to tell investigators what really happened and when, have divided themselves into pro- and anti-Olivieri camps; and depending on which side any new investigator appears to be on, one group will talk with her and the other will refuse to be interviewed. My tentative conclusion is that while the CAUT report is very well documented and persuasive on its face, any account of the Olivieri case based on that report will have to have an asterisk next to it, like the home run record of a baseball slugger accused of taking steroids" (http://brodyhooked.blogspot.com/2007/02/olivieri-case-she-said-they-said.html—accessed July 7, 2010).
8 Olivieri, quoted in the *Globe and Mail*, September 3, 2005.
9 Shuchman (2005) suggests that, at least in this case, it may take "a flawed and problematic character" to take a stand on some issues (cited by Brody, 2007). Schafer (2007), on the other hand, argues: "The veritable cornucopia of discredit which Shuchman heaps on

Introduction

For Nancy Olivieri, John le Carré's story of *The Constant Gardener* was not a "thriller" but a realistic account of the situation that individuals can find themselves in when confronting institutions and large corporations. The story of what was to become the "Olivieri case" began in 1989 when Dr. Nancy Olivieri became involved in an initial pilot study of an experimental drug developed to deal with a potentially fatal blood disorder called thalassemia. Initial promising results at the Hospital for Sick Children (HSC) in Toronto encouraged Olivieri to seek funding to continue research on the drug. An extension of the clinical drug trials was supported by Apotex Inc., a private pharmaceutical manufacturer, and in 1993 Olivieri and HSC's associate director for clinical research, Dr. Gideon Koren, signed a contract with Apotex. The contract included confidentiality, communication and intellectual rights clauses and the level of profits that would accrue to the company in exchange for continued funding for the clinical trials. The unexpected effects of the trial drug (Deferiprone) ultimately changed the direction of this story. The effects included the "toxicity" of the drug (i.e., it had poisonous effects on some patients) and the "inefficacious" nature of the drug (i.e., the drug's positive effects were reversed in some cases).[10] In other words, the drug appeared to *increase* some patient's health problems and in others ceased to be effective after a period of time.

Problems arose when Olivieri set out to report her findings to the university's Research Ethics Board (REB) and to inform her patients—i.e., the parents of the sick children involved—of the changing "risk/benefit" ratio as required under the REB's ethics codes.[11]

Under contractual obligations to Apotex, Olivieri began by trying to convince the company of her need to report her adverse findings. Apotex disagreed with her findings and her request to notify the REB, placing Olivieri in an ethical dilemma of honouring either her contractual obligations to Apotex or her broader commitment to uphold the ethics of medical practice in general and those of the REB in particular. She chose the latter and ended up embroiled in a series of disputes in which she found herself confronted by legal challenges from Apotex, institutional pressures from the University of Toronto and the

Nancy Olivieri is, I'm sorry to say, standard punishment for those who have the temerity to challenge powerful vested interests. In the popular imagination David bravely slays Goliath. Alas, in the real world, the whistle-blower's issue of principle is easily re-described as an act of private disloyalty and, worse, as evidence of professional incompetence and psychological disturbance" (http://brodyhooked.blogspot.com/2007/02/olivieri-case-she-said-they-said.html—accessed July 7, 2010).

10 http://en.wikipedia.org/wiki/Nancy_Fern_Olivieri.

11 Note that, in Canada, all research involving human subjects must be pre-approved by a university's Research Ethics Board and changes in the process must be reported to the REB (see Bryman, Bell, Mills and Yue, 2011).

HSC and attacks on her character from various people, including her colleague Dr. Gideon Koren.

To put it in terms of le Carré's novel, Koren was Olivieri's Kovac, KVH was her Apotex, and Dypraxa was her Deferiprone. But fiction merged with fact when Olivieri found her reputation as a scientist, a researcher and a person was attacked on all fronts. In the novel, under severe pressures, Lara Emrich chose to run away from the issues involved. Nancy Olivieri chose to make a stand. The case, as we shall show, raises important questions about ethics at work and issues of the contexts in which organizational members attempt to make decisions. Knowing some of the key facts of the case, one wonders whether Olivieri would do it again if she had to. The case highlights the ethical dilemmas involved and asks students to consider how they would respond if placed in a similar situation.

The 'facts' of the case[12]

The "Olivieri case" was a high-profile series of ethical disputes concerning multiple institutions and individual researchers involved in the clinical research on a new drug. The drug was developed during the period of the mid-1980s to the mid-1990s to treat an inherited, potentially fatal blood disorder called thalassemia.

The initial dispute over the drug's potential use arose from an attempt to advise patients of potential side effects of Deferiprone (L1) and was compounded by oversights, mistakes or misjudgements by individuals, public institutions, a private corporation and inquiry panels. The focus of this case revolves around issues of research ethics and academic freedom so important to the public interest that it attracted national and international attention.[13]

---

12 It is important to note that *all* business cases are works of fiction—they attempt to encourage critical thought and engagement through the development of carefully constructed stories based on selective accounts of events. These selective accounts are often focused on discussions around organizational effectiveness and success, but mask the fact that they are based on fictionalized accounts. This case study has at its base an attempt to encourage discussion around the problem of ethical practices in organizations. We readily admit that, *like all cases*, ours is a story based on selected accounts, but we provide reference to different accounts to allow the student to critically assess the various accounts used. For discussion of the influence of writing genres on the development of scholarly accounts, see White (1985) and Czarniawska and Gagliardi (2003).

13 See Thompson, Baird and Downie, 2001.

FIGURE 1 The core players in the Olivieri case

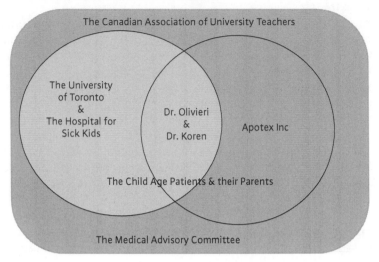

The University
of Toronto
&
The Hospital for
Sick Kids

Dr. Olivieri
&
Dr. Koren

Apotex Inc

The Canadian Association of University Teachers

The Child Age Patients & their Parents

The Medical Advisory Committee

The Olivieri Report

The primary conflict involved Apotex Inc., a private pharmaceutical manufacturer; the Hospital for Sick Children (HSC) in Toronto, a teaching hospital affiliated with the University of Toronto; Dr. Nancy Olivieri, a clinical researcher; and Dr. Gideon Koren, associate director for clinical research at the HSC. Drs. Olivieri and Koren were both associated with the University of Toronto. Additional parties are the Hospital Medical Advisory Committee (MAC), the Canadian Association of University Teachers (CAUT) and, not least, the sick children and their parents who constituted the patient group primarily affected by the drug trials.

The L1 drug trials and contractual agreements

In 1989, an initial pilot study of a new (experimental iron chelation) drug called Deferiprone (L1) was initiated to assess its long-term efficacy and safety at the Hospital for Sick Children (HSC), one of the fully affiliated teaching hospitals of the University of Toronto. In the early 1990s, Dr. Nancy Olivieri, a specialist in the treatment of hereditary blood diseases, wished to further study the L1 drug, as it had shown promise in the pilot study. It appeared to reduce tissue iron loading in a group of transfusion-dependent thalassemia patients.[14] The funding requirements were exceptionally high and could only be fulfilled through a corporate sponsor. Dr. Koren negotiated an arrangement with Apotex Incorporated, which

---

14   Ibid., p. 4.

agreed to acquire the commercial development rights for L1 and to sponsor the clinical drug trials.

In April 1993, Dr. Olivieri and Dr. Koren signed a contract with Apotex to conduct a new randomized trial to compare L1 with the standard treatment, the drug Deferoxamine (DFO) with child-age patients. This contract contained a confidentiality clause giving Apotex the right to control communication of trial data for one year after the termination of the trial, and Apotex had the right to terminate the trial at any time. This provision was fully in accordance with the University of Toronto's policy on contract research.

The 1989 pilot study was continued with the support of Apotex, although the contract for this new trial, in 1993, was signed two years later in October of 1995, which did not contain the confidentiality clause for the continued pilot study. The hope was that the trials would lead to the licensing of L1 for therapeutic use and Apotex would be able to market the drug as an alternate to the current DFO treatment that was known to be very hard on patients. These two studies were the only two clinical trials in any centre that included baseline assessments of liver iron concentration and liver histology, the most accurate measures of the long-term efficacy and safety of an iron chelation drug.[15]

Apotex's investment meant the trial was eligible for matching funding from the Medical Research Council (MRC) under its university-industry program, which Dr. Olivieri was able to secure with the approval of the HSC and the University of Toronto. Around the same time, the University of Toronto and Apotex had been engaged in discussions for a multimillion-dollar donation, intended to allow a new biomedical research centre to be built that would benefit the university and its affiliated health care institutions.

The beginning of the conflict

In early 1996, Dr. Olivieri identified an unexpected risk of the L1 drug related to growth retardation in youth and moved to disclose the findings to her patient's parents. Apotex issued warnings of legal action if she disclosed the risk to family members of the child patients or to anyone else, as she was under a confidentiality agreement. However, HSC's Research Ethics Board (REB) accepted that Dr. Olivieri had an obligation to inform patients of the risk and issued a directive from the REB chair to that effect. In May, when Dr. Olivieri moved to inform the patients and their parents, Apotex terminated the trials and simultaneously issued warnings of legal action if she disclosed the risk to her patients or anyone else because it "could not allow such information to be transmitted to

15   Ibid.

patients."[16] The termination of the trials caused significant concern for patients for whom the L1 drug was working well during the trials.

The university was drawn into the conflict between Dr. Olivieri and Apotex because two key ethics principles were in contention: (i) academic freedom and (ii) the rights of participants in a clinical trial and their parents to be informed of risk. In June, University of Toronto's Dean of Medicine, Dr. Arnold Aberman, mediated a new arrangement between Dr. Olivieri and Apotex under the Emergency Drug Release program of Health Canada. Apotex agreed to reinstate the supply of its L1 drug for those patients who appeared to be benefitting. Dr. Olivieri agreed to administer it to those particular patients on condition that they and their parents were informed of and accepted the new risk, and agreed to monitoring tests for safety. The patients were no longer in a research trial and so were not under the jurisdiction of the hospital's Research Ethics Board. It was also agreed that Apotex would continue very substantial research funding to Dr. Koren.

It would later be revealed—during the CAUT review of the Olivieri case—that Koren gave repeated reassurances to Olivieri that he agreed with her findings while also telling Apotex that he agreed with the company's position that there was no risk of loss of sustained efficacy of its drug.[17] Unknown to Olivieri until after the fact, Koren subsequently re-analyzed data from the terminated L1 trials and published findings that the drug was effective and safe. Koren's publications did not disclose Apotex's financial support for his research, made no reference to the risks of the L1 drug identified by Olivieri and did not acknowledge her contributions to generating the data he used. Consequently, Apotex used Koren's statements about the L1 drug to counter Olivieri's adverse findings on its drug.

In the fall of 1996, Apotex stopped supplying the drug for a second time, causing concern to the patients and their parents. Following another intervention by Dr. Arnold Aberman, Apotex again agreed to reinstate the supply, but the supply of L1 nevertheless remained irregular into early 1997. In February 1997, Dr. Olivieri identified a second, more serious risk (that the drug may cause progression of liver fibrosis)[18] through reviews of patients' charts. Apotex issued legal warnings against disclosure again. Despite the possible legal action by the company and the lack of effective assistance from her university and hospital, Olivieri informed her child-age patients, their parents and the scientific community of the risks she had identified.

---

16   Ibid., p. 5.
17   See the Olivieri Report (Thompson, Baird and Downie, 2001).
18   Liver fibrosis is the scarring process that represents the liver's response to injury. In the same way as skin and other organs heal wounds through deposition of collagen and other matrix constituents, so the liver repairs injury through the deposition of new collagen. Over time, this process can result in cirrhosis of the liver in which the architectural organization of the functional units of the liver becomes so disrupted that blood flow through the liver and liver function become disrupted. Once cirrhosis has developed, the serious complications of liver disease may occur, including portal hypertension, liver failure and liver cancer.

Dr. Olivieri began the process of transitioning her patients back to the standard treatment, a complex process that takes a number of weeks. The newly identified risk related to liver fibrosis was not an acute one, so there was time for a safe and orderly transition. During the transition period, a dispute developed between Olivieri and Dr. Hugh O'Brodovich, HSC's Paediatrician-in-Chief. Following discussions with Apotex and Koren, O'Brodovich appeared to have drawn the incorrect conclusion that the newly identified risk was one of acute toxicity. It is possible that he drew this conclusion because his expertise was not in the specific field in question –haematology. O'Brodovich also incorrectly supposed that the hospital's Research Ethics Board had jurisdiction over the matter and that Dr. Olivieri was obligated to notify the REB of the risk. Later, these errors would play a further role in the dispute (see below). Meanwhile, in March, this latter dispute was resolved through discussion between the two doctors.

At the same time, Apotex began efforts to persuade medical administrators and patients in Toronto, as well as regulatory agencies and the scientific community, that L1 was effective and safe and should be in wider use. Apotex proposed a new treatment arrangement for Toronto thalassemia patients in which an annual liver biopsy, the test that had led to the identification of both of the unexpected risks of L1, would not be an integral part of the safety monitoring regime for all patients. Olivieri did not accept this proposal, as she had phased out L1 in the clinics she directed. She had the support of haematologist Dr. Michael Baker, Physician-in-Chief of the Toronto Hospital, where adult thalassemia patients received their care under her supervision.

The scientific community concerns

In 1997 and 1998, increasing numbers of medical scientists expressed concerns over the lack of effective action by HSC and the university to assist Dr. Olivieri in contending with Apotex's actions against her. This led to calls for an independent inquiry into the controversy.

In early 1998, Apotex submitted licensing applications for L1 in several jurisdictions and alleged that data from the terminated Toronto trials had been compromised by protocol violations by Dr. Olivieri. The company used the short-term trials conducted by Dr. Olivieri at sites outside Canada to meet the licensing requirements for the U.S. FDA. The trials' primary objective was an assessment of known acute-toxicity effects of L1 and used this as the pivotal efficacy and safety trial. Unlike the randomized and long-term trials conducted in Toronto, the short-term trial did not include baseline and annual determination of liver iron concentration and liver histology for all participants.

This all occurred against a background where, in the spring of 1998, agreement in principle was reached between the University of Toronto and Apotex for what would have been the largest donation the university had ever received. Through matching funding from other sources, it would have been approximately $92 million. However, in the wake of the controversy, the university and Apotex decided to suspend discussions until the dispute involving Dr. Olivieri and Apotex was resolved.

The issue goes public

In August 1998, more than two years after the controversy began, it became public. Without giving Olivieri an opportunity to respond, the HSC executive issued a public statement repeating many allegations made privately to it by Apotex against the quality of Dr. Olivieri's scientific work. One week later, the hospital unilaterally established a review of the controversy and appointed Dr. Arnold Naimark of the University of Manitoba as its reviewer. This became known as the Naimark Review, but Nancy Olivieri and her supporters, suspecting the biases of Naimark and what they saw as the narrow focus of the review, declined to participate in it.

The Naimark Review

During the Naimark Review, Koren and O'Brodovich put forward testimony against Olivieri on several topics that would later prove to be incorrect. Worse, it was later proven that Koren was sending anonymous letters to the media and to colleagues disparaging Olivieri and others. Dr. Aideen Moore, who became Chair of the HSC Research Ethics Board shortly after the Toronto trials were terminated, also wrongly claimed in testimony that Olivieri had failed in her obligations to report new risks to the REB in later drug trials. The Naimark Review accepted the testimony of these witnesses as true and castigated Olivieri for dereliction of duty.

In December 1998, HSC's Board of Trustees, acting on the Naimark Review, declared that Olivieri had "failed" in a reporting obligation—namely, to notify the REB of an unexpected risk in a timely way. The Board directed the hospital's Medical Advisory Committee to inquire further into Olivieri's conduct. During this follow-up inquiry, Koren and O'Brodovich introduced new allegations concerning Olivieri's care of thalassemia patients during the period in early 1997, when the second risk of L1 was identified and patients were being transferred to standard therapy. They had alleged that a test (liver biopsy) that Olivieri had performed on some patients was a risky procedure and was not clinically indicated. On January 6, 1999, following an unrelated event,[19] Olivieri was removed from her post as director of the HSC hemoglobinopathy program with no opportunity to respond to HSC's charges against her. HSC issued directives that Dr. Olivieri and her colleagues—Drs. Chan, Durie and Gallie—were not to

---

19   Olivieri had protested against the decentralization of the Toronto Hospital's sickle cell disease (SCD) program and was supported by patient support groups.

discuss their concerns publicly. As a result of these two HSC actions, legal counsel for Olivieri, distinguished scientists from abroad, the Canadian Association of University Teachers (CAUT), the University of Toronto Faculty Association and the University of Toronto administration intervened. This would result in a CAUT Report of the Committee of Inquiry, or the "Olivieri Report."

On January 25, 1999, University of Toronto President Robert Prichard mediated an agreement that was signed by HSC and Dr. Olivieri to resolve a range of issues. The agreement restored Olivieri's authority over research and clinical care of HSC hemoglobinopathy patients, and affirmed the right to academic freedom for university faculty working at HSC. It also provided assurance of HSC's financial support for Dr. Olivieri in the event of legal action against her by Apotex.

Dr. Gideon Koren takes a front-row seat in the conflict

In May 1999, Drs. Olivieri, Chan, Durie and Gallie lodged a complaint against Dr. Koren on the basis of substantial forensic evidence identifying him as the author of a series of anonymous letters to the press which, arguably, presented a false impression of Olivieri and others' role in the L1 trials. Koren initially denied his involvement, until additional DNA evidence was obtained identifying him as the author. He was provided with all the details and given a chance to respond before the disciplinary action was imposed on him in April 2000.

By this time, Apotex and the university had resumed discussions about the multimillion-dollar donation and the company requested assistance from university President Prichard in lobbying the government of Canada against proposed changes to drug patent regulations that would adversely affect the company's revenues. Prichard wrote to the prime minister, stating the proposed government action could jeopardize the building of the university's proposed new medical sciences centre. He later apologized to the university community, saying he had acted inappropriately. The lobbying efforts were unsuccessful and Apotex withdrew from the 1998 agreement in principle on the donation. Nonetheless, for reasons that are not clear, in 2000, Apotex made a substantial, albeit smaller, multi-million dollar donation to the university.

In April 2000, HSC and the University of Toronto disciplined Koren for gross misconduct—namely, sending anonymous letters disparaging the personal and professional integrity of Drs. Olivieri, Chan, Durie and Gallie, and persistently lying to conceal his actions. In a press conference after the disciplinary actions were taken against Dr. Koren, the hospital Board and MAC announced they were referring the allegations against Dr. Olivieri, cast in the form of publicly expressed concerns, to the College of Physicians and Surgeons of Ontario and the University of Toronto for investigation. Nonetheless, the MAC and the university still persisted with some of the allegations against Olivieri, not taking the time to review the contradictions in Koren's own correspondence before going public with the actions against Olivieri. Apotex used the allegations against Dr. Olivieri and the MAC allegations to the College of Physicians and Surgeons of Ontario (CPSO) to defend the reputation of its L1 drug in legal proceedings.

The CAUT Report of the Committee of Inquiry

Reporting in 2001, the CAUT review of the Olivieri case[20] concluded that Olivieri had in fact fulfilled all her reporting obligations and that she had rightly put the patients' right to be informed ahead of concerns of possible legal action against her by Apotex. The report noted that the Naimark Review had mistakenly characterized Olivieri's later work on patients as "drug trials" and thus covered by REB requirements. This was not the case, and therefore the charges against her were unfounded. Equally, the report dismissed the allegations that Olivieri had performed risky procedures. They found the allegations were incorrect and could have been corrected if anyone on the MAC had checked the literature or well-established practices at the hospital. In fact, O'Brodovich had been repeatedly advised by Olivieri in writing that these biopsies were being scheduled and of the clinical indication for them, and he had not opposed them at the time. Dr. Olivieri was not aware of the case against her and had no opportunity to respond. Non-experts in the field made the decision without checking relevant facts. The report cleared Olivieri of any wrongdoing and, as a result, she was able continue her work as a clinical researcher with the university and the hospital.

The aftermath

So where do we find Dr. Olivieri five years after the Olivieri Report? She has been honoured and recognized for her contributions to medical research by receiving the 2009 Scientific Freedom and Responsibility Award by the American Association for Advancement from Science, "for her indefatigable determination that patient safety and research integrity come before institutional and commercial interests" (*CAUT Bulletin*, 2010).

Nonetheless, the controversy continues. A recent book claims that Olivieri's activities were less than heroic and have left patients in dire need of a proper treatment (Shuchman, 2005). The author, Miriam Shuchman, also contends that "there are people who would be alive if L1 had continued to be available in North America and had they stayed on it" (quoted in Gatehouse, 2005). Olivieri has since responded that Shuchman fails to disclose her association with one of the people who gave incorrect evidence against her at the Naimark Review— namely, her husband Dr. Donald Redelmeier (Olivieri, 2006).[21]

---

20 See the Olivieri Report (Thompson, Baird and Downie, 2001, 9).
21 The answer to this question is unclear, but in the scientific world, the facts supporting Dr. Olivieri *et al.*'s case against the efficacy of Deferiprone (L1) are mounting, with recent

In the meantime, Dr. Gideon Koren, who was found guilty of gross misconduct at one university, has nonetheless managed to find a distinguished place in the medical profession. In 2010, he received the Canadian Society for Clinical Investigation Distinguished Scientist Award, and he holds several important positions in the field.[22]

The Constant Gardener comes to life

As was stated at the opening of the case, some aspects of the Olivieri case bear uncanny resemblance to John le Carré's *The Constant Gardener*. Both involve "heroic" women whose efforts to expose aspects of the use and production of certain drugs lead them into serious conflict with a powerful drug manufacturer. However, there are important points of departure that make the Olivieri case more complex. Unlike the fictitious KVH, Apotex is not some conspiratorial organization that operates outside the law. On the contrary, it is the very legal processes involved that reveal the complex ethical issues involved. That Nancy Olivieri found herself fighting to save her reputation and career speaks to the complex and contextual nature of business ethics; a context that saw her and other medical doctors knowingly placing themselves in a potential conflict of interest and ethical dilemma. The ethical decision making of the various players involved—Olivieri, Gideon, Apotex, members of the relevant Research Ethics Board and senior administrators at the University of Toronto and the Hospital

evidence from investigators in the U.K. supporting the North-American findings. "In parallel, investigators in the U.K. reported the results of deferiprone therapy over 42.5 months (range, 8 to 56 months) in 42 patients with Cooley's anemia aged 29.9 years (range, 20 to 58 years) *(22, 23)*. No significant declines in serum ferritin concentration were reported in these patients over this period of therapy. In the 17 patients in whom hepatic iron concentrations were determined after therapy, concentrations exceeded the threshold for cardiac disease and early death *(4)* in ten patients. The conclusion of this analysis is similar to those in the Canadian study *(19)*: the U.K. investigators have now concluded that 'long-term therapy with deferiprone may not provide adequate control of body iron in a substantial proportion of patients with thalassaemia major' *(22, 23)*. In summary, two interpretations of the results obtained from the only centres to quantitatively determine body iron burden in patients receiving long-term deferiprone therapy raise concerns that long-term deferiprone may not provide adequate sustained control of body iron in a substantial proportion of patients with Cooley's anemia" (http://sickle.bwh.harvard.edu/l1_olivieri.html).

22 These include Founder and Director, Motherisk Program, Hospital for Sick Children; the Ivey Chair in Molecular Toxicology, University of Western Ontario; Holder, The Research Leadership for Better Pharmacotherapy during Pregnancy and Lactation, Hospital for Sick Children; Founder and Head, Fetal Alcohol Canadian Expertise (FACE); Chair, Steering Committee, Breaking the Cycle, Toronto; Editor in Chief (North America), Therapeutic Drug Monitoring; Editor in Chief, Fetal Alcohol Research (FAR); Scientific Director, Canadian Foundation for Fetal Alcohol Syndrome, 2008–present (http://www.clinpharmtox.utoronto .ca/faculty/Koren_Biosketch.htm).

for Sick Children—reveals a process bounded by competing interests. What those competing interests are and how they shape ethical decision making is the subject of this case.

Bibliography

Brody, Howard (2006). *Hooked: Ethics, the Medical Profession, and the Pharmaceutical Industry*, Lanham, MD, Rowman and Littlefield Publishers Inc.

Brody, Howard (2007). "The Olivieri Case: She Said, They Said…" *Hooked: Ethics, Medicine and Pharma* (blog). http://brodyhooked.blogspot.co.uk/2007/02/olivieri-case-she-said-they-said.html.

Bryman, Alan, Emma Bell, Albert J. Mills and Anthony R. Yue (2011). *Business Research Methods. First Canadian Edition*, Toronto, Oxford University Press.

Caut Bulletin (2010). "Oilivieri Honoured with Prestigious Award," *C.A.U.T. Bulletin*, March, p. B-57-53.

Czarniawska, Barbara, and Pasquale Gagliardi (Eds.) (2003). *Narratives We Organize By*, Amsterdam, John Benjamins Publishing Company.

Gatehouse, Jonathon (2005). "Book Review: The Drug Trial," *The Canadian Encyclopedia/The Encyclopedia of Music in Canada,* Retrieved from http://www.canadianencyclopedia.ca/index.cfm?PgNm=TCE&Params=M1ARTM0012767

Olivieri, Nancy (2006). "A Response from Dr. Nancy Olivieri," *Canadian Medical Association Journal*, Vol. 174, No. 5, p. 661-662.

Shuchman, Miriam (2005). *The Drug Trial: Nancy Olivieri and the Science Scandal that Rocked the Hospital for Sick Children*, Toronto, Random House Canada.

Schafer, Arthur (2007). "Commentary: Science Scandal or Ethics Scandal? Olivieri Redux," *Bioethics*, Vol. 21. No. 2, p. 111-115.

Thompson, Jon, Patricia Baird and Jocelyn Downie (2001). *The Olivieri Report: The Complete Text of the Report of the Independent Inquiry Commissioned by the Canadian Association of University Teachers*, Toronto, Lorimer.

White, Hayden (1985). *Tropics of Discourse. Essays in Cultural Criticism*, Baltimore, Johns Hopkins University Press.

About the authors

Albert J. Mills is Director of the PhD (Management) program and Professor of Management in the Sobey School of Business, Saint Mary's University, Canada. He is the author and editor of 35 books and special issues. His forthcoming books include *Gender and Aviation International Perspectives* (London: Ashgate); *The Oxford Handbook of Diversity in Organizations* (Oxford, Oxford University Press); *The Routledge Companion to Management and Organizational History* (London: Routledge); and *The Routledge Companion to Critical Management Studies* (London: Routledge). He is currently working on two SSHRC (Social Sciences & Humanities Research Council of Canada) funded projects to study (i) intersectionity over time and (ii) the development and dispersement of management theory. Albert is a former co-divisional chair of the Critical Management Studies of the Academy of Management and currently serves as the Co-Chair of the International CMS Executive.

Authors Albert J. Mills and Heidi Weigand receiving their finalist plaque for this case study.

Heidi A. Weigand is a PhD Candidate in the Management Department, Sobey School of Business, at Saint Mary's University, Canada. She also serves as a Director at the Centre for the Study of Sport and Health working with businesses, athletes and students in Atlantic Canada focusing on building mental resiliency to help bounce back from setbacks. Heidi has been a part-time instructor in both the marketing and management departments at Saint Mary's University as well as the Public Relations department at Mount Saint Vincent University with a focus on human resources and organizational behaviour. Her research is in the areas of sport, mental health, positive leadership, employee engagement, motivation, intersectional discrimination studies, and youth at risk goal setting practices. She is currently investigating if positive leadership can be taught and the impacts on employee and leader work behaviours. Heidi is on the board of directors for the Canadian Centre of Ethics in Public Affairs and serves as part of the research committee. She comes from a private sector background with over 20 years of management experience in the USA and Canada with Xerox and IBM.

Teaching notes for this case are available from Greenleaf Publishing. These are free of charge and available only to teaching staff. They can be requested by going to:
www.greenleaf-publishing.com/darkside2notes